Bargaining Behavior

Bargaining Behavior

LAWRENCE E. FOURAKER
Professor of Business
Administration
Harvard Graduate School
of Business Administration

SIDNEY SIEGEL
Late Research
Professor of Psychology
The Pennsylvania
State University

McGraw-Hill Book Company, Inc.

New York   San Francisco   Toronto   London

338.5
F 773

Bargaining Behavior

Preface

Sidney Siegel and I have collaborated in a research program concerned with testing economic models by means of controlled laboratory experimentation. We began our work in 1958, and the first results, for equal-strength bilateral monopoly, were published in 1960 (*Bargaining and Group Decision Making*, McGraw-Hill). We devoted the 1960–1961 academic year to the experiments presented here. In the summer of 1961 we prepared and distributed mimeographed reports of these experiments, under the titles: *Bargaining Behavior I* (with D. Harnett), *Bargaining Behavior II*, and *Oligopoly Bargaining: the Quantity Adjuster Models* (with Martin Shubik). Our purpose was to obtain the reaction of our colleagues. We also wished to have available complete sets of data while Sid was at the Center for Advanced Study in the Behavioral Sciences and I was at the Harvard Business School. Our plan was to devote the summer of 1962 to the completion of the bargaining behavior manuscript. Sid's untimely death in November, 1961, disrupted this plan.

With the assistance of Mrs. Siegel I have attempted to complete the manuscript. In general I followed the reporting plan we initially constructed. Some of the interpretation came after November, 1961, but it is such a logical extension of the discussions, conjectures, and analysis in which Sid and I had participated that I feel reasonably certain he would have concurred. The major exception to this statement is the statistical methodology. I am not a statistician, and our division of research labor always placed such analysis in Sid's hands. Unfortunately, the joining of our various experimental results required that I revise some of the statistical analysis, to provide some amount of methodological consistency over the set of experiments. In general I chose the simplest and least elegant test available and reported the full set of data so that those interested in more sophisticated analysis could follow their own preferences.

We were most fortunate in having generous financial support for this program of research. The basic grant was from the National Science Foundation to Sid (NSF-G16423). I have received support at various stages of the research from the Office of Naval Research (NONR-G00012), the National Science Foundation (NSF-G23814), and the Ford Foundation. We received the willing cooperation of the administration and staff at The Pennsylvania State University throughout the research program.

Professor Martin Shubik worked closely with us on several studies testing the quantity adjuster models. Some of these results have been reported elsewhere [Fouraker, Shubik, and Siegel (1961)] and some appear here. Our collaboration with Professor Shubik has been most helpful to us in our work.

In the execution of the studies we have been assisted by a number of students. In particular, Donald L. Harnett worked closely with us throughout the research. Important assistance also was provided by Julia McMichael Andrews, Jay Siegel, Alan Parker, and Richard Zeckhauser.

My secretaries, Helen Smith and Eleanor Hodges, combined patience and competence in the proper proportions.

Several colleagues have offered suggestions and criticism. Howard Raiffa, John Pratt, A. J. Goldman, and Vernon Smith are among them. Robert Bishop was kind enough to provide an extensive, detailed evaluation of our initial work and the preliminary reports of the results presented here. Alberta E. Siegel is responsible in large measure for any instances of clear exposition and organization the reader may come upon. Any ambiguities and errors remaining in the book are there notwithstanding the most welcome efforts of these people. The responsibility for this residue is mine.

Lawrence E. Fouraker

Contents

PART ONE

Introduction

CHAPTER 1

Introduction

Over the past several years we have conducted, at The Pennsylvania State University, a series of controlled experiments regarding the decision behavior of human subjects. This decision behavior has been studied in the context of a simulated conflict situation. We chose economic conflict models because:

1. Economic models are quite sophisticated. Of all the social sciences, economics has developed the most impressive body of theory. Many economic situations, such as bilateral monopoly (one buyer and one seller) and oligopoly (a few

3

sellers), have attracted the interest of economic theorists for over a century. The discipline has emphasized the abstraction process by which hypotheses are formed and has encouraged the restatement and analysis of such hypotheses in more elegant form. These propositions come to us with the best credentials; their consistency has been verified by a series of scholars over several generations.

2. Economic variables may be measured with relative ease. The ability to give critical variables a quantitative representation is virtually a precondition for speculating about relations among the variables and for verifying such relations. Many economic variables are subject to measurement on the same scale: money.

3. Our culture is so oriented to economic institutions that subjects can grasp the essential nature of an economic situation without too much difficulty. The subject can imagine himself in such a situation and can identify with a role as an economic actor, for he knows that he either has been or will be in comparable circumstances in his career. Further, in our culture it is relatively easy to induce and control the motivation of subjects in a simulated economic situation. This is done by using money as a reward.

4. Since the decisions of the subjects will be related to some monetary reward they will receive, it is possible to keep a quantitative record of their decision processes. This is necessary for testing hypotheses about such decision behavior and quite useful for formulating new hypotheses.

The initial studies we conducted were concerned with bilateral monopoly, a circumstance where a single buyer is confronted by a unique seller. The results for the equal-strength case were reported in *Bargaining and Group Decision Making* [which will be referred to as Siegel and Fouraker (1960)]. The unequal-strength bilateral monopoly situation is considered in the first section of this book (Chapters 2 to 6). The last part of the book is concerned with oligopoly models (Chapters 7 to 10).

We have several objectives in this study. First, we have a continuing interest in the ability of the experimental method to yield consistent and reasonable results. If the methodology employed in our previous work yields consistent results in the present setting, it will enable the experimenter to choose among alternative theories of bargaining behavior with some degree of reliability. Second, the process of giving a theory an experimental manifestation requires that some new variables be considered in an orderly fashion. The experimental method, by its very nature, requires the modification of some economic models. Finally, we have an interest in the implications of this work for the broader questions of human conflict. Each of these points will be considered at more length.

DISCRIMINATING AMONG ECONOMIC THEORIES BY MEANS OF EXPERIMENTATION

Economic conflict involving a few principals, such as occurs in bilateral monopoly and oligopoly, has attracted the interest of economists over an extended period of time. The result has been a rather confusing welter of theoretical propositions about such behavior. This is less the fault of economists than of businessmen; the adjustment of empirical oligopolies and bilateral monopolies has generated a confusing mass of configurations, mores, and customs. The absence of empirical uniformity has prevented the emergence of simple, unique generalizations that command everyone's acceptance. The basic problem in such a conflict situation is that an individual cannot adopt a simple maximizing strategy in an invariant environment. His decision will alter the fortunes of others, thus changing the environment in which they take action. As others make appropriate adjustments, these changes affect the original participant. The parties are independent in their roles as decision makers, yet their welfare is mutually dependent. The phenomenon is a group adjustment process among sovereign parts, with a minimum of communication and coordination.

This is the same type of relation that received so much attention in the work of von Neumann and Morgenstern, *The Theory of Games and Economic Behavior* (1947).   The reinforcement of economic theory with the mathematics and general methodology of that magnificent work has provided the impetus for a broad front of new research; we hope this book is a proper element of that movement.

The various theoretical models are all *correct* in the sense that the conclusions follow logically from the premises.   Economic theory is usually presented in the classical scientific form: if A, B, and C are true, then D will follow.   The task is to identify the correct set of assumptions for a particular situation so that reliable predictions can be made.

Since logic alone is insufficient to help the economist choose among alternative models, he must either (1) make an empirical, naturalistic study of the actual means by which such adjustments are achieved or (2) attempt to simulate the phenomenon in a laboratory, where appropriate controls may help him understand the relation between certain critical variables and the resulting adjustments.   Since the relevant field data were not available to test the conflict models, we turned to the method of controlled experimentation.

MODIFICATION OF THE ECONOMIC MODELS

The experimental manifestation of an economic theory requires that some conditions not previously considered be given more specific recognition as variables.   The prime example is the type and amount of communication allowed among participants.   We tried to minimize the amount of social interaction among the participants in our experimental work: The subject did not know with whom he was bargaining, and he was allowed to communicate only by means of written bids.   This enabled us to (1) keep a record of the communications among subjects, (2) use the amount and type of communication as an independent variable, and (3) isolate the effect of other variables more precisely than would have been possible if subjects had been given an opportunity to communicate freely and directly. For our experimental work on bilateral monopoly we identified two information states: incomplete, where the subject knew only his own profits resulting from any decision; and complete, where the subject knew the decision and amount of profits accruing to his rival as well as his own profit position.

Controlled experimentation is conducive to hypothesis formation. Experimental results normally display more dispersion than is suggested by the theory under test, even when the central tendency of those results is consistent with the theoretical solution. The experimenter's explanation or interpretation of such dispersion constitutes hypotheses; these propositions suggest additional independent experimentation. The experimental process is a continuous one.

Some of the hypotheses we derived from the first experiments on bilateral monopoly involved the psychological characteristics of the bargainers. The major example is the level-of-aspiration phenomenon involved in bargaining; we are concerned with its role in the new bilateral monopoly and oligopoly settings.

CONFLICT AND ITS RESOLUTION

Our ultimate objective is an increased understanding of the nature of human conflict and how such conflict may be resolved in a constructive manner. Economic models, in addition to having the advantages sketched above, contain the essence of the conflict situation: It is in the mutual interest of the participants to come to *some* agreement, and this provides a cooperative aspect; however, given that an agreement will be achieved, the interests of the participants are opposed, and this is a basis for rivalry. It is our hope that continued controlled experiments in this setting will suggest some useful generalizations about the problem. It may be dangerous to employ such generalizations in an empirical situation without modifications, for our experimental models are quite austere. However, the effects of information conditions have been observed over enough experiments (here and elsewhere), and have exhibited sufficient consistency, to provide a strong basis for working hypotheses. The need is to develop more propositions of this nature. The process is a slow and costly one, but the progress is likely to be on a sound basis and therefore cumulative.

PART TWO

Bilateral Monopoly

CHAPTER 2

Theoretical Formulation

THE EQUAL-STRENGTH CASE

Perhaps the most general bilateral monopoly situation is one in which neither party has a structural advantage. We report in Siegel and Fouraker (1960) the results of experiments conducted under such simulated conditions. Those results may be summarized as follows:

Let the seller of the commodity have an average cost of production represented by the linear function

$$\frac{C}{Q} = A' + B'Q \tag{2.1}$$

where Q = quantity produced
C = total cost
A' and B' = parameters
Any contract which satisfies (2.1) will yield zero profits to the seller. Let the buyer's demand curve be represented by the linear function

$$\frac{R}{Q} = A - BQ \qquad (2.2)$$

where R = total revenue
A and B = parameters
Any contract which satisfies (2.2) will yield zero profit to the buyer. We assume that the buyer and seller attempt to maximize their respective profits π_b and π_s.

Negotiations were conducted as follows: One party proposed a price and quantity contract; the other party would either accept the proposal or make a counteroffer. Most pairs of buyers and sellers succeeded in arriving at a contract after protracted negotiation. The central tendency of such contracts was to the quantity which maximized joint profits and to the price which divided those joint profits equally. This solution is shown in Figure 2.1.

Joint profits are defined as

$$\pi_b + \pi_s = R - C$$
$$= AQ - BQ^2 - A'Q - B'Q^2. \qquad (2.3)$$

This function is maximized by that value of Q which makes the first derivative zero and the second derivative negative:

$$\frac{d(\pi_b + \pi_s)}{dQ} = A - 2BQ - A' - 2B'Q = 0$$
$$\frac{d^2(\pi_b + \pi_s)}{dQ^2} = -2B - 2B' < 0.$$

The resulting quantity, which maximizes joint payoff, is designated Q_p and is

$$Q_p = \frac{A - A'}{2B + 2B'}. \qquad (2.4)$$

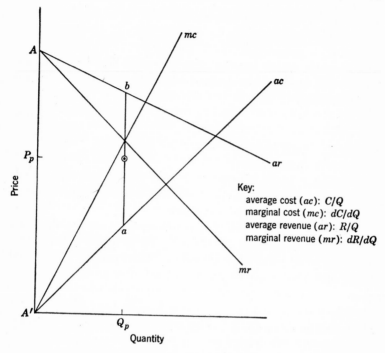

FIGURE 2.1   Central tendency (P_p, Q_p) of contracts under equal-strength bilateral monopoly.

The set of prices between the average revenue and the average cost functions associated with this quantity is defined as the Paretian optima (line segment ab in Figure 2.1).   Any contract which is an element of this set has the following characteristic: It is impossible to move to any other contract and improve the profit position of both parties; indeed, any change will worsen the profit position of at least one of the parties.   Our observed central tendency was to the midpoint of the Paretian optimal set (contract P_p, Q_p in Figure 2.1); price P_p results in an equal division of the maximum joint profits and is defined

$$P_p = \frac{AB' + A'B}{B + B'}. \qquad (2.5)$$

THE UNEQUAL–STRENGTH CASE: PRICE LEADERSHIP MODELS

In view of the results from the equal-strength bilateral monopoly models, the price leadership case suggested by Bowley (1928) is of particular interest. Under this structure one of the parties has the power to establish the price at which the exchange will take place; the other party has the power to choose the quantity which will be exchanged at the established price. The role of price leader is a privileged one: for normal linear functions the price leader will receive between two-thirds and all of the joint profits, according to the Bowley model. This asymmetric power relationship results in an equilibrium solution that is *not* an element of the Paretian optima.

Assume that both parties seek to maximize their individual profits and that the seller is the price leader. The buyer's profits are defined as

$$\pi_b = R - PQ$$
$$= AQ - BQ^2 - PQ \qquad (2.6)$$

where P is the price set by the seller and Q is the quantity selected by the buyer. The buyer's profits, within the constraints of the established price, are maximized when he selects a quantity so that the first derivative of Equation (2.6) is zero, provided the second derivative is negative. That is,

$$\frac{d\pi_b}{dQ} = A - 2BQ - P = 0$$
$$Q = \frac{A - P}{2B}. \qquad (2.7)$$

This adjustment equates the buyer's marginal revenue ($A - 2BQ$) with his marginal cost (P). The seller's profit is defined as

$$\pi_s = PQ - C$$
$$= PQ - A'Q - B'Q^2. \qquad (2.8)$$

It is assumed that the seller either knows or will discover that the buyer's quantity selection will be as indicated in Equation

(2.7). If we substitute this value for Q in Equation (2.8), we may write the seller's profit as

$$\pi_s = \frac{1}{2B}\left(AP - P^2 - A'A + A'P - \frac{B'A^2}{2B} + \frac{AB'P}{B} - \frac{B'P^2}{2B}\right).$$
$$(2.9)$$

To derive the price choice which renders Equation (2.9) a maximum, take the first derivative of π_s with respect to P, equate this function to zero, and solve for P (noting that the second derivative is negative). That is,

$$\frac{d\pi_s}{dP} = \frac{1}{2B}\left(A - 2P + A' + \frac{AB'}{B} - \frac{B'P}{B}\right) = 0. \quad (2.10)$$

Since $1/2B > 0$, the Bowley price is

$$P_b = \frac{AB + A'B + AB'}{2B + B'}. \quad (2.11)$$

If the seller chooses this price, the buyer will respond with the Bowley quantity selection of

$$Q_b = \frac{A - A'}{2B' + 4B}. \quad (2.12)$$

The price and quantity strategies indicated by (2.11) and (2.12) are equilibrium strategies in the game-theory sense. If the seller chooses the price P_b shown in (2.11), the buyer maximizes on that transaction by choosing the quantity Q_b shown in (2.12). If the buyer is going to choose a maximizing quantity, the highest profit accrues to the seller when he chooses price P_b.

It follows that the Bowley quantity is less than the Pareto quantity:

$$Q_b = \frac{A - A'}{2B' + 4B} < Q_p = \frac{A - A'}{2B' + 2B}. \quad (2.13)$$

It would be possible for bilateral monopolists who had reached an agreement at the Bowley point to increase their profits by moving to some contract that was an element on a subset of the

Paretian optima.   This condition led Fellner (1947) to reject the
Bowley solution in favor of some solution on the Paretian optima.
Since we had established a tendency to the midpoint of the
Paretian optimal set under equal-strength bilateral monopoly
[Siegel and Fouraker (1960)], we took this contract (P_p, Q_p) as
the basis for an alternative hypothesis to the Bowley contract
(P_b, Q_b).   We shall call the contract (P_p, Q_p) the Pareto solution
for purposes of simplicity.

These considerations may be summarized by means of Figure
2.2.   The seller, in the role of the price leader, assumes that the

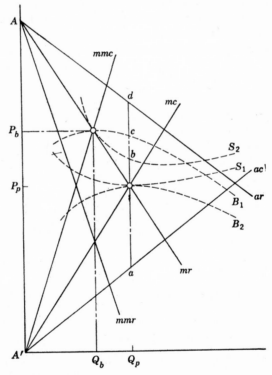

FIGURE 2.2   The bilateral monopoly model for price
leadership.

buyer will choose the quantity determined by the intersection of the established price and the buyer's marginal revenue function, according to the Bowley model. The seller considers mr as the demand confronting his concern and maximizes by choosing the price P_b, since the resulting quantity Q_b is associated with the intersection of his marginal cost and what he considers to be his marginal revenue mmr. (This function is marginal to the marginal revenue curve.) If the buyer always maximizes in response to a price quotation (i.e., chooses a contract that is on mr), the most favorable contract to the seller is (P_b, Q_b), where mr is tangent to the highest feasible isoprofit curve of the seller S_2. This solution results in a profit to the buyer associated with his isoprofit curve B_1. It would be possible for both buyer and seller to move to more favorable isoprofit curves if they could exchange Q_p at some price in the subset cb of the Paretian optimal set of prices ad.

An alternative solution is (P_p, Q_p), the contract which yields an equal division of maximum joint profits, indicated by the intersection of the marginal functions in this example. This is a quasi-equilibrium point, for the isoprofit curves S_1 and B_2 are tangent at (P_p, Q_p) and have slopes of zero at the point of tangency. If the seller quotes P_p, the buyer responds with Q_p, which is the best choice for both parties, given that P_p has been chosen [see Fouraker (1957)]. Note that the minima of the seller's isoprofit curves generate his marginal cost function, while the maxima of the buyer's isoprofit curves generate his marginal revenue function.

THE EXPERIMENTAL CONDITIONS AND STATEMENT OF HYPOTHESES

To obtain an experimental representation of an economic model, it is often necessary to incorporate variables which are not present in the original theory. From our previous work on bilateral monopoly and from our pilot work for the present experiments, it appeared that three experimental variables might affect the central tendency of contracts negotiated within the structure of price leadership. These variables were (1) amount of information, (2) form of the bidding, (3) incidence of culturally reinforced or prominent contracts, such as one involving an equal division of profits. It was decided to allow each of these variables to take on two states, one expected to be favorable to the Bowley solution and one expected to be favorable to the Paretian optimal solution.

In general we expected the Bowley solution to obtain because of its strong equilibrium properties. Relative to the information variable, it appeared that the condition of *incomplete* information (in which a participant knows only his own profit resulting from a contract) would tend to favor the Bowley solution. The equilibrium structure of the situation could be identified under incomplete information, while Pareto optimal nonequilibrium solutions could be identified only under *complete* information (in which the participant knows the profits accruing to both parties as the result of a contract). Therefore complete information does not favor the Bowley solution. Complete information makes it possible to identify some non-Bowley solution, such as (P_p, Q_p), and conceivably to move toward it; so this condition is designated as favoring the Pareto solution.

The form of the negotiations might be either a single, once-and-for-all transaction or a sequence of price and quantity transactions having profits associated with each bid. The single transaction would seem to favor equilibrium behavior (and thus the Bowley solution), for there is no opportunity for effective communication in the market. Repeated bidding makes it possible for the parties to communicate [Luce and Raiffa (1957)] and possibly to achieve some nonequilibrium solution by a learning process. The probability of the parties' arriving at a Paretian optimal solution seems greater with repeated bidding.

Pigou (1908) and Schelling (1957) indicate that a contract involving an equal division of joint profits has an ethical appeal in our culture. If a feasible contract on the Paretian optima involves an equal division of profits, and the Bowley solution

TABLE 2.1   Combinations of Experimental Conditions and Related Hypotheses

Experiment	Information	Form of bidding	Position of equal split	Predicted solution
1	C	S	E_b	Bowley point
2	C	S	E_p	Bowley point
3	I	R	E_p	Bowley point
4	C	R	E_b	Bowley point
5	C	R	E_p	Pareto point
6	I	S	E_b*	
7	I	S	E_p*	
8	I	R	$E_b\dagger$	

* Eliminated because I and S are incompatible.

† Unnecessary in that altering the position of the equal split (from experiment 3) should not affect the results under incomplete information.

Key: I = incomplete information
       C = complete information
       S = single transaction
       R = repeated transactions
       E_b = equal-split payoff at Bowley point
       E_p = equal-split payoff on the Paretian optima

does not, the contract (P_p, Q_p) will be favored. If the profits are transformed so that the payoff at the Bowley point is in equal parts, while no such contract appears as an element of the (discrete) Paretian optimal set, the Bowley solution is favored.*

With three experimental variables, each taking on two states, $2^3 = 8$ possible experiments may be conducted. These combinations of experimental variables are listed in Table 2.1. Only five of the possible eight combinations were conducted as experiments. The sixth and seventh were dropped because one-shot

* There is always some price which would divide the maximum joint profits equally, but it does not have to be offered as a possible choice in an experiment if discrete prices are listed and interpolation is not permitted. All profit transformations to make the Bowley contract yield equal profits must, of necessity, make the implied revenue and cost functions nonlinear.

price bids under incomplete information would be pointless: the situation would contain no guide to intelligent behavior. The eighth combination, IRE_b (incomplete information, repeated bidding, equal-split at Bowley point), was dropped because it was hypothesized that IRE_p would lead to the Bowley solution, and this expected result would not be changed by altering the equal-split position to favor the Bowley solution. Indeed, the incidence of the equal-split is unimportant under incomplete information, for the participants cannot identify which contract is thus ethically reinforced. Therefore, condition E_p is likely to become effective only in conjunction with C; complete information enables the parties mutually to identify a specific non-Bowley contract. Even so, the parties may need some means, such as sequential bidding, to move toward such a contract once it is identified.

In the next chapter the procedures of the experiments are discussed in detail.

CHAPTER 3

Experimental Procedures

To test the hypotheses of the research concerning bilateral monopoly, we conducted a series of five experiments. Each experiment in the series was designed to test one or more different hypotheses, and therefore each one had certain distinctive controls, distinctive procedures related to the various independent and dependent variables, and so forth. The common features of the experiments, however, loom larger than the differences among them. The purpose of this chapter is to describe those features of the experimental procedures which were common to all the experiments concerning bilateral monopoly. The distinctive procedures of particular experiments will be presented and discussed in later chapters, where the experiments are reported.

SUBJECTS

In all, 106 individual subjects participated in the various bilateral monopoly experiments, serving in 53 different bargaining pairs. All subjects were male undergraduates from The Pennsylvania State University; at the time of recruitment, they were told only that they would be paid for participating in a research project. They were assured that they would not be exposed to noxious stimuli. The amount of money that could be earned was not specified, nor was the nature of their participation. Each experimental session was conducted with different subjects; no subject participated in more than one session.

PROCEDURES

An experimental session began with the subjects coming to an assigned room, where they were met individually by the experimenters. Each subject was given a number corresponding to the order of his arrival. After all subjects for the session had arrived, each exchanged his number for a second one, randomly drawn. This second number identified the subject in the experiment. Thus, the order in which the various subjects arrived did not determine their identifying number in the experiment.

Before the subjects arrived at the experimental session, a list of numbers from 1 to n was set up for that session. (The n's in the various sessions varied from 20 to 24.) Then, by use of a table of random numbers, these numbers were paired. The paired numbers represented the various bargaining teams. On the basis of the toss of a coin, one of the numbers in each pair was designated as the buyer and the other as the seller.* For

---

* The price leadership role was not randomized over the buyer-seller conditions. From Siegel and Fouraker (1960) it was concluded that the buyer-seller classification did not exercise a significant influence on the

all experimental sessions in which information levels were to be compared, another toss of a coin determined whether the pair was assigned to have complete or incomplete information.

Reference to this prepared list determined whether each subject was a buyer or a seller, the identity of his bargaining partner, and whether, in the appropriate circumstances, he was to bargain under complete or incomplete information. That is, each of these subject assignments was determined by random procedures.

After the subjects had received their identifying numbers and the experimenter had determined their assignments by referring to the prepared sheet, the buyers were sent to one room and the sellers to another. When information level was varied, four rooms were used in order to separate the buyers and sellers with complete information from those with incomplete information. Once in their rooms, subjects were told whether they were buyers or sellers. Each subject was given printed instructions, a profit table,* and a sheet for recording the price and quantity bids and his profits. The instructions were read, and each subject had his own copy of them to use throughout the experimental session.

After hearing the instructions read, the subjects were given the opportunity to ask questions. Most of the questions centered on interpreting and using the profit tables. Specific examples were presented to clarify the use of the tables. The fact was emphasized that any profit earned during the session would become the subject's personal property.

The period of instructions lasted about 20 minutes. Then the

---

division of profits in the equal-strength case. In all the following experiments the seller was allowed to be the price leader because in our culture this is more often the case.

* The appendixes contain the various instructions and profit tables used by buyers and sellers in the different experiments. The functions on which the tables are based are presented in the following chapters in connection with discussions of specific hypotheses and their tests. References to specific sets of instructions and profit tables in the appendixes are made at appropriate places in the following chapters.

subjects were taken individually into a large room containing separate cubicles, each furnished with a desk and a chair. These cubicles were formed by partitions extending about halfway to the ceiling. Once in his assigned cubicle, a subject could not see anyone except the research personnel; nor could he be seen by anyone but them. Negotiations were conducted in silence, with no communication permitted between the participants other than the written bids.

After all subjects had been directed to their assigned cubicles, a general announcement was made calling for the bargaining to begin. The seller, as price leader, initiated the process by writing a price bid on the sheet provided for that purpose. This price was recorded by a research assistant, who then informed the buyer of the price which would prevail for the transaction. In the light of this information, the buyer made his quantity selection, thus establishing the profit for himself and the seller.

When the bargaining was in the form of a single transaction, it was ended as soon as the buyer made his quantity choice and the seller was informed of this decision. After the transaction the buyers and sellers remained in their cubicles until they were paid the actual amounts they had negotiated; they were then dismissed from separate exits so that they would not come into contact with their bargaining opponent.

When the bargaining was in the form of repeated transactions, the bidding process was identical for each transaction in the series. The seller was always informed of the buyer's quantity choice before he was required to make the next price offer of the series. When repeated bidding was used, the first three transactions were practice trials and were provided to let the subjects become accustomed to the use of the profit table; the profit from these trials was not included in determining the cash payoff. After the practice trials, the sessions consisted of 19 regular transactions, an announced final trial, plus a special twenty-first trial, run under slightly different conditions. In a general announcement preceding the twentieth trial, all subjects were told that the following bid would be their final one; the objective was to hold end effects constant on both the twentieth and twenty-first trials. After the twentieth trial, however, it was announced that an additional transaction was to be run under the condition that all entries in the profit table were to be tripled—i.e., all profits and losses for this one transaction were to be three times the amount shown on the table. After this transaction was completed, the buyers and sellers were led to separate rooms where their profits were totaled, and each was paid in cash.

For each experiment in the series, each subject, upon being paid, was asked not to divulge the nature of the study or the amount of money earned, as doing so might affect the results of future experiments. Subsequent analysis indicated that subjects were probably keeping this trust.

THE PAYOFF MATRIX

The payoff tables given to the subjects showed the levels of profit corresponding to the various combinations of price and quantity choices. Quantity choices ranged from 0 to 18, and price choices from 1 to 16. The prices that the seller might select were listed along the left margin, while the top row consisted of possible quantity selections for the buyer. Entered in the body of the table, at the intersection of each price row and quantity column, were the profits associated with these bids. For subjects bargaining under complete information each entry in the profit table (see Appendix I) contained the payoff to both buyer and seller, while the bargaining pairs under incomplete information were furnished with tables which contained only the payoff to the subject making the decision, not showing the payoff to his rival (see Appendix III).

The payoff matrices were derived from hypothetical cost and revenue functions. If the buyer chose a quantity of zero, it was assumed that he wished to maintain the status quo; such a contract was given the arbitrary value $\pi_b = 0$, $\pi_s = 0$ and held constant over the several experiments, regardless of the transformation involved.

DISCUSSION OF THE PROCEDURES

One purpose of the experimental procedures was to minimize interpersonal reactions between subjects. Thus, the bargainers were physically separated, and they communicated only through an intermediary. Subjects did not know the identities of their bargaining rivals. The bargaining was conducted in silence, to preclude the possibility that a subject might identify his opponent by recognizing his voice. Moreover, the buyers and sellers were given instructions in separate rooms so that they could not see their possible bargaining rivals during the instruction period.

This procedure eliminates certain variables which may well be important in bargaining—variables connected with interpersonal perceptions, prejudices, incompatibilities, etc. It is our belief that such variables should be either systematically studied or controlled in the experimentation on bargaining. It cannot be assumed that such variables may simply be neglected. We have chosen to control these variables at this stage of our research program, with the intention of manipulating and studying them systematically in future studies.

Another purpose of our experimental procedures was to randomize the effects of certain variables which were not of interest to us at the present stage of our research. We used randomization procedures to cancel any possible effects of arrival of subjects, thinking that early and late comers might differ in strength of motivation to participate, utility of money, compulsiveness, etc.—variables we did not wish to study systematically at this time. We also used randomization procedures to control those preferences which may draw particular sellers and buyers together in the marketplace.

CHAPTER 4

Experimental Tests of Alternative Models

The theoretical models presented in Chapter 2 offer two distinct solutions to the price leadership bilateral monopoly bargaining situation. It was shown that if

A = price axis intercept of average revenue function
A' = price axis intercept of average cost function
B = slope (negative) of average revenue function
B' = slope of average cost function
Q = quantity

then the price and quantity predicted by Bowley are

$$P_b = \frac{AB + A'B + AB'}{2B + B'} \qquad (2.11)$$

$$Q_b = \frac{A - A'}{2B' + 4B} \qquad (2.12)$$

whereas the quantity which maximizes joint profits Q_p is

$$Q_p = \frac{A - A'}{2B' + 2B}. \qquad (2.4)$$

When the even division of payoff appears explicitly on the Paretian optimal set the equal-split price P_p is a feasible choice and is defined as

$$P_p = \frac{AB' + A'B}{B + B'}. \qquad (2.5)$$

This chapter presents the experiments which were designed to test the prediction that price leadership bilateral monopoly contracts would support either the Bowley or the Pareto solution, depending on the combination of three experimental variables. The three relevant variables—information conditions, form of the bidding, and position of the equal payoff—were experimentally manipulated in order to test the hypotheses.

The following combinations of experimental conditions were studied:

Experiment 1. Complete information, single transaction, and equal-split payoff at the Bowley point: CSE_b

Experiment 2. Complete information, single transaction, and equal-split payoff on the Paretian optima: CSE_p

Experiment 3. Incomplete information, repeated transactions, and equal-split payoff on the Paretian optima: IRE_p

Experiment 4. Complete information, repeated transactions, and equal-split payoff at the Bowley point: CRE_b

Experiment 5. Complete information, repeated transactions, and equal-split payoff on the Paretian optima: CRE_p

The order of the experiments reported here starts with the set of conditions thought to most strongly favor the Bowley solution (experiment 1 above) and ends with the only set of conditions thought to be favorable to a Pareto solution (experiment 5 above).

In the studies reported below, the following set of parameters was used initially in deriving the expected values associated with the alternative theories: $A = 19$, $A' = -11$, $B = 0.5$, $B' = 0.5$. Thus, for each study, the operational statements of the Bowley point and the joint maximum (Paretian optimal set) in terms of the parameters are as follows:

The Bowley point:

$$P_b = \frac{AB + A'B + AB'}{2B + B'} = \frac{19(0.5) + (-11)(0.5) + 19(0.5)}{2(0.5) + 0.5} = 9$$

$$Q_b = \frac{A - A'}{2B' + 4B} = \frac{19 - (-11)}{2(0.5) + 4(0.5)} = 10.$$

The Paretian optimal set:

$$Q_p = \frac{A - A'}{2B' + 2B} = \frac{19 - (-11)}{2(0.5) + 2(0.5)} = 15.$$

For those studies for which the Pareto set $Q_p = 15$ includes an even division of joint payoff, the equal-split price P_p is operationally defined as follows:

$$P_p = \frac{AB' + A'B}{B + B'} = \frac{19(0.5) + (-11)(0.5)}{0.5 + 0.5} = 4.$$

It should be noted that although the Bowley point ($P_b = 9$, $Q_b = 10$) and the joint maximum ($Q_p = 15$) do not vary from study to study, the payoffs to the bargainers cannot remain constant because they are affected by manipulation of the position of the equal-split, the form of the bidding, etc. Therefore, for each study, a linear transformation was applied to all payoffs resulting from the above parameters. This transformation, which did not change the quantity predictions, was used to (1) manipulate the equal-split point and (2) keep the total possible amount of joint profit equal for all studies.

EXPERIMENT 1: COMPLETE INFORMATION, A SINGLE TRANSACTION, AND EQUAL–SPLIT PAYOFF AT THE BOWLEY POINT

Introduction

According to the theoretical formulation in Chapter 2, the set of conditions which should lead bargainers to show the greatest tendency to the Bowley solution is the CSE_b combination.   For all the experiments under consideration, this particular combination of conditions is unique in that it contains *two* forces favorable to the Bowley solution, whereas all other combinations contain only one.   The two conditions favoring this solution are:

1. Single transaction: The lack of opportunity for communication through a series of transactions eliminates the possibility of using threat of punishment, or reward, in order to reach a solution on the Paretian optimal set.
2. Equal payoff at the Bowley point: Under this condition the Bowley point, besides being a strong equilibrium solution in itself, is given the added appeal of being an ethical or "fair" solution, in that the participants can divide joint profits equally at that point.

The Experimental Test

Subjects and Procedure.   Twenty male undergraduate students (10 bargaining pairs) participated in this experiment.   Each subject was given a double-entry profit table* containing both his own and his rival's payoffs, and a set of printed instructions.

* Entries in the profit table are shown in dollars, the following transformations having been applied:

Seller's profits: $\pi_s = .04\pi_s - 1.56$
Buyer's profits: $\pi_b = .04\pi_b + 2.44.$

An exception to this transformation was the zero payoff to the buyer and seller for the contracts involving a zero quantity choice by the buyer, as noted above.

The profit table is shown in Appendix I. The instructions were as follows:

Instructions

The National Science Foundation and the Ford Foundation have provided funds for the conduct of research regarding economic decisions. If you follow instructions carefully and make an appropriate decision, you will earn an appreciable amount of money. *You may keep all the money you earn.* You cannot lose your own money, but a poor choice can result in small or no profit to you.

You will be paired, at random, with another person. You will not see this person or speak with him at any time. You will never know the identity of your opponent, nor will he be aware of yours.

You and your anonymous partner will engage in a single transaction by means of a written bid. Imagine that you and he are exchanging some commodity. One of you will be selected (at random) to act as the seller of this commodity, the other will act as the buyer. You must deal only with your unknown counterpart and he must deal only with you.

You will be furnished with a table showing the various levels of profit you can attain. Prices are listed on the left hand side of the table, quantities across the top. The upper figure in each box of the body of the table represents the profit the *buyer* will receive, depending upon the price and quantity selected. The lower figure in each box represents the profit the *seller* receives for the associated price and quantity choices. For example, at a price of 16 and a quantity of 8, the buyer's profit is $2.12 and the seller's profit is $5.80. All figures in the body of the table are in dollars.

The *seller* will start the transaction by quoting a price. He may select any one of the prices on the left hand side of the table. The price he has selected will be recorded by an experimental assistant on a yellow sheet provided for that purpose.

The yellow sheet then is taken by the assistant to the *buyer*. He sees the price which has been established for the transaction. In the light of this information he selects the quantity to be exchanged at this price. He may choose any of the quantities across the top of the table. In other words, the seller chooses the price line, the buyer chooses the quantity column. The box where these choices intersect indicates the amount of profit you receive for the transaction, the upper figure being the buyer's profit, the lower figure being the seller's profit.

After the buyer has made his quantity choice the seller will be informed of the decision and both buyer and seller will be paid the amount of money (profit) indicated in the table.   This will be done in separate counting rooms, so you will not see the person with whom you have been bidding.

Are there any questions?

As was explained in Chapter 3, subjects were randomized into pairs and into the roles of buyer and seller and were taken individually to cubicles where they were isolated from all persons other than the experimenters and other research personnel. Each bargaining pair participated in a single transaction, the seller setting the price at which the exchange would take place, the buyer naming the quantity to be exchanged at this price. Negotiations were conducted in silence by means of written bids transmitted by the research personnel.

TABLE 4.1   Price and Quantity Agreed upon in Contracts Reached by Bargaining Pairs
(Experiment 1, CSE_b)

Bargaining pair	Price	Quantity	Observation supports, Bowley: B, Pareto: P
1	11	7	B
2	9	10	B
3	9	10	B
4	9	10	B
5	9	10	B
6	9	10	B
7	9	10	B
8	9	11	B
9	9	11	B
10	7	12	P, B
Mean	9.00	10.10	
Median	9	10	

Results.   Table 4.1 contains the price and quantity observations for the 10 bargaining pairs.

The hypothesis under test here is that contracts will support the Bowley solution ($P_b = 9$, $Q_b = 10$) rather than the Pareto solution ($Q_p = 15$, $7 < P_p < 8$).   If a bargaining pair negotiates a contract with both a price and a quantity closer to one of the solutions, it is counted as an observation in support of that solution; if the quoted price supports one model but the quantity selection supports the other, it is counted as one-half an observation in support of each solution.   Thus, the first nine bargaining pairs had contracts closer to the Bowley solution than to the Pareto solution; in the tenth pair the seller named a price closer to the Pareto solution, but the buyer chose a quantity closer to the Bowley solution.   With 9.5 observations in support of the Bowley prediction and .5 in support of the Pareto alternative, it is apparent that the first experiment supports the Bowley model.   The incidence is significant against the null hypothesis (one-tailed binomial test, $p < .01$).   The null hypothesis in this situation would be that each model had an equal chance of being supported by an observation.

This conclusion is supported by the sample averages: the mean and median prices are 9, the Bowley prediction; the mean quantity is 10.10, only .10 units from the Bowley prediction but 4.9 units from the Pareto amount.   The median quantity is precisely the Bowley amount.

Discussion

The data are consistent with the hypothesis drawn from the Bowley model that, with the parameters used, contracts will tend to be negotiated at a price of 9 and a quantity of 10.   It is interesting to note that while 8 of 10 sellers named exactly the Bowley price, only 6 of 10 buyers chose the Bowley quantity.   Two cooperative buyers chose quantities of 11 rather than the maximizing quantity of 10; thus, by imposing only a 2-cent loss on themselves, they gave their unknown opponent an extra 38 cents. Additional discussion of these data will be given in Chapter 6.

EXPERIMENT 2: COMPLETE INFORMATION, A SINGLE TRANSACTION, AND EQUAL–SPLIT PAYOFF ON THE PARETIAN OPTIMA

Introduction

In the second experiment, as in the first, subjects bargained under complete information, and the negotiations consisted of a single transaction. Experiment 2 differed from experiment 1 in the location of the equal-split payoff; in experiment 2 the equal-split payoff was located on the Paretian optima. Although it is true for this experiment that a "fair," "ethical," or "prominent" solution exists on the Paretian optima, it is also true that a seller would prefer a Bowley contract, for at the Bowley solution he makes a larger profit than at the equal-split price of 4. The set of conditions contains only one condition specifically favorable to a Bowley solution: the single transaction condition, which eliminates the possibility of "communication" between bargainers such as can be achieved in repeated transactions. The hypothesis guiding the experiment is that this force alone would be strong enough to produce results consistent with the Bowley solution.

The Experimental Test

Subjects and Procedure. The subjects whose contracts provided a test of the hypothesis were 20 male undergraduates (none of whom participated in previous studies), serving in 10 bargaining pairs. Instructions and a double-entry profit table* containing the profits to both buyer and seller were given to each subject (see Appendix II). Subjects were randomized into pairs and into buyer and seller roles. Buyers were given instructions in one room and sellers in another, to preserve the anonymity of

---

* Buyer and seller profit entries, shown in dollars, were arrived at by means of the following transformations (except for the arbitrary value assigned to zero buyer responses):

$$\pi_b = 0.04\pi_b + 0.44$$
$$\pi_s = 0.04\pi_s + 0.44.$$

TABLE 4.2   Price and Quantity Agreed upon in Contracts Reached by Bargaining Pairs
(Experiment 2, CSE_p)

Pair	Price	Quantity	Observation supports
11	9	7	B
12	9	8	B
13	11	8	B
14	10	9	B
15	9	10	B
16	9	10	B
17	9	10	B
18	9	10	B
19	9	10	B
20	10	10	B
Mean	9.40	9.20	
Median	9	10	

the pairs. Subjects were taken individually to their assigned cubicles, where they participated in a single transaction. No communications other than the written bids were permitted between the participants.

Results. Table 4.2 presents the data relevant to the research hypothesis. The price and quantity contracts agreed upon by all bargaining pairs are shown in this table.

The hypothesis under test here is that contracts will support the Bowley solution ($P_b = 9$, $Q_b = 10$) rather than the Pareto solution ($P_p = 4$, $Q_p = 15$). All 10 pairs negotiated contracts closer to the Bowley point, providing strong support for this solution. The difference from the null hypothesis is significant (one-tailed binomial test, $p < .001$).

Again the median price and median quantity have exactly the Bowley values; the mean price and quantity are closer to the Bowley than to the Pareto predictions, as expected.

Discussion

The data of the experimental test offer strong support for the Bowley hypothesis.

The buyers, in general, indicated displeasure upon being informed of the seller's price choices, but most of them chose quantities to maximize their own profits. Several buyers, however, chose to punish the sellers by taking a loss for themselves in such a manner that they would inflict even greater losses on their anonymous counterparts. In pair 11, for example, the buyer cut his own profit by 18 cents when he chose a quantity of 7 instead of 10, but in so doing he reduced his seller's profit by $1.38. Only one buyer took a loss so that the seller could earn more; the buyer in pair 20 chose a quantity of 10 rather than 9, reducing his profits by 2 cents but increasing the seller's profits by 46 cents (see Appendix II). Additional discussion of these data will be given in Chapter 6.

EXPERIMENT 3: INCOMPLETE INFORMATION, REPEATED TRANSACTIONS, AND EQUAL-SPLIT PAYOFF ON THE PARETIAN OPTIMA

Introduction

In the first two experiments, negotiations consisted of a single transaction. In experiment 3, in contrast, repeated transactions were used. Bargainers negotiated under incomplete information, and the equal-split payoff was on the Paretian optima.

It is hypothesized that the incomplete-information condition in experiment 3 would dominate the other two conditions, and that the contracts therefore would stabilize at the Bowley solution. The significance of the condition of incomplete information is that neither party can identify the equal-split price P_p nor the fact that a "fair" solution exists along the Paretian optima. For that matter, neither can even identify the joint maximizing quantity. Thus it seemed unlikely that a contract would be reached along this optimal set, especially since a strong equilibrium is available as an alternative. In the light of the information afforded them, the buyer and seller have no a priori reason for not being satisfied with Bowley strategies.

The Experimental Test

Subjects and Procedure.   The subjects of the third experimental session were 22 male undergraduate students (11 bargaining pairs).*   None of them had participated in any of the previous bargaining experiments.

Subjects were randomized into pairs and into buyer and seller roles and were given sets of instructions and profit tables† (see Appendix III).   The profit table furnished to each buyer showed only the profits to a buyer; a seller's profit table showed only the profits to a seller.   After the instruction period the buyers and sellers were led individually to their assigned cubicles.   The experimental session consisted of a total of 24 transactions; the seller first named a price, and the buyer then named a quantity for each transaction.   The 24 transactions consisted of 3 practice trials, 19 regular transactions, an announced final regular transaction, and a special transaction which will be considered later.

Results.   The last regular transaction, number 19, is taken to represent the relevant statistic,‡ and contracts from this trans-

---

* Although 22 subjects (11 pairs) started the experiment, 2 pairs had to be dropped since 1 person in each of 2 bargaining pairs indicated that he did not understand the instructions; these pairs therefore are not included in the analysis.

† Profit table entries are in hundredths of a cent and were arrived at by means of the following transformations:

$$\pi_b = 20\pi_b + 220$$
$$\pi_s = 20\pi_s + 220.$$

‡ Inspection of the data revealed, in general, few differences among the average results of transactions 18, 19, and 20.   The number of transactions to be used was decided prior to the collection of data on the basis of pilot studies which indicated that 20 transactions would be sufficient for the average subject to reach equilibrium behavior.

The determination of the proper length for such an experiment is difficult. Some subjects need more transactions to approach equilibrium behavior— they are still engaged in a learning process when the experiment is terminated. If the experiment continues too long, however, subjects are likely to grow bored and begin to amuse themselves with unusual choice patterns. This is particularly true for some subjects who quickly identify and follow some equilibrium strategy.   The termination point is an attempt at compromise between these two sources of variation.

TABLE 4.3   Price and Quantity Agreed upon for the
Nineteenth Transaction
(Experiment 3, IRE_p)

Pair	Price	Quantity	Observation supports
21	8	11	B
22	8	12	B
23	8	11	B
24	10	10	B
25	8	11	B
26	8	11	B
27	7	12	B
28	14	5	B
29	5	14	P
Mean	8.44	10.78	
Median	8	11	

action were used to test the hypothesis that the Bowley price of 9
and quantity of 10 would be supported. The results of this
transaction are presented in Table 4.3. Complete protocols for
all nine bargaining pairs are presented in Appendix III.

The hypothesis under test here is that contracts resulting from
the nineteenth transaction will support the Bowley solution
($P_b = 9$, $Q_b = 10$) rather than the Pareto solution ($P_p = 4$,
$Q_p = 15$). Eight of the nine pairs performed in accordance with
this expectation. These results provide strong support for the
Bowley model. The variation from the null prediction is significant (binomial test, $p < .02$). However, one pair, 29, did
approximate the Pareto solution as a result of some rivalrous
signals on the buyer's part.* This tendency to defect from the
Bowley point is continued on the twentieth transaction, which
includes end effects. There, seven of the nine pairs supported

---

* A rivalrous signal by a buyer would take the form of a quantity response
which fell short of the amount required to maximize the buyer's profit.
This action reduces the buyer's profits, but it generally reduces the seller's
profits by an even larger amount. Further discussion is presented in
Chapter 6.

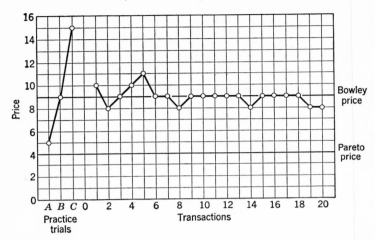

FIGURE 4.1   Median price bid for each transaction in experimental session 3: IRE_p.

the Bowley prediction, while two pairs (28 and 29) negotiated contracts closer to the Pareto solution.

The averages continue to support the Bowley values, however. The median price is 8, the median quantity 11. This is true on the twentieth transaction as well as the nineteenth. The mean contract of $\bar{P} = 8.44$, $\bar{Q} = 10.78$ on the nineteenth transaction supports the Bowley point; on the twentieth transaction the mean values are even closer: $\bar{P} = 8.78$, $\bar{Q} = 10.22$. Median price and quantity bids are shown in Figures 4.1 and 4.2. Note that after the fifth transaction the median prices never deviate by more than one unit from the Bowley prediction.

Discussion

The variability of price and quantity bids in this experiment was greater than in the studies reported earlier, probably because of the limited information possessed by the subjects. Toward the end of the session, the quantity chooser was generally content to maximize his profits on each trial by choosing his optimal quantity. (This is reflected in the median choices shown in

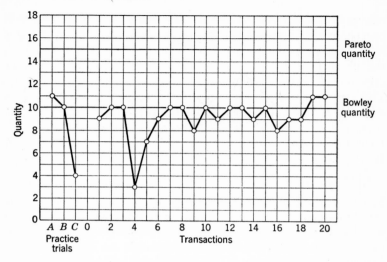

FIGURE 4.2   Median quantity bid for each transaction in experimental session 3: IRE_p.

Figure 4.2.)   From these choices, the price leader seemed able to behave as though he could discern the nature of the demand curve facing him and tended toward maximizing his own profits by approaching the Bowley point.   Additional discussion of these data will be given in Chapter 6.

EXPERIMENT 4: COMPLETE INFORMATION, REPEATED TRANSACTIONS, AND EQUAL–SPLIT PAYOFF AT THE BOWLEY POINT

Introduction

In experiment 4, subjects again negotiated via repeated transactions.   This experiment differs from the third, however, in two important respects: bargainers had complete information, and the equal-split payoff was at the Bowley point.   It seems that the Bowley solution is somewhat weaker for experiment 4 than for the first three, since both complete information and repeated transactions allow the possibility of communication by means of punishment and reward.   However, even though both buyer and seller might prefer some contract along the Paretian optimal set, the absence of a discrete "prominent" solution (i.e., an equal division of profits) along this set makes agreement difficult. Thus, while it was hypothesized that the Bowley solution should still obtain, it was recognized that the prediction was a weak one since the pull of the possibility for greater profits along the Paretian optima might offset somewhat the strength of the Bowley solution.

The Experimental Test

Subjects and Procedure.   The hypotheses concerning the fourth experimental session were tested with 20 male undergraduate subjects (10 bargaining pairs), none of whom participated in previous studies.   Subjects were randomly assigned into pairs and randomly designated as buyers or sellers.   Buyers and sellers were instructed in separate rooms, where each received a double-entry profit table,* containing the profits of both buyer and seller, and a set of printed instructions (see Appendix IV). The bargaining session consisted of 24 transactions (3 practice trials, 19 regular trials, a final trial, and a special final trial); the same procedure was used as in the third experimental session, and it is outlined in Chapter 3.

Results.   Table 4.4 contains the prices and quantities resulting from the nineteenth transaction in the fourth experimental session.   Complete protocols for all 10 bargaining pairs are presented in Appendix IV.

The hypothesis under test is that the Bowley solution ($P_b = 9$, $Q_b = 10$) will be supported.   Of the 10 contracts, 6.5 were closer

---

* Buyer and seller profit entries, in hundredths of a cent, were arrived at by means of the following transformations:

$$\pi_s = 20\pi_s - 780$$
$$\pi_b = 20\pi_b + 1220.$$

Again the buyer's quantity choice of zero was assigned the payoff of $\pi_b = 0$, $\pi_s = 0$.

TABLE 4.4   Price and Quantity Agreed upon for the Nineteenth Transaction
(Experiment 4, CRE_b)

Pair	Price	Quantity	Observation supports
30	9	9	B
31	7	11	P, B
32	9	9	B
33	16	1	B
34	8	11	P, B
35	8	13	P
36	13	3	B
37	7	16	P
38	8	12	P, B
39	9	10	B
Mean	9.4	9.5	
Median	8.5	10.5	

to the Bowley solution than to the Pareto solution, while 3.5 were closer to the Pareto solution. These results do not differ significantly from the null prediction; according to the binomial test, $p < .38$.

As expected, the model tendency is still toward the Bowley solution, but there is much more variability among the contracts than was the case in the first three experiments, suggesting that the strength of the Bowley solution is diminished under the conditions of experiment 4.

This tendency continues through the twentieth transaction, in which the support for the two theories is evenly divided.

The sample averages reflect the same considerations. The median contract for the nineteenth transaction was at a price of 8.5 and a quantity of 10.5; for the twentieth transaction, the comparable figures were 8 and 11.5. The mean contract for the nineteenth transaction was $\bar{P} = 9.4$, $\bar{Q} = 9.5$, amounts which are close to the Bowley amounts. For the twentieth transaction, the means moved toward the Pareto amounts: $\bar{P} = 7.4$, $\bar{Q} = 12.0$.

Figures 4.3 and 4.4 display the median price and quantity bids on each of the transactions in experiment 4.

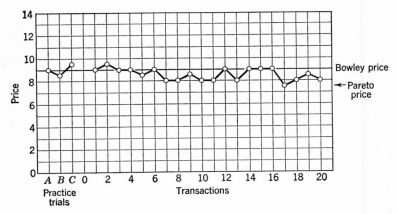

FIGURE 4.3   Median price bid for each transaction in experimental session 4: CRE_b.

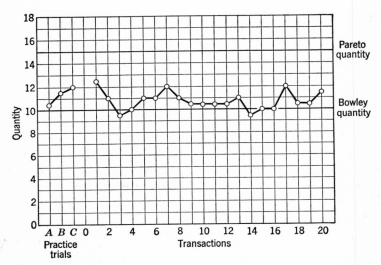

FIGURE 4.4   Median quantity bid for each transaction in experimental session 4: CRE_b.

Discussion

While these results, on balance, support the Bowley solution, the support is not strong.   The repeated transactions, in conjunction with complete information, tended to induce an increased attempt on the part of buyers to communicate by their quantity choices.   The absence of a prominent Pareto optimal contract made it difficult to communicate effectively, however.   Three pairs (35, 37, and 38) did manage to approximate the Pareto point; they created three different patterns in moving away from the Bowley point.   Additional discussion of these data will be given in Chapter 6.

EXPERIMENT 5: COMPLETE INFORMATION, REPEATED TRANSACTIONS, AND EQUAL-SPLIT PAYOFF ON THE PARETIAN OPTIMA

Introduction

If the Paretian optimal solution is to obtain for any experimental situation of bilateral monopoly with price leadership, it should obtain when negotiators have complete information, when they negotiate via repeated transactions, and when the equal-split payoff is located on the Paretian optima.   These were the circumstances in experiment 5, and thus the experiment was a test of the prediction that bargainers would negotiate contracts on the joint optimal solution.   The condition of complete information allows both the buyer and the seller to identify the "fair," equal division of profits associated with the Pareto solution, while repetitive bidding gives the buyer an opportunity to communicate through punishment and reward—to "teach" the seller which price he considers acceptable.

The Experimental Test

Subjects and Procedure.   Twenty-four male undergraduates (twelve bargaining pairs), none of whom participated in previous studies, served as subjects for the fifth experimental session.

TABLE 4.5   Price and Quantity Agreed upon for the
Nineteenth Transaction
(Experiment 5, CRE_p)

Pair	Price	Quantity	Observation supports
40	9	10	B
41	9	10	B
42	11	4	B
43	4	15	P
44	5	14	P
45	5	0	P, B
46	5	0	P, B
47	4	15	P
48	4	15	P
49	4	15	P
50	4	8	P, B
51	9	14	B, P
Mean	6.08	10.00	
Median	5.00	12.00	

The procedures followed in the execution of this session were precisely the same as those followed in the immediately previous two
sessions (described earlier).   Randomly paired buyers and sellers
were isolated and given instructions and a double-entry profit
table* containing the profits both to the buyer and to the seller
(see Appendix V).   Negotiations were conducted in silence, with
each bargaining pair participating in 24 transactions by means of
written bids.   As in the immediately previous two sessions, there
were 3 practice trials, 19 regular trials, a final trial, and a special
final trial.

Results.   Table 4.5 shows the price and quantity bids resulting
from the nineteenth transaction.   Complete protocols for all 12
bargaining pairs are presented in Appendix V.

* Profit entries, in hundredths of a cent, were arrived at by means of the
following transformations:
$$\pi_b = 20\pi_b + 220$$
$$\pi_s = 20\pi_s + 220.$$

The hypothesis under test here is that contracts resulting from the nineteenth transaction will support the Pareto contract ($P_p = 4$, $Q_p = 15$) rather than the Bowley solution ($P_b = 9$, $Q_b = 10$).

Of the 12 contracts, 5 support the Bowley prediction and 7 support the Pareto prediction. This is the only experiment of the five which yielded a preponderance of contracts closer to the Pareto solution. While this result is not significant against the null hypothesis (according to the binomial test, $p < .4$), it does indicate the direction of change resulting from the altered state of the control variables.

This conclusion is reinforced when the contracts negotiated on the twentieth trial are examined. Only 2.5 observations support the Bowley prediction, while the remaining 9.5 support the Pareto prediction. According to the binomial test, this result is significant against the null hypothesis at $p < .08$.

The averages support no simple interpretation. On the nineteenth transaction, the mean price $\bar{P} = 6.08$ is nearer the Pareto value $P_p = 4$ than the Bowley value $P_b = 9$. The median price, 5, also supports the Pareto prediction. The mean quantity on the

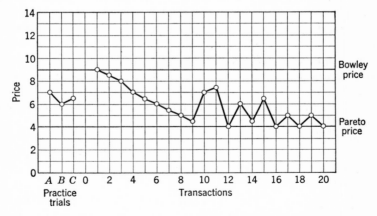

FIGURE 4.5 Median price bid for each transaction in experimental session 5: CRE_p.

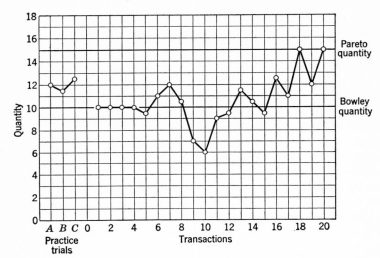

FIGURE 4.6   Median quantity bid for each transaction in experimental
session 5: CRE_p.

nineteenth transaction, however, is $\bar{Q} = 10$, precisely the Bowley
amount.   This mean is perhaps not representative since it is dis-
torted by the fact that two of the values were zero (see Table 4.5).
The median quantity, 12, falls between the Pareto and the Bowley
predictions.

On the twentieth transaction, the mean contract supported
the Pareto prediction more closely: $\bar{P} = 5.00$, $\bar{Q} = 13.91$.   The
medians were also closer to the Pareto prediction: the median
price 4 was precisely the Pareto value, as was the median
quantity 15.

Median price and quantity bids for each transaction are shown
in Figures 4.5 and 4.6.

Discussion

Examination of the individual protocols contributes to the
interpretation of these results.

The protocols of two pairs, 40 and 41, provide clear support for the Bowley solution. The bargaining conducted by pair 42, in contrast, was quite erratic, producing a pattern which does not provide support for either theory.

The next eight pairs, 43 through 50, conducted negotiations which seem to provide support for the Pareto solution. Either the bargainers had identified the equal-profit contract at the outset, as was the case for pair 43, or the buyer engaged in considerable "teaching activity" to induce the seller to lower his price. Among these pairs, there were five price bids of 4 and three of 5 on the nineteenth transaction. The quantity responses were optimal in all but three of these eight cases. The exceptions were pairs 45, 46, and 50; in these cases each buyer was still trying to induce the seller to lower his price.

The final pair, 51, oscillated between a contract with a price of 9 and a quantity of 14, yielding high profits to the seller, and a contract with a price of 1 and a quantity of 18, yielding high profits to the buyer. This seemingly irrational behavior was clarified by a postexperimental interview with the subjects concerned; they indicated that they were trying to split maximum joint profits and somehow felt this strategy would be most profitable.

The results of experiment 5 suggest that when a prominent Pareto optimal contract is available, many buyers are able to use repeated bids under complete information to force the sellers (the price leaders) away from the Bowley point to a more mutually advantageous contract.

GENERAL DISCUSSION

The purpose of the experiments reported in this chapter was to investigate the effect of various combinations of three experimental conditions—amount of information, form of bidding, and position of the equal-split payoff—and to test specific predictions of the results of experiments involving combinations of these conditions. The general hypothesis underlying these experiments was that either the Bowley or the Pareto solution would obtain,

TABLE 4.6   Observations Supporting the Bowley or Pareto Solutions
(Summary of the Experiments)

Experiment	Conditions	I		II	
		Bowley	*Pareto*	*Bowley*	*Pareto*
1	CSE_b	9.5	0.5		
2	CSE_p	10.0	0.0		
3	IRE_p	8.0	1.0	7.0	2.0
4	CRE_b	6.5	3.5	5.0	5.0
5	CRE_p	5.0	7.0	2.5	9.5

Note: I represents observations for the single-transaction experiments and on the nineteenth transaction for the repeated-transaction experiments; II represents observations on the twentieth transaction for the repeated-transaction experiments.

depending on the particular combination of conditions. The results of the experiments are summarized in Table 4.6.

It was suggested initially that four out of the five experimental sessions involved conditions that would favor the Bowley solution, but that the sessions would differ predictably in their strength of support for this solution. These experiments were presented in the order of the strength of their predicted tendency toward the Bowley point, starting with the set of conditions most strongly favoring a Bowley solution and ending with those least strongly favoring that solution. Since a trend toward a particular solution was predicted, it was thought appropriate to perform an overall test on the data. Toward that end, the Jonckheere test (1954), a nonparametric test for ordered alternatives, was applied to the differences between the observed contracts and the predicted Bowley contract. The hypothesis was that the size of these differences would tend to be smallest for the CSE_b combination of conditions, larger for the CSE_p combination, larger for the IRE_p, and larger still for CRE_b.

Table 4.7 presents the absolute differences between each contract and the Bowley quantity for the four experimental sessions

TABLE 4.7   Differences in Absolute Value between Observed
Quantity Contracts and the Bowley Quantity
(Four Combinations of Conditions)

CSE_b	CSE_p	IRE_p	CRE_b
3	3	1	1
0	2	2	1
0	2	1	1
0	1	0	9
0	0	1	1
0	0	1	3
0	0	2	7
1	0	5	6
1	0	4	2
2	0		0

under discussion.   The results of the Jonckheere test on the data
in Table 4.7 permit rejection of the null hypothesis in favor
of the hypothesis that the difference scores show this trend:
$CSE_b < CSE_p < IRE_p < CRE_b$.   (In performing this statistical test, we were faced with the problem created by ties.   If every
single tie is counted against the hypothesis, surely a conservative
procedure, the probability level yielded by the Jonckheere test is
$p < .12$.   If one-half the ties are counted against the hypothesis
and one-half for it, perhaps a more sensible procedure, then
$p < .005$.)

This finding may be interpreted to mean that when bargainers
have single-shot bids and when the equal-split payoff is at the
Bowley point, there is considerable force toward a Bowley solution.   Contracts deviate little from this point when the equal-
split payoff is at the Paretian optima, however.   Indeed, the
difference between the results of the first and second experiments
appears insignificant by any standards.   However, the support
for the Bowley solution is weakened when repeated bids are
allowed, rather than a single-shot bid, since with repeated bids
the bargainer in the weaker position (here, the quantity chooser)
can communicate by means of his choices and attempt to influ-

ence the choices of his opponent.   The use of repeated bids forces a movement of the contracts away from the Bowley point.   This tendency is particularly strong under complete information, as opposed to incomplete information.

In the chapter which follows, attention is given to comparisons across conditions.   Analysis is focused on the effect each of the following has on the bargaining outcome: amount of information, form of the bidding, and location of the prominent contract.

CHAPTER 5

Comparison of Treatments

We concluded in Chapter 4 that the Bowley model is a reasonably good predictor of contracts negotiated under conditions of price leadership bilateral monopoly, except in experiment 5. In that experiment we chose the states for the three treatment variables that favored the Pareto solution and saw that this combination of forces was sufficient to shift the incidence of the observations away from the Bowley point. It is our purpose in this chapter to assess the relative strength of these forces by means of cross comparisons of experiments. For example, the first two experiments involved complete information and one transaction; they

54   Bilateral Monopoly

TABLE 5.1   Summary of Experimental Results

Experiment	Conditions	Number of observations closer to			
		Bowley price	*Pareto price*	*Bowley quantity*	*Pareto quantity*
1	CSE_b	9	1	10	0
2	CSE_p	10	0	10	0
3	IRE_p	8 (7)	1 (2)	8 (7)	1 (2)
4	CRE_b	5 (4)	5 (6)	8 (6)	2 (4)
5	CRE_p	4 (2)	8 (10)	6 (3)	6 (9)

Note: Figures in parentheses are the count on the twentieth transaction and include end effects; other figures are for the nineteenth transaction for repeated-bid experiments.

differed only in the location of the prominent contract. A comparison between the data from experiments 1 and 2 should indicate the influence of this treatment variable. Further, experiments 4 and 5 also differed only in the location of the prominent contract, so a replication is available.

The results of the experiments are summarized in Table 5.1. This table differs from the summary (Table 4.6) in the last chapter; here we have separated the decisions made by the buyers and sellers and recorded the number of price observations closer to the Bowley or the Pareto price and the number of quantity observations closer to the Bowley or the Pareto quantity. The major purpose of this finer classification is to obtain data in integer form so the cross comparisons may be made by the Fisher exact probability test [Siegel (1956)].

EFFECT OF THE LOCATION OF A PROMINENT CONTRACT

The first comparisons concern the importance of the location of the equal-split contract. The hypothesis is that state E_b, an equal division of profits at the Bowley point, will favor the Bowley solution; state E_p, a discrete Pareto optimal equal-split

TABLE 5.2   Effect of Variables E_p and E_b

Experiment	Conditions	Price		Quantity	
		Bowley	Pareto	Bowley	Pareto
1	CSE_b	9	1	10	0
2	CSE_p	10	0	10	0

contract, will favor the Pareto parameters.   Table 5.2 shows the results of the first comparison, between experiments 1 and 2.

It is apparent that the hypothesis is not supported by the data: there is not a significant shift in the observations as a result of the changed state of E (for price, $p < .5$; for quantity, $p < 1.0$ by the Fisher test).   Indeed, the only difference between the experiments is in the opposite direction from that predicted by the hypothesis: the price observations provide stronger support for the Bowley model in experiment 2 than they do in experiment 1.

Another comparison regarding the effect of the prominent contract is possible, however.   Experiments 4 and 5 involve complete information and repeated bids and differ only with respect to E.   The results are shown in Table 5.3 for the nineteenth transaction.

Again the result is not significant (for price, $p < .4$; for quantity, $p < .16$).   However, the changes are in the direction predicted by the hypothesis for both price and quantity, and the probabilities have been reduced.   This trend is continued on the

TABLE 5.3   Effect of Variables E_p and E_b
(A Replication)

Experiment	Conditions	Price		Quantity	
		Bowley	Pareto	Bowley	Pareto
4	CRE_b	5	5	8	2
5	CRE_p	4	8	6	6

twentieth transaction, where the probability that E exercises no influence on price is reduced to $p < .25$, and for quantity, $p < .12$. It must be concluded, however, that the location of the prominent contract is not a powerful experimental condition; such influence as it does have on the results is activated by the repeated form of bidding.

EFFECT OF THE FORM OF THE BIDDING

The first and the fourth experiments provide an opportunity to test for the influence of the form of bidding since the experiments are similar in other respects. The hypothesis is that single bids will tend to favor the Bowley solution (because of its strong equilibrium properties), while repeated bids will tend to favor the Pareto solution (for they provide a means for communication regarding non-Bowley contracts). The results are shown in Table 5.4 for the nineteenth transaction.

The changes in the supporting observations are in the predicted direction; however, the probabilities that such changes resulted from chance, rather than the altered form of bidding, are still fairly large ($p < .07$ for price, $p < .24$ for quantity). The twentieth transaction (experiment 4), which the subjects knew to be the last, reduced these probabilities rather sharply ($p < .033$ for price, $p < .044$ for quantity).

It is possible, with experiments 2 and 5, to make another comparison of the form of the bidding. These results, for the nineteenth transaction, are shown in Table 5.5.

TABLE 5.4   Effect of Variables R and S

Experiment	Conditions	Price		Quantity	
		Bowley	Pareto	Bowley	Pareto
1	CSE_b	9	1	10	0
4	CRE_b	5	5	8	2

TABLE 5.5   Effect of Variables R and S
(A Replication)

Experiment	Conditions	Price		Quantity	
		Bowley	Pareto	Bowley	Pareto
2	CSE_p	10	0	10	0
5	CRE_p	4	8	6	6

Once more the changes are in the expected direction; the probabilities that they resulted from chance are quite small (for price, $p < .002$; for quantity, $p < .012$).   These probabilities are reduced even further if the relevant observations are assumed to occur on the twentieth transaction ($p < .0001$ for price and quantity).

It would seem to follow from these considerations that the form of the bidding is an important experimental condition.   Single-shot bids provide strong support for the Bowley contract—there is little chance for other institutional factors to interfere with the equilibrium properties of that solution.   Repeated bidding permits exchange of information, and there is some tendency to move away from the Bowley solution toward the Paretian optima; this tendency is greatly strengthened when the Paretian optima contain a prominent contract as a discrete element.

EFFECT OF THE AMOUNT OF INFORMATION

Since we conducted only one experiment under conditions of incomplete information (number 3), we can make only one comparison; this is shown in Table 5.6, for the nineteenth transaction.   This comparison is between experiments 3 and 5, which differed only in the amount of information available to the bargainers.   The hypothesis is that incomplete information will act as noise in the channel of communication and thus will tend to support the Bowley solution; complete information will enable the parties to use the repeated bids more effectively as a communication device and will tend to assist the Pareto solution.

58   Bilateral Monopoly

TABLE 5.6   Effect of the Variables I and C

Experiment	Conditions	Price		Quantity	
		Bowley	*Pareto*	*Bowley*	*Pareto*
3	IRE_p	8	1	8	1
5	CRE_p	4	8	6	6

The observed changes are in the expected direction and, quite probably, are a result of the altered experimental circumstance ($p < .02$ for price; $p < .08$ for quantity). Once again these probabilities are contracted when based on the twentieth transaction (for price, $p < .01$; for quantity, $p < .025$). This conclusion is reinforced by Figure 5.1, which shows the pattern of median price bids on each transaction for the third and fifth experiments.

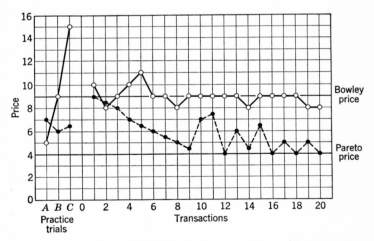

FIGURE 5.1   Median price bid for each transaction under incomplete information (IRE_p) and complete information (CRE_p). White circles represent incomplete information; black circles represent complete information.

It seems appropriate to conclude that the amount of information is a significant experimental variable, falling between the form of the bidding and the location of the prominent contract in the degree of its importance.

SUMMARY

We conclude that the following experimental variables do influence (in the order listed) the results of negotiations under price leadership bilateral monopoly:

1. Form of bidding
2. Amount of information
3. Location of a prominent (equal-split) contract

The states S, I, and E_b favor the Bowley solution; in fact, the Bowley solution is so robust that the presence of any one of these states in an experiment tended to produce Bowley results. The states R, C, and E_p favor the Pareto solution. However, the Pareto solution is contingent upon these three favorable conditions being brought together in concert.

CHAPTER 6

Sources of Variability
in Bargaining

In our work on equal-strength bilateral monopoly we observed a tendency for contracts to be Pareto optimal and to involve an equal division of the maximum joint profits. When we changed the structure to price leadership, where the power relationship is asymmetrical, we observed that the agreements were not Pareto optimal under most experimental conditions; rather, they tended to converge on the solution predicted by Bowley. This solution has strong equilibrium properties in the game-theory as well as the economic sense. It was possible, by appropriate experimental controls, to induce a substantial portion of subjects to shift toward the Pareto set, but this required a combination of conditions favorable to such a result.

One task remains. We must attempt to explain the deviations around the supported solutions. If consistent sources of such deviations can be identified, it may be possible to modify the surviving theoretical model and thus set the stage for further experimentation. Three possible sources of such variation will be considered: (1) the lack of discriminability in the payoff table, (2) variation in psychological attributes of the subjects, (3) the immaturity and lack of business experience of the subjects. We shall start with the question of discriminability.

DISCRIMINABILITY

It is important to note that the nature of the payoff structure for the present series of experiments was unfortunately one in which adjacent profit entries often differed by only very small amounts. Bargaining experiments conducted by Siegel and Fouraker (1960) showed a decrease in response variability as the difference between adjacent entries was increased. Therefore, to test for such behavior in the present series of experiments a special transaction was added to the experiments with repeated bids. This special transaction was the final triple-payoff transaction mentioned in Chapter 3.

The purpose of the final triple-payoff transaction in experiments 3, 4, and 5 was to determine whether the increase in discriminability between adjacent units in the payoff function which was created by the use of triple payoffs led to a reduction in the variability of contracts around the predicted point. For a test of this, comparisons are made between the contracts negotiated on the triple-payoff transaction (the twenty-first) and the final regular transaction (the twentieth).

The reader will remember that experiments 3, 4, and 5 were all repeated-transaction experiments. The subjects were 62 male undergraduates (31 bargaining pairs), randomized into information conditions, buyer and seller roles, and membership pairs.

In experiment 3, bargainers negotiated under incomplete information, whereas in 4 and 5 they had complete information.   In experiments 3 and 4, the Bowley point was the equal-split contract.   The profit sheets used in these experiments, and the data, are presented in Appendixes III, IV, and V.

Buyers and sellers were instructed separately.   Once in their isolated cubicles, each bargainer participated in three practice trials, followed by 19 regular transactions.   It was announced that the twentieth transaction was to be the final transaction. After it was completed, another general announcement was made, calling for a final triple-payoff transaction.

Subjects were informed that for this final transaction all profits (and losses) in their tables were to be three times the amount shown.   Each profit entry in the payoff tables was therefore increased by a multiple of three, thus tripling the difference between each profit entry.

The hypothesis under test here is that increasing the discriminability of the payoff table will result in a decrease in response variability about the predicted outcomes (the Bowley point for subjects in experiments 3 and 4 and the Pareto solution for subjects in experiment 5).   Table 6.1 shows the prices and quantities resulting from the twentieth and twenty-first transactions for the three experiments.

As can be seen from Table 6.1, the price and quantity bids resulting from the twenty-first (triple-payoff) transaction show differences from those of the twentieth.   The changes are counted as being for or against the predicted solution, depending upon whether they are toward the Bowley contract ($P_b = 9$, $Q_b = 10$) in experiments 3 and 4 or toward the Pareto contract ($P_p = 4$, $Q_p = 15$) in experiment 5.   The results are summarized in Table 6.2.

As Table 6.2 reveals, 11 pairs changed in the direction predicted, while 5 changed in the opposite direction.   This difference is significant against the null hypothesis at $p < .105$, according to the binomial test.   Thus these data confirm the prediction that an increase in the discriminability of the payoff function will

TABLE 6.1   Prices and Quantities Resulting from the Twentieth and Twenty-first (Triple-payoff) Transactions

Experiment 3				Experiment 4				Experiment 5			
Price		*Quantity*		*Price*		*Quantity*		*Price*		*Quantity*	
20th	*21st*	*20th*	*21st*	*20th*	*21st*	*20th*	*21st*	*20th*	*21st*	*20th*	*21st*
16	9	3	10	9	6	6	12	9	9	10	10
11	9	8	10	9	9	7	7	9	9	10	10
9	9	10	10	9	8	10	12	6	6	12	13
8	9	11	10	9	9	10	10	6	4	13	15
8	8	11	11	8	9	11	8	4	5	15	0
8	9	11	10	8	8	12	13	4	4	15	9
8	8	11	11	7	9	14	12	5	5	14	14
6	10	13	9	7	7	16	16	4	4	15	15
5	5	14	14	7	7	16	16	4	4	15	15
				1	9	18	10	4	4	15	15
								4	4	15	15
								1	4	18	15
Mean 8.78	8.44	10.22	10.56	7.40	8.10	12	11.60	5.00	5.17	13.92	12.17
Median 8	9	11	10	8	8.5	11.5	12	4	4	15	14.5

increase the tendency of bargainers to negotiate contracts at the predicted solution, though the confirmation is weak.

It should be noted that the interpretation supported by this analysis is not supported by an examination of the means (Table 6.1). In experiments 3 and 5, the mean price and the mean

TABLE 6.2   Direction of Changes between Twentieth and Twenty-first Contracts in Relation to Predicted Solution

Experiment	Number of pairs changing toward predicted solution	Number of pairs changing away from predicted solution
3	5	0
4	3	3
5	3	2
Total	11	5

quantity changed but little between transactions 20 and 21, but the direction of the change was away from the predicted solution. In experiment 4, the direction of the change was as predicted.

Of particular interest is the bargaining pair under complete information (pair 46, Appendix V) whose triple-payoff price and quantity bids both moved away from the equal-split, joint maximum solution. For this final transaction the seller, realizing that the threat of punishment was no longer of use to the buyer, raised his price from 4 to 5 in the hope of gaining extra profit for himself. If the buyer maximized at the higher price, this strategy would give the seller an additional 8.10 cents (for a total of 82.20 cents) and would result in a decrease of 9.90 cents for the buyer (for a total of 65.40 cents). The buyer negotiating with this seller had "taught" his opponent, at considerable expense, that bids of 4 or lower were the *only* acceptable prices. Thus, when offered a price of 5 for the triple-payoff transaction, he seemed to become angry and chose to give a zero response, imposing zero profit on both parties. He commented in the interview that the seller "tried to mess around."

We turn now to another explanation for the observed variation around the predicted solutions. It is quite likely that varying psychological attributes of subjects will influence the results of bargaining and negotiation. For example, we found in our first work on bilateral monopoly that the level of aspiration was a useful explanatory variable. We shall attempt to relate this phenomenon to the present series of experiments.

BARGAINING TYPES AND SIGNALS

Consider the first experiment. The subjects had complete information regarding a prospective single transaction; the Bowley prediction, based on the assumption that each player seeks his own self-interest, is reinforced in that it involves an equal split of profits. The subjects seemed to understand the situation prior to the decision. Why then did only 6 of the 10 pairs come to precisely the Bowley contract of $P_b = 9$, $Q_b = 10$, where each made $4.44? We conducted interviews with each of the deviating subjects at the end of the experiment. Their comments were as follows:

> Pair 1, SELLER (who quoted a price bid of 11):
> "I'll give him a chance to take a 2-cent cut and give me a lot more by taking a quantity of 9."

> Pair 1, BUYER (who responded with a quantity of 7, giving them profits of $\pi_s = \$3.62$, $\pi_b = \$3.70$):
> "He could have gone to about 9, but as long as he didn't I'll take a 2-cent cut and cost him a lot more."

> Pair 8, BUYER (who responded with a quantity of 11 to a price of 9):
> "For only 2 cents less for me he gets 38 cents more."

> Pair 9, BUYER (who responded with a quantity of 11 to a price of 9):
> "He could have gone to a higher price. He was a pretty square shooter and stayed in the middle."

> Pair 10, SELLER (who quoted a price of 7):
> "If I took 7, there was a chance we could both do better if he went out."

There would seem to be at least two interpretations of such behavior. First, there may be differences in the objectives of bargainers; second, the bargainers may employ different means to achieve similar ends.

Bargaining Types

There may be different bargaining types. Some subjects appear to be concerned only with their own rewards, as assumed by Bowley; they seem indifferent to the fortunes of their opponents. Such a subject might be called a *simple maximizer* (M): it is assumed that his objective is to maximize his own profits, π_b for buyers, π_s for sellers.

Other subjects do seem concerned about the fortunes of the people with whom they are paired. This concern may take two forms. First, there is the person, such as the buyer in pair 8, who apparently derives satisfaction from the success of his partner and is willing to take a small loss to give the other person a large gain. We define such a bargainer as a *cooperator* (*C*) and assume that his objective, at the limit, is to maximize the joint profits, $\pi_s + \pi_b$, of his pair. Second, there is the person, such as the buyer in pair 1, who seems to derive satisfaction from inflicting losses on his opponent. Typically, such a bargainer wants to beat his rival; we assume that such a *rivalist* (*R*) has as a limiting objective the maximization of the difference in profits ($\pi_b - \pi_s$ if he is a buyer, $\pi_s - \pi_b$ if he is a seller).

There have been many similar classifications of personality types by psychologists [for example, the work of Deutsch (1949)]. Indeed, such categorization has ancient origins. Witness the following selection from the *Sabbath and Festival Prayer Book* on social responsibility (p. 335):

> There are four characters among men: he who says, what is mine is mine, and what is thine is thine; his is a neutral character. He who says, what is mine is thine and what is thine is mine; he is a boor. He who says, what is mine is thine and what is thine is thine; he is a saint. He who says, what is thine is mine and what is mine is mine; he is wicked.

In these terms, our simple maximizer is a neutral man; our cooperator a saint; and our rivalist wicked. Perhaps the closest thing to boors in our experiments were those subjects who attempted to establish alternating patterns.

In our preliminary report of these experiments we considered only these behavioral classifications. However, the incidence of these types varied substantially among the five experiments (see Table 6.4), and we concluded that the various behavioral patterns apparently could be induced by the bargaining process as well as by the individual's prior experience. There must be something in the dynamics of the bargaining situation to induce buyers to be cooperative, on balance, in experiment 4 and rivalistic, on balance, in experiment 5. Since subjects were assigned to these experiments at random, it would be most unlikely that these results reflect intrinsic differences in personality.

Communication Signals

The only mode of communication between these subjects is their price and quantity bidding. The subject may deviate from a simple maximizing bid as a signal to his partner. In the first experiment the seller in pair 10 chose a price below 9 (see Appendix I), apparently hoping that the buyer would recognize this as a signal to improve both profit positions over that implied by the Bowley contract. The buyer responded as a simple maximizer, and the seller had no way of signaling his dissatisfaction with such a response, for it was a single-transaction experiment.

The second experiment induced more rivalistic responses in the subjects than the first. This probably resulted from the shift of the equal division of profit away from the Bowley solution. We had seen in our previous work that, under complete information, subjects behaved as if they set their aspiration levels at an equal division of profits. The asymmetry of the payoff at the Bowley point in the second experiment may have induced a tendency toward rivalistic signals on the part of both buyers and sellers.

Signals in a single-transaction game are little more than a gesture, a parting shot. There are no further decisions to be made, so the signal cannot alter the state of the world. They may serve a constructive purpose in a repeated-transaction game, however, for the signals may influence the future choices of the other player. To be consistent with our classification of bargaining types, let us define a maximizing response as a neutral signal (M). Relative to this, if a response reduces the opponent's profit, it is a rivalistic signal (R). If it increases the profit to the opponent, in comparison with a simple maximizing response, it is defined as a cooperative signal (C). The rationale for such signals might be taken from level-of-aspiration theory. If a player wants to reduce his opponent's level of aspiration, he might succeed by giving him a series of failure experiences [Simon (1957)]. This could be done by giving a sequence of rivalistic signals, which would reduce the opponent's profits in comparison with either a maximizing or a cooperative strategy.   If a player wants to raise the opponent's level of aspiration, he might do so by giving him a series of success experiences [Simon (1957)], i.e., cooperative signals.   This would increase the opponent's profit in comparison with either maximizing or rivalistic responses.   Depending upon the setting, a subject motivated solely by desire for personal profit might decide to send any of the three signals.   Therefore it is impossible to determine whether a given decision reflects a certain personality type or an attempt to communicate in a certain way.

Whether we think of a rivalistic bid as representing a rivalistic personality or as representing an attempt to communicate in a rivalistic way, however, its significance for the model is the same. This is true as well for cooperative and maximizing bids.

Significance for the Model

There are nine possible combinations of bargaining types or classes of communicators.   (Order is important for mixed pairs because of the asymmetry of the price leadership situation.) Only in cases of two simple maximizers and two communicators sending neutral (i.e., maximizing) signals and combinations of these does the Bowley solution obtain.   Table 6.3 indicates the relationship between the Bowley contract and contracts resulting from the other combinations.

Circumstances which encourage the emergence of these personality types or attempts to communicate in these terms will result in substantial dispersion of negotiated contracts.   Complete information is necessary if the parties are to be able to distinguish between a cooperative act, a rivalistic act, or a maximizing act; in the absence of information, it is much more likely that responses will be of the simple maximizing variety.   Similarly, repeated transactions are required for the parties to be able to communicate with each other and attempt to induce changes in behavior patterns.   Let us analyze the experimental results to see if consistent patterns of this sort emerge.

TABLE 6.3   Combinations of Types and
Resulting Contracts under Bilateral
Monopoly with Price Leadership

Combination*	Solution	
MM	Bowley contract: P_b, Q_b	
RM	$P > P_b$	$Q < Q_b$
CM	$P < P_b$	$Q > Q_b$
CC	$P < P_b$	$Q > Q_b$
MC	$P \geq P_b$	$Q > Q_b$
RC	$P \geq P_b$	$Q > Q_b$
CR	$P < P_b$	$Q > Q_b$
MR	$P \leq P_b$	$Q \gtrless Q_b$
RR	$P \geq P_b$	$Q < Q_b$

* The first symbol represents the seller; the second, the buyer.
Key: M = simple maximizer
      R = rivalist
      C = cooperator

Classification of Subjects

For the single-shot experiments (1 and 2) if a seller named a
price in excess of $P_b = 9$, he is classified as a rivalistic type; if he
named a price less than 9, he is classed as a cooperator; if he
quoted 9, he is classed as a simple maximizer. An index of his
behavior is $I_s = P - 9$, where P is his price choice; a positive
value indicates a rivalistic price choice; a negative value indicates a cooperative price choice. Similarly, if the buyer chose
the quantity which maximized his profits in light of the price
established by the seller, he is designated as type M; a larger
quantity selection signifies a cooperative type, for it reduces his
profits and helps his opponent; a smaller quantity choice is indicative of rivalistic behavior. An index of the buyer's behavior is
$I_b = Q - Q_m$, where Q is his quantity choice and Q_m is the
maximizing quantity choice; a negative value is indicative of
rivalistic behavior, a positive value of cooperative behavior.

Table 6.4 shows the frequency of bids of the various types on
the final trial. In experiments 1 and 2, as this table indicates,
simple maximizing behavior is the dominant type observed.
There is slightly more rivalistic behavior in the second experi-

TABLE 6.4   Contracts on the Final Trial and Indexes of Bargaining
Behavior
(Experiments 1–5)

Experiment	Pair number	Price	Quantity	I_s	I_b	Seller type	Buyer type
1	1	11	7	2	−1	R	R
	2	9	10	0	0	M	M
	3	9	10	0	0	M	M
	4	9	10	0	0	M	M
	5	9	10	0	0	M	M
	6	9	10	0	0	M	M
	7	9	10	0	0	M	M
	8	9	11	0	1	M	C
	9	9	11	0	1	M	C
	10	7	12	−2	0	C	M
2	11	9	7	0	−3	M	R
	12	9	8	0	−2	M	R
	13	11	8	2	0	R	M
	14	10	9	1	0	R	M
	15	9	10	0	0	M	M
	16	9	10	0	0	M	M
	17	9	10	0	0	M	M
	18	9	10	0	0	M	M
	19	9	10	0	0	M	M
	20	10	10	1	1	R	C
3	21	8	11	7	−2	R	R
	22	8	12	−3	6	C	C
	23	8	11	34	−3	R	R
	24	10	10	1	7	R	C
	25	8	11	20	−23	R	R
	26	8	11	−21	−85	C	R
	27	7	12	20	−36	R	R
	28	14	5	4	−33	R	R
	29	5	14	−6	−64	C	R
	Σ			56	−233		

TABLE 6.4   Contracts on the Final Trial and Indexes of Bargaining Behavior (Continued)

Experiment	Pair number	Price	Quantity	I_s	I_b	Seller type	Buyer type
4	30	9	9	−4	−79	C	R
	31	7	11	−5	−12	C	R
	32	9	9	1	−1	R	R
	33	16	1	37	5	R	C
	34	8	11	−6	−15	C	R
	35	8	13	−18	31	C	C
	36	13	3	22	4	R	C
	37	7	16	−36	72	C	C
	38	8	12	−21	35	C	C
	39	9	10	6	−6	R	R
	Σ			−24	34		
5	40	9	10	4	−9	R	R
	41	9	10	−24	−40	C	R
	42	11	4	−11	−39	C	R
	43	4	15	−95	0	C	M
	44	5	14	−24	−61	C	R
	45	5	0	−85	−184	C	R
	46	5	0	−58	−133	C	R
	47	4	15	−95	0	C	M
	48	4	15	−87	−20	C	R
	49	4	15	−32	−63	C	R
	50	4	8	−53	−105	C	R
	51	9	14	−45	+3	C	C
	Σ			−605	−651		

ment than in the first; this probably reflects the change in the equal-profit contract from the Bowley point to the Paretian optima.

For the repeated trial experiments, another index of cooperative or rivalistic behavior, a logical extension of the one just described, was constructed. For the seller the index consisted of the sum of the deviations around 9, the Bowley price. That is,

$$I_s = \sum_{i=1}^{19} (P_i - 9).$$

If this index equals zero, the seller has behaved, on balance, as a simple maximizer, as is assumed by the Bowley model. If this index is positive, the seller has, on balance, sent rivalistic signals to his buyer.   Price bids above 9 reduce the seller's profit from that associated with the Bowley strategy, but they reduce the buyer's profits as well, and often by considerably more.   If the index is negative, the seller has, on balance, sent cooperative signals to the buyer.   Such price concessions will reduce the seller's profits if the buyer responds as a simple maximizer. However, if the buyer also makes cooperative responses, it may be possible for them both to improve upon their expected profits imputed by Bowley behavior.

For the buyer the index was calculated by taking the sum of the deviations from the quantity choice which would have maximized his profits on each transaction, given the price quoted by the seller.   That is,

$$I_b = \sum_{i=1}^{19} (Q_i - Q_{im}).$$

If this index is zero, the buyer has responded as a simple maximizer, on balance.   This is the behavior pattern upon which the Bowley model is constructed.   If this index is positive, the buyer has in general selected quantities in excess of those which would have maximized his profits.   Since such choices yield a windfall profit to the seller, in comparison with the maximizing choice Q_{im}, they are indicative of cooperative behavior.   If I_b is negative, on the other hand, this signifies rivalistic signals: The buyer has reduced his own profit from time to time in order to impose (probably) a greater loss on the seller.

The indexes for all five experiments are presented in Table 6.4, with the implied strategy identified for each bargainer.   The relevant contracts are also reproduced in this table: the single bid for the first two experiments, the contract on the nineteenth trial for the last three experiments.   Finally, the indexes for experiments 3 to 5—the experiments with repeated transactions—are shown graphically in Figures 6.1 to 6.3. In these figures, the indexes computed for each pair are shown as a point, with the pair's number identifying that point.

The indexes of bargaining behavior for the last three experiments were given special representation because these repeated-bid experiments presented an opportunity for communication between buyer and seller. They had the opportunity to learn more equilibrium strategies and move away from the Bowley solution, which characterized the first two experiments so well. Hopefully the bargaining indexes will suggest the learning and teaching process which some subjects employed to escape the Bowley constraints. This suggests some qualifications concerning the interpretation of Figures 6.1 to 6.3:

1. If I_b has a value near zero, the buyer has sent Bowley responses on balance; the expected learning pattern of the seller is also the Bowley pattern, or an I_s value near zero.

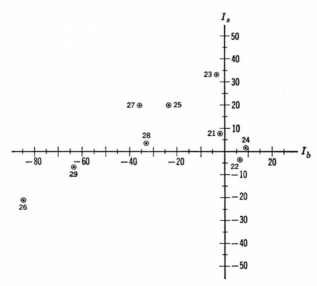

FIGURE 6.1   Bargaining behavior indexes, experiment 3.

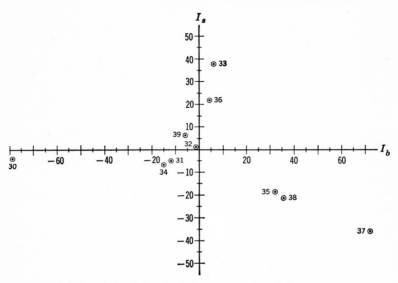

FIGURE 6.2   Bargaining behavior indexes, experiment 4.

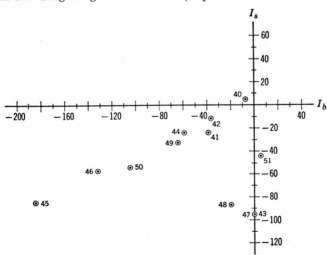

FIGURE 6.3   Bargaining behavior indexes, experiment 5.

This seems to be the experience of pairs 21 and 22 in experiment 3, pairs 32 and 39 in experiment 4, and pair 40 in the last experiment.

2. There is an exception to this consideration, since the cooperative solution to experiments 3 and 5 implies a maximizing response from the buyer to the seller's price of 4; this also implies a zero value for I_b. If a pair quickly identified the cooperative solution (say in the practice trials) and followed it throughout the experiment, we would get the indexes $I_b = 0$, $I_s = -95$. This happened with pairs 43 and 47 in experiment 5; it was approximately true for pair 48 in the same experiment. These fast learners and teachers also fail to give a representative picture of the mechanism by which other subjects *moved* from contracts in the Bowley region to contracts in the Pareto region during the progress of the experiment.

3. Finally, the alternators generate indexes that have little relation to the other patterns. Such pairs as 24, 33, and 51 may be identified as alternators from the protocols in the Appendixes.

Let us consider each experiment in turn. In experiment 3 the incomplete-information condition tends to block the communication channel. However, a least-squares trend line fitted to the observations in Figure 6.1 has a positive slope, suggesting that a buyer can force a seller to lower his aspiration level, and his price, by giving him failure experiences in the form of rivalistic quantity choices. This conclusion is reinforced by a study of the bargaining protocols (Appendix III). In pair 21 the buyer sent only one nonmaximizing signal to the seller, a two-unit rivalistic bid on transaction 17, so there was very little non-Bowley behavior in this pair; to some extent the same may be said for the next pair, number 22. The buyer sent several signals, but they were all so weak (a deviation of only one unit) that his behavior is quite close to maximizing.

Pair 24 provides an example of a buyer attempting to use a

rewarding, cooperative strategy to get the seller to a lower price policy, and perhaps to approach the Pareto solution. The buyer started with a cooperative signal, maximized when the seller raised his price, rewarded him when the seller lowered his price (bid 3), signaled mild displeasure when the price rose once more, but eventually returned to a cooperative strategy when the price fell. The buyer could not get concessions from the Bowley price with any regularity, however, and must be judged a failure in his instructional effort. Toward the end it appears that he may have shifted to an alternating strategy.

The remainder of the pairs in experiment 3 display a fairly consistent relationship between the willingness of the buyer to punish the seller with rivalistic quantity choices and the seller's price concessions. The buyer in pair 26 gave the most rivalistic responses and received the most cooperative price concessions; of the remaining pairs, the buyer in 23 gave the least rivalrous responses and suffered the highest price bids. The other observations fell within this range.

In experiment 5 the same payoff structure was used as in experiment 3. The complete-information condition in experiment 5, however, permitted the identification of the prominent Pareto solution. Again a least-squares trend line fitted to the observations in Figure 6.3 has a positive slope, suggesting that rivalistic responses are effective in forcing the seller to make price concessions. With the exception of the pairs that quickly identified and stabilized at the Pareto solution (43, 47, and 48) and the alternating pair (51), the remaining eight observations form a pattern consistent with that observed in experiment 3. The most punitive buyer (pair 45) secured the greatest price concessions. (Indeed, he even made more money than his rival, who had substantial structural advantages.) The least punitive buyer (pair 40) gave only two rivalistic bids, maximizing on all others. As a consequence the learning process for pair 40 followed the Bowley forecast and yielded the fewest price concessions. The other pairs fall in a near-linear relationship between these extremes.

The effect of the change in information on the degree of rivalistic bidding by buyers is quite marked, as is revealed in a comparison of experiments 3 and 5. It also appears that in experiment 5 sellers were more willing to make price concessions toward the Pareto contract. It seems reasonable to hypothesize that in this experiment the buyers could identify the Pareto contract and acquired an aspiration level of 24.7 cents for each transaction. Many of the sellers started with higher aspirations than that imputed to them at the Pareto contract, perhaps in the neighborhood of the 32.2 cents accorded to them by the Bowley solution. To lower the sellers' levels of aspiration, the buyers had to give them repeated failure experiences in the form of less-than-maximizing quantity responses. The buyers were successful in experiment 5, we believe, because the seller could identify a reasonable alternative: the Pareto solution; they had somewhere to go. The buyers were not successful in experiment 3 because no clear alternative to the Bowley position was available; the Pareto solution was masked by incomplete information.

Experiment 4 provides an interesting contrast to what has gone before. Here the Bowley point involves an equal division of profits; there is no prominent contract on the Paretian optima. However, it is possible for each party to improve upon his share of 22.2 cents at the Bowley solution; in experiment 4 there are nine such contracts. Each involves a price of 7 or 8, and quantities of 12 or more. None of these quantity responses is a maximizing response of the buyer to a quoted price of 7 or 8; each is in excess of the maximizing choice. The buyer must communicate to the seller his willingness to cooperate by means of these excess quantity choices if they are to leave the Bowley equilibrium. In this instance the buyer wants to raise the seller's aspiration above the 22.2 cent Bowley profit. The buyer can do so by cooperative bids, giving the seller a series of successful experiences (i.e., making more money than the seller might expect to, if the seller assumed he was paired with a maximizer).

Such reasoning is consistent, in part, with the observations in experiment 4. A least-squares trend line has a negative slope, suggesting that cooperative bids by the buyer will induce similar behavior by the seller. Again some comments are required. The buyers in pairs 32 and 39 used mostly maximizing responses, so the sellers learned the Bowley strategy (approximately). Pair 33, and perhaps 36, displayed alternating tendencies. The buyers in pairs 35, 37, and 38 gave the most cooperative signals; they received the most price concessions, and made the most money. In every instance, when their seller quoted a price of 7 or 8, they gave a nonmaximizing response that improved the profits of both buyer and seller over the Bowley point. They were the only cases in which both buyer and seller made more than the predicted Bowley profit of $5.11. This experience should be compared with the would-be cooperative buyer in pair 24, experiment 3, who ended with less profit than predicted by Bowley.

Although in experiment 5 the buyers were able to improve on their Bowley profits by rivalrous bids, the use of rivalrous bids in experiment 4 produced less than Bowley profits: The buyer in pair 30 gave a substantial number of punitive responses (even in comparison with buyers in experiments 3 and 5), but there was really no place to drive his opponent, who eventually grew rather balky.

This buyer indicated in a postexperiment interview that he wanted to beat the other man; he would seem to be an example of an individual who has a rivalistic personality.

LEVEL OF ASPIRATION

Our experiments on equal-strength bilateral monopoly [Siegel and Fouraker (1960)] suggested that subjects tended to set their level of aspiration at an equal share of the maximum joint profit, assuming the information condition was such that this contract could be identified. The only experiment in this series which replicates such a circumstance is experiment 5: complete information allows both bargainers to identify the Pareto contract of (4, 15) and the related profits of $\pi_s = 24.7$ cents and $\pi_b = 24.7$

cents for each transaction.   If the buyer identified such a share
as his level of aspiration, he would be frustrated by any price bid
in excess of 4; such a bid would prevent him from achieving his
level of aspiration.   Psychological theory suggests that a frustrated person will search for some means of altering the situation
which prevents the achievement of the desired goal [Simon
(1957)].   About the only mechanism available for such a search
in this experiment is the rivalrous response: it signifies displeasure
with the current price bid and a willingness to prevent the seller
from realizing a share in excess of 24.7 cents.   Such bids may
induce sufficient failure experiences to cause the seller to lower
his level of aspiration and offer the price of 4.   These considerations suggest the following proposition: If the quoted price on a
given transaction is in excess of 4, the quantity response will be
rivalrous; if the quoted price is equal to or less than 4, the quantity response will be maximizing.   Several points need to be made
with respect to this proposition:

1. Psychological theories other than the level-of-aspiration
    model may be consistent with such a proposition.
2. Since this proposition was stated after the data were col-
    lected, any analysis of the data in terms of this proposition is
    by way of an interpretation of the experiments, not a test of
    the level-of-aspiration hypothesis.
3. The proposition calls for maximizing responses to price bids
    less than 4.   There is another explanation for such bids:
    A seller might be dilatory in identifying the equitable con-
    tract and offer the lower price (which yields greater profit
    to the buyer) to offset an earlier price that exceeded 4.

Each of 12 pairs negotiated a sequence of 19 contracts in
experiment 5.   This produced a set of 228 observations.   There
were 160 observations consistent with the level-of-aspiration
hypothesis described above; 68 of the observations were not
consistent with that hypothesis.   Since these observations are
not independent, a probability statement should not be made
regarding these results.   Of the 12 pairs, 9 provided more obser-

vations in support of the hypothesis than against it.   This result is significant against the null hypothesis at $p < .08$ (binomial test).

Corollary propositions might also be considered.   For example, it would be expected that any price increase on the seller's part would induce a rivalrous response from the buyer.   (We will call this the R hypothesis.)   That is, if

$$P_{t+1} > P_t$$

then $$Q_{t+1} < Q_{t+1\text{max}}$$

where t represents the transaction number and $Q_{t+1\text{max}}$ represents a maximizing quantity response to a price of P_{t+1}.   This proposition has the same support from level-of-aspiration theory that the first proposition does: a price increase is a frustrating strategy from the buyer's point of view.   Of 51 price increases (in experiment 5) 38 elicited a rivalrous response.

In two of the pairs there were no price increases.   For the remaining 10 pairs, 7 provided more observations in support of the hypothesis than observations opposed to it.

The companion version of this proposition would be that if price is reduced by the seller, the buyer will give a cooperative response.   (This is the S hypothesis.)   This proposition, which is not necessarily supported by level-of-aspiration theory, finds no encouragement in experiment 5: There is no supporting observation out of 57 instances of price reductions; the buyers responded with a maximizing choice 27 times and with a rivalrous choice 30 times.

Propositions related to these will be considered in conjunction with the oligopoly experiments.

AMOUNT OF EXPERIENCE

One possible source of variation around the bilateral monopoly solutions is the lack of experience in business matters that characterizes most undergraduates.   Indeed, some people question the generality of experimental results derived from naïve subjects. For these reasons, and as a check on our results, Siegel and Harnett (1961) replicated experiments 3 and 5 with mature subjects possessing some experience in business relationships. This replication will be designated as experiment 6.

The replication by Siegel and Harnett took place in New York City in 1961. Thirty-two employees of the industrial sales operation of the General Electric Company served as subjects. There was some variation in the procedures of the replication from our procedures already reported. The most important variations are:

1. The profit tables were transformed to increase the payoff for each decision; it was felt the business people required larger payoffs to hold their interest. (As in experiments 3 and 5 the equal division of profits was an element of the Paretian optima.)

2. The subjects were informed in advance that there would be 10 trials. After the tenth trial, an eleventh was announced and transacted. The purpose of this procedure was to hold end effects constant on trials 10 and 11. The reader will note that there were fewer transactions in experiment 6 than in experiments 3 and 5.

The 32 men were paired at random and the pairs were assigned on a random basis to two information conditions: eight pairs bargained under complete information and eight bargained under incomplete information.

For analysis purposes, the next-to-last regular transaction was taken to provide the relevant data, as in experiments 3 and 5. In experiment 6, this was the ninth transaction.

The contracts negotiated by the eight pairs of businessmen bargaining under complete information are presented in Table 6.5. It will be noted that seven of the eight pairs negotiated contracts closer to the Pareto solution than to the Bowley solution. By the binomial test, this result deviates significantly from chance expectation: $p < .04$.

Of twelve pairs of student subjects who bargained under comparable conditions (in experiment 5), seven arrived at trans-

TABLE 6.5   Replication of Experiment 5, Complete Information, Contract on the Ninth Transaction

Pair	Price	Quantity	Supports, Bowley, Pareto	I_s	I_b	Seller type	Buyer type
1	4	15	P	−24	−16	C	R
2	4	14	P	−31	−58	C	R
3	4	15	P	−39	−21	C	R
4	4	15	P	−29	−10	C	R
5	2	17	P	−38	0	C	M
6	4	15	P	−46	0	C	M
7	4	15	P	−30	−41	C	R
8	10	11	B	12	2	R	C
Mean	4.5	14.6					

actions closer to the Pareto solution while five were closer to the Bowley solution.

The buyers in both groups employed rivalistic signals, on balance, to achieve the same results: price concessions from the sellers. Table 6.7 shows a comparison of the incidence of bargaining types in experiments 3 and 5 and their replications.

TABLE 6.6   Replication of Experiment 3, Incomplete Information, Contract on the Ninth Transaction

Pair	Price	Quantity	Supports, Bowley, Pareto	I_s	I_b	Seller type	Buyer type
9	9	10	B	10	−9	R	R
10	9	10	B	0	0	M	M
11	12	7	B	15	0	R	M
12	11	9	B	4	0	R	M
13	10	3	B	10	−21	R	R
14	13	2	B	4	−16	R	R
15	8	11	B	25	14	R	C
16	8	5	B	4	−20	R	R
Mean	10	7.1					

TABLE 6.7   Percentage of Student and Businessman Subjects
Adopting Various Bargaining Strategies

Combination of strategies		Incomplete information		Complete information	
Seller	Buyer	Students (experiment 3)	Businessmen (experiment 6)	Students (experiment 5)	Businessmen (experiment 6)
R	R	55.5	50.0	8.3	
R	M		25.0		
R	C	11.1	12.5		12.5
M	R				
M	M		12.5		
M	C				
C	R	22.2		66.7	62.5
C	M			16.7	25.0
C	C	11.1		8.3	

The contracts negotiated by the eight pairs of businessmen bargaining under incomplete information are presented in Table 6.6.   All eight pairs of businessmen negotiated contracts closer to the Bowley prediction than to the Pareto prediction.   This result is significant against the null hypothesis at $p < .005$.   It is also consistent with the results of experiment 3, where eight pairs of students negotiated contracts closer to the Bowley point and one pair came closer to the Pareto alternative.   Also, the dynamics of the bargaining were similar to those observed in our third experiment: the businessmen sellers were slightly rivalistic, on balance; the buyers also were rivalistic but less so than under complete information.

Siegel and Harnett concluded that the business subjects were more perceptive and aggressive than the student subjects; this is supported by their tendency to move to the Pareto point under complete information, and by the substantial increase in end play when under complete information.   There was little end play among the students.   In general, however, the same conclusions hold for both groups: With repeated bids, a prominent Pareto optimal contract, and incomplete information, the parties will tend to negotiate Bowley contracts; an increase in the amount of information will enable the buyers to communicate more readily, and there will be a tendency to shift to the Pareto solution.

The propositions regarding level of aspiration experienced mixed support from the replications. The first proposition, that price bids in excess of 4 would receive rivalrous responses, was supported in 52 out of 72 observations in the complete-information experiment with businessmen. This is almost exactly the same proportion as was observed in experiment 5. Of the eight pairs, six provided more supporting than opposing observations.

The other propositions did not fare as well. The notion that a price increase will receive a rivalrous response was supported but 9 times in 21 observations; 10 times the response was a maximizing one and twice it was a cooperative bid. This is not a significant result. The companion proposition fared even worse, as would be expected. There were only 3 cooperative responses to price reduction; there were 19 maximizing responses to such behavior and 9 rivalrous responses.

From the replication with businessmen as subjects, it seems reasonable to think that the inexperience of our subjects in experiments 1 to 5 is one source of the variability in the contracts they negotiated. Under complete information, the mature and experienced men negotiated contracts more consistently close to the predicted solution than did men students. Although it is true that the student subjects appear to conform more closely to the prediction under incomplete information, we think this is so largely because the mature subjects were still engaged in extensive signaling activity on the ninth transaction.

We would not wish to view experiment 6 as providing a definitive contrast between businessmen and students as subjects, not only because the experiments differ in the amount of the payoff (it was increased in experiment 6) and in the number of transactions executed (fewer in experiment 6), but also because no effort was made to "match" the businessmen and the students on other relevant variables, such as intelligence and level of education.   At most, the comparison is suggestive.   The principal conclusion to be drawn from experiment 6 is that our findings in the other experiments appear to have some generality; the pattern of negotiations observed among students may also be observed in negotiations among more mature and experienced men.

CONCLUSION

In the five experiments we conducted on bilateral monopoly under conditions of price leadership, the Bowley solution provided the norm for the dyadic adjustments.   This solution is not Pareto optimal.   The incidence of negotiated contracts could be shifted toward the Pareto solution by altering the experimental conditions (form of bidding, location of prominent contract, amount of information) to states favoring that solution.   The mechanism by which this shift occurred appeared to involve certain psychological attributes of the subjects: levels of aspiration, rivalistic or cooperative proclivities, and willingness and ability to send and receive appropriate signals.   Since these psychological properties apparently varied among subjects, they were a source of some of the dispersion that was observed around predicted solutions.   Another source of such dispersion was the small differences in payoff associated with different choices made by a subject; this weak reinforcement appeared to reduce a subject's discriminability among acts.

Further, the subjects' lack of experience in such economic bargaining may have contributed to the dispersion of observations around expected solutions.   It was of interest, however, that a replication of two of the experiments, using mature subjects, produced results that supported the expected solutions to about the same degree as the student-subject data.

PART THREE

Oligopoly

CHAPTER 7

Theoretical Formulation

Oligopoly, a market structure characterized by a few sellers, is the classic situation of economic conflict. The independent decisions of the participants determine the mutual benefits. Once again it is in the player's interest to come to some adjustment, thus providing a cooperative aspect. Until an adjustment is reached, however, the interests of the participants are opposed. This section of the book will be devoted to a consideration of oligopoly.

The oligopolistic phenomenon has generated numerous conceptual models, many offering contradictory predictions for the resolution of the conflict. This diversity stems from varying assumptions regarding the mode of behavior of the participants. Our primary purpose in this section is to see whether experimental data will be consistent with the predictions of various oligopolistic theories when we attempt to simulate the appropriate economic structure in the laboratory.* We are once more concerned with hypothesis testing; this chapter will be devoted to a derivation of the relevant propositions.

Our experience with bilateral monopoly experimentation suggested some relationships which might be anticipated. These forecasts were made before the oligopoly experiments were conducted.

1. Incomplete-information conditions will tend to favor those solutions which are based on the assumption that the participants are simple maximizers. Since most traditional economic models incorporate this assumption, the solutions offered by such models would be expected to obtain in conjunction with the incomplete-information condition.
2. A corollary of the first proposition concerns the other information state: complete information. This condition is favorable to the emergence of the diverse psychological attributes of the bargainers, which tend to increase the dispersion of negotiated contracts.

Initially we had assumed that subjects could be classed as bargaining types: rivalistic (R), cooperative (C), or simple maximizers (M). However, the bilateral monopoly experiments established that the nature of the conflict situation could induce changes in these patterns of bargaining behavior: Under some circumstances subjects tend to send rivalistic signals to their opponents; other circumstances elicit cooperative or maximizing signals. Now, complete information is favorable to such diverse

---

* For more extensive treatment of the various oligopoly theories, see Fellner (1949), Shubik (1959), Zeuthen (1930), Stackleberg (1952), Bishop (1961), Chamberlin (1933), and Schneider (1952). The solutions presented in this chapter are by no means original; they find many predecessors in the above writings and other sources.

attempts at communication. Further, it is quite impossible to tell whether an isolated act, say a rivalistic bid, indicates that the bargainer is one who is intent upon beating his opponent (a rivalistic type) or represents an act of strategy by a simple maximizer who feels that such behavior will increase his total profits in the long run. However, it is not necessary for our argument that we make such a distinction : Complete information activates both types of behavior, and both types tend to increase the dispersion of contracts in conflict situations.* We assume then that the following bargaining types (or communicators) will affect the bargaining under oligopoly :

1. The simple maximizer (M), who is concerned solely with his own profit.
2. The rivalist (R), who makes punitive choices either to reduce his opponent's profit aspirations in such a manner that his own profits may be increased or because he derives satisfaction from reducing the gain accorded to the opposition and desires to surpass his rival.
3. The cooperator (C), who makes rewarding choices either in hopes of enhancing his own profits in the long run or because he derives satisfaction from the prosperity of his opponent.

For the laboratory simulation of oligopoly, we established two basic experimental situations. In each, the individual producers had but one decision variable. In the first group of experiments, the decision variable was the *quantity* they would produce, indi-

---

* This was not the case in the equal-strength bilateral monopoly experiments reported in Siegel and Fouraker (1960). There complete information tended to reduce dispersion around the contract which yielded an equal division of maximum joint profits (which we have called, for convenience, the Pareto contract). The form of those negotiations was conducive to such a result : each party had a veto over any proposed contract. That is, a contract had to be mutually acceptable before it became effective. Under complete information the subjects tended to set their aspiration levels at half the maximum joint profits, so that the Pareto contract became the only solution which was mutually acceptable. The veto power was not present in the experiments reported in this book.

vidually, during the next period.   In the second group, the decision variable was the *price* they would charge for the product,
individually, during the next period.   The quantity adjuster
version of the oligopoly problem originated with Cournot (1838)
as did the following solution.

QUANTITY ADJUSTER OLIGOPOLY

The Cournot Model

Assume there are N independent producers of a homogeneous
commodity.   (The product is homogeneous in the sense that
consumers do not differentiate among the products of the N producers.)   Say the demand for the commodity is represented by
the linear equation

$$P = A - BQ$$

where P = price
  A = price axis intercept of the function
  B = slope of the function
  Q = aggregate output of the N producers.

That is, $Q = \sum_{j=1}^{N} q_j$, where q_j is the output choice of the jth producer.   It simplifies the problem, without detracting from its
essential nature, if we assume costs to equal zero (as Cournot did
initially).

Cournot assumed that the individual firms would adjust their
outputs to maximize their individual profits.   Firm 1 would
choose that level of production q_1 which maximized its profits, π_1.
Now π_1 is defined as follows:

$$\pi_1 = Pq_1 = Aq_1 - Bq_1 \sum_{j=1}^{N} q_j. \tag{7.1}$$

The q_1 value which maximizes this expression depends upon the
assumed relation between q_1 and the production decisions of other
producers, summarized by the variable $\sum_{j=2}^{N} q_j$.   Cournot assumed

that there was no relation between q_1 and $\sum\limits_{j=2}^{N} q_j$; he assumed that each producer ignored the effect of his own production decision on the production decisions of the other oligopolists. The output of the other firms, $\sum\limits_{j=2}^{N} q_j$, was assumed to be invariant with respect to q_1 and could therefore be treated as a constant. Under this assumption, π_1 is maximized by setting the first derivative of Equation (7.1) equal to zero,

$$\frac{d\pi_1}{dq_1} = A - Bq_1 - B\sum_{j=1}^{N} q_j = 0. \tag{7.2}$$

Since the second-order condition is satisfied

$$\frac{d^2\pi_1}{dq_1^2} = -2B < 0$$

the solution of (7.2) provides the quantity decision that maximizes π_1:

$$q_1 = \frac{A - B\sum\limits_{j=2}^{N} q_j}{2B}. \tag{7.3}$$

There are N of these unknown individual quantities, and N independent equations, as indicated by (7.3). Thus, a unique, nontrivial solution exists [Murdoch (1957)]. By the appropriate matrix inversion we may identify the output of any entrepreneur as

$$q_1 = \frac{1}{N+1}\frac{A}{B}. \tag{7.4}$$

Thus, the aggregate output is

$$Q = \frac{N}{N+1}\frac{A}{B}. \tag{7.5}$$

The amount A/B is the quantity axis intercept of the demand function. It is the aggregate output which yields a price of zero.

Since there are no costs, a price of zero yields zero profits to the producers. The absence of profits or losses characterizes the competitive adjustment in economics, so A/B is identified as the aggregate competitive output. Cournot's oligopoly solution is for each firm to produce $1/(N + 1)$ of this competitive output. In the aggregate the N firms would produce $\dfrac{N}{N+1}\dfrac{A}{B}$. When $N = 1$, the aggregate (and individual) output would be $\dfrac{1}{2}\dfrac{A}{B}$, or one-half the competitive output. This adjustment yields the greatest possible profit, within the constraints of a linear, negatively sloping demand curve, and zero costs. Therefore the production of $\dfrac{1}{2}\dfrac{A}{B}$ is defined as the monopoly output. As N increases, the aggregate output increases, approaching the competitive adjustment for very large numbers of firms. It should be noted that the Cournot model dictates that, as N increases:

1. The aggregate output, $\dfrac{N}{N+1}\dfrac{A}{B}$, *increases.*

2. The individual output, $\dfrac{1}{N+1}\dfrac{A}{B}$, *decreases.*

Thus a rather stringent relation between individual and aggregate output is implied by the Cournot model.

The Condition of Incomplete Information

The crucial assumption in Cournot's model is that entrepreneurs are quantity adjusters; and further, that $\sum_{j=2}^{N} q_j$, the production of other firms, is invariant with respect to q_1, the output of the firm under consideration. This latter assumption seems most reasonable when the circumstances are such that the individual cannot identify the effect on the profits of his competitors of changes in his own production. If the individual entrepreneur does not know the relation between his output and the profit of his competitors, he may act as if those profits, $\sum_{j=2}^{N} \pi_j$, are some constant, and concentrate on maximizing his own net returns. Under these Cournot conditions it is of no consequence whether the participant is trying to (1) act as a simple maximizer and increase his own profits π_1, (2) act as a rivalist and make more profit than his opponent, (3) act as a cooperator and increase the joint profits to himself and his opponents; for $\sum_{j=2}^{N} \pi_j$ is treated as a constant. Further, there is little purpose in sending anything but maximizing signals in repeated-bid games. The same strategy indicated by Equation (7.4) will maximize all the objective variables under consideration when $\sum_{j=2}^{N} \pi_j$ is a constant. If we are successful in creating an experimental representation of the Cournot conditions, we would expect the following:

1. The central tendency of results would approximate the Cournot solution because of its strong equilibrium properties.
2. There would be relatively little dispersion around this central tendency based on personality differences.

We felt that the closest approximation to the Cournot condition would be obtained by informing the participant only of the profits accruing to him as a result of a particular production decision and not providing him with any indication of the profits going to his opponents. We have defined this experimental condition as *incomplete information.* Our assumption here is that the condition of incomplete information will lead each participant to act as if the sum of his rival's profits were a constant, so that he will behave the same, regardless of his objective.

The Condition of Complete Information

If each participant can identify some relation between his production choice and the profits accruing to his rivals, the Cournot assumptions will no longer be as generally applicable. This condition would obtain if each participant were informed not only of his own profits resulting from a production choice, but also of the profits and production choices of his rivals.   We define this condition as *complete information*.   We have suggested that the naïve profit maximizer will be indifferent to the relation between q_1 and $\sum\limits_{j=2}^{N} \pi_j$ and will continue to follow a Cournot strategy, with his objective remaining the maximization of π_1.   If he is a sophisticated profit maximizer, or if his objective is the cooperative one of increasing his opponent's profits as well as his own, he will abandon the Cournot strategy, as the following calculations indicate.

The Paretian Optimal (Joint Profit Maximization) Model

Joint profits are defined as

$$\pi_1 + \sum_{j=2}^{N} \pi_j = A \sum_{j=1}^{N} q_j - B \left(\sum_{j=1}^{N} q_j \right)^2. \tag{7.6}$$

They are maximized when the second-order condition is met and

$$\frac{d \left(\pi_1 + \sum\limits_{j=2}^{N} \pi_j \right)}{dq_1} = A - 2B \sum_{j=1}^{N} q_j = 0. \tag{7.7}$$

This may be accomplished by choosing q_1 so that, solving (7.6) for q_1,

$$q_1 = \frac{A - 2B \sum\limits_{j=2}^{N} q_j}{2B} = \frac{1}{2} \frac{A}{B} - \sum_{j=2}^{N} q_j. \tag{7.8}$$

This is the equivalent of each participant's choosing his output in such a manner that the total output of the industry is always that which maximizes joint profits:

$$Q = \sum_{j=1}^{N} q_j = \frac{1}{2} \frac{A}{B}. \tag{7.9}$$

In this case, N cooperative producers would have the same aggregate output as a single monopolistic firm.   A cooperative signal then is an individual production decision designed to shift total production toward that amount which maximizes joint profits. A sophisticated profit maximizer might send such a signal if he thought he might receive the same sort of signal in response; such a strategy might lead to his sharing the maximum joint profit, the assumed goal of the sophisticated maximizer.

The Competitive Model

The competitive solution is for each participant to choose a quantity output such that the aggregate output yields zero profits to each of the oligopolists. The competitive solution implies that under zero cost conditions the expected output of the representative firm would be

$$q_k = \frac{1}{N}\frac{A}{B}. \tag{7.10}$$

The aggregate output under the competitive model is

$$Q = \frac{A}{B}. \tag{7.11}$$

A variation of the competitive model, which we have termed the *rivalistic model*, yields some interesting behavioral implications. In the rivalistic model it is assumed that each participant has as his objective the maximization of the difference between his profit and profits accruing to his rivals. His objective is defined as

$$\pi_1 - \sum_{j=2}^{N} \pi_j = Aq_1 - Bq_1 \sum_{j=1}^{N} q_j - A \sum_{j=2}^{N} q_j + B \sum_{j=1}^{N} q_j \sum_{j=2}^{N} q_j. \tag{7.12}$$

It will be at a maximum when the second-order condition is satisfied and

$$\frac{d\left(\pi_1 - \sum_{j=2}^{N} \pi_j\right)}{dq_1} = A - Bq_1 - B \sum_{j=1}^{N} q_j + B \sum_{j=2}^{N} q_j = 0. \tag{7.13}$$

This adjustment may be achieved by selecting the quantity which satisfies Equation (7.13):

$$q_1 = \frac{1}{2}\frac{A}{B}. \tag{7.14}$$

As we have seen above, this is the aggregate output which maximizes joint profits; it is the output a monopoly would select. Moreover, this solution is invariant with respect to N; so the individual whose objective is to maximize the difference between his profits and those of his opponents would produce the monopoly output, regardless of the number of competitors. If the competitors are motivated by similar objectives, they too will produce $\frac{1}{2}\frac{A}{B}$ units. So the aggregate output for two competitors will be A/B (the competitive result); for three competitors it will be $\frac{3}{2}\frac{A}{B}$; for four competitors it will be $2A/B$, and so forth.

Under complete information, the dispersion of contracts and the central tendency of contracts will depend upon the incidence of the different bargaining types and the incidence of various signals. If all the participants in a certain market use cooperative signals, and each is trying to increase the joint profits of all, the result is likely to be a total output of $\frac{1}{2}\frac{A}{B}$, with each participant producing $\frac{1}{2N}\frac{A}{B}$. If all the participants are simple maximizers, they will follow Cournot strategies and produce $\frac{N}{N+1}\frac{A}{B}$ in the aggregate. If all the participants are rivalistic and are striving to increase the difference between their profits and those of their opponents, the individual output will tend toward $\frac{1}{2}\frac{A}{B}$, and the aggregate output will approximate $\frac{N}{2}\frac{A}{B}$. It is apparent that, unless all of the bargainers are of the same type or employ similar signals, a change in the information condition from incomplete to complete will increase the dispersion of negotiated contracts.

The possible combinations of bargaining types or signals and the associated prediction of the outcome will depend upon the number of participants. It follows from this, and other considerations, that N is an important experimental variable, as is the information condition.

THE CONDITION OF NUMBER OF PARTICIPANTS

When $N = 1$, the monopoly output of $\frac{1}{2}\frac{A}{B}$ will result, regardless of the psychological makeup of the participant. For $N > 1$, the conceptual solution no longer is trivial.

For our experiments we allowed N to take on two values, 2 and 3. The Cournot prediction is that the individual output would be $\frac{1}{N+1}\frac{A}{B}$ and the aggregate output $\frac{N}{N+1}\frac{A}{B}$. An increase in N would reduce the individual output but increase the aggregate output. Our expectation is that the Cournot result will obtain under conditions of incomplete information for the reasons discussed above. Under complete information the increase in N may induce a change in the results: cooperative behavior becomes much more difficult as the number of participants increases [Luce and Raiffa (1957)]. This may be seen from the structure of the conflict situation: With $N = 2$, the cooperative player dominates the result; for regardless of the characteristic of his opponent (cooperative, rivalistic, or simple maximizer), the cooperative solution will obtain (see Table 7.1). The cooperative player will reduce his output against either a rivalistic or simple maximizing opponent. The opponent, in turn, will select a larger output. When two cooperative players bargain, each will tend to produce one-half the monopoly output [Schelling (1957)]. In any event the cooperative result tends to obtain for $N = 2$, provided only one of the players is so disposed; for he can always adjust his output so that the aggregate production will maximize joint profits.

This is not true for $N = 3$. In this situation, at least two of the players must be cooperative to dominate the result and produce a cooperative solution. If there is only one cooperative player, the solution will vary depending upon the types or the signals employed by the other two players. The Cournot prediction for triopoly, $\dfrac{3}{4}\dfrac{A}{B}$, might obtain from either a combination of three simple maximizers or from a combination of one cooperative, one maximizing, and one rivalistic bargainer (see Table 7.1). Further, tacit agreements are much harder to establish and maintain with three players than with only two. Thus an increase in N from 2 to 3 will tend to work against the cooperative solution and for the rivalistic one.

Derivation of Predictions under Various Experimental Conditions

We identified two important experimental conditions, information and the size of N, and decided to let these conditions take on each of two states. The two information conditions are complete information and incomplete information; the two values of N are $N = 2$ (duopoly) and $N = 3$ (triopoly). There are four combinations of conditions: incomplete-information duopoly, complete-information duopoly, incomplete-information triopoly, and complete-information triopoly. Our purpose in this section is to derive the appropriate theoretical prediction for each of these oligopoly combinations, taking into consideration the effect of the various groupings of bargaining types and signals. These predictions are summarized in Table 7.1.

Under incomplete information we assumed the solution would be invariant with respect to the combination of bargaining types or signals, and predicted the Cournot result. For $N = 2$ the Cournot result would be $\dfrac{2}{3}\dfrac{A}{B}$; for $N = 3$ the Cournot result would be $\dfrac{3}{4}\dfrac{A}{B}$.

The complete-information condition activates the effect of the possible combinations of bargaining types on the predicted result. For $N = 2$, the presence of one or more cooperative types ensures

TABLE 7.1   Possible Oligopolistic Combinations of Bargaining Types or Signals and Related Predictions

Number of bargainers	Possible combinations of bargaining types or signals	Predicted aggregate output Q	
		Incomplete information	*Complete information*
$N = 2$	CC	$Q = \dfrac{2}{3}\dfrac{A}{B}$	$Q < \dfrac{2}{3}\dfrac{A}{B}$
	CM	$Q = \dfrac{2}{3}\dfrac{A}{B}$	$Q < \dfrac{2}{3}\dfrac{A}{B}$
	CR	$Q = \dfrac{2}{3}\dfrac{A}{B}$	$Q < \dfrac{2}{3}\dfrac{A}{B}$
	MM	$Q = \dfrac{2}{3}\dfrac{A}{B}$	$Q = \dfrac{2}{3}\dfrac{A}{B}$
	MR	$Q = \dfrac{2}{3}\dfrac{A}{B}$	$Q > \dfrac{2}{3}\dfrac{A}{B}$
	RR	$Q = \dfrac{2}{3}\dfrac{A}{B}$	$Q > \dfrac{2}{3}\dfrac{A}{B}$
$N = 3$	CCC	$Q = \dfrac{3}{4}\dfrac{A}{B}$	$Q < \dfrac{3}{4}\dfrac{A}{B}$
	CCM	$Q = \dfrac{3}{4}\dfrac{A}{B}$	$Q < \dfrac{3}{4}\dfrac{A}{B}$
	CCR	$Q = \dfrac{3}{4}\dfrac{A}{B}$	$Q < \dfrac{3}{4}\dfrac{A}{B}$
	CMM	$Q = \dfrac{3}{4}\dfrac{A}{B}$	$Q < \dfrac{3}{4}\dfrac{A}{B}$
	CMR	$Q = \dfrac{3}{4}\dfrac{A}{B}$	$Q = \dfrac{3}{4}\dfrac{A}{B}$
	CRR	$Q = \dfrac{3}{4}\dfrac{A}{B}$	$Q > \dfrac{3}{4}\dfrac{A}{B}$
	MMM	$Q = \dfrac{3}{4}\dfrac{A}{B}$	$Q = \dfrac{3}{4}\dfrac{A}{B}$
	MMR	$Q = \dfrac{3}{4}\dfrac{A}{B}$	$Q > \dfrac{3}{4}\dfrac{A}{B}$
	MRR	$Q = \dfrac{3}{4}\dfrac{A}{B}$	$Q > \dfrac{3}{4}\dfrac{A}{B}$
	RRR	$Q = \dfrac{3}{4}\dfrac{A}{B}$	$Q > \dfrac{3}{4}\dfrac{A}{B}$

Key: C = cooperative
  M = simple maximizer
  R = rivalistic

an aggregate output less than the Cournot amount.   This adjustment may be Pareto optimal, where neither producer can alter his production decision without having an adverse effect on the profits of at least one of the participants.

If both bargainers are simple maximizers, the Cournot result obtains, even under complete information.   If only one of the bargainers is a simple maximizer, and the other is a rivalistic type, the expected aggregate output is greater than the Cournot amount.

If both bargainers are of the rivalistic type, each will tend to produce $\frac{1}{2}\frac{A}{B}$, with an aggregate output of A/B when $N = 2$. This is the same output that would obtain under competitive economic conditions (i.e., when there is a very large number of independent producers, each trying to maximize his own profits).

For complete-information triopoly it is necessary for at least two of the participants to be cooperators to approximate the Paretian optimal result.   As we noted above, this is probably a difficult condition to acquire, so the cooperative solution is less likely under triopoly than under duopoly.

If two simple maximizers are paired with a cooperator, they will force the cooperator to reduce his output and perhaps keep aggregate output less than the Cournot prediction.   A simple maximizer and a rivalist will also force a cooperator to reduce his output if they are paired with such a person; the expected aggregate output for such a combination would be the Cournot quantity.

Two rivalists will encroach upon the output of a cooperator, forcing total production beyond the Cournot amount.

Three simple maximizers will yield the Cournot prediction, each producing an expected $\frac{1}{4}\frac{A}{B}$ in the aggregate.   If one of their members is transformed into a rivalist, he will go toward the rivalist's invariant output $\frac{1}{2}\frac{A}{B}$; the two remaining simple maximizers will reduce their production toward $\frac{1}{6}\frac{A}{B}$ each, and total output will exceed the Cournot prediction.   If two of the members are rivalists, they will tend to produce A/B together, leaving the simple maximizer to choose a zero output.   In effect, two rivalists will drive either a cooperator or a simple maximizer out of the market; or they may transform the third member into a rivalist.   In that case, the aggregate output would exceed the competitive production and each producer would be incurring a loss.

In this section we have derived a series of predictions for duopolistic bargaining about quantity decisions under conditions of both complete and incomplete information.   These predictions were tested in a series of experiments which will be reported in Chapter 9.

PRICE ADJUSTER OLIGOPOLY

Cournot's contribution was largely ignored until it was reviewed by the French mathematician Bertrand (1883).   Bertrand criticized Cournot's assumption that the sellers would act as quantity adjusters, and he suggested that they would consider price as the relevant decision variable.   Under this assumption, Bertrand indicated that the Cournot solution was not appropriate; rather, the rivals would engage in successive price cutting until they reached that level of prices where further cuts would reduce individual profits rather than increase them.   This followed from the assumption that the product was homogeneous, so that the producer who offered the lower price would obtain all of the trade.

At the other extreme, a number of economists suggested that the oligopolists would foresee the ultimate consequences of a price war and recognize that their long run interests were best served by tacitly agreeing on letting the monopoly price rule in the market, so that they could share this maximum *joint* profit.*   This is the Paretian optimal solution.

Thus, even if we reject the Cournot assumption regarding the

* See Fisher (1898), Moore (1906), Young (1925), Schumpeter (1928), Wicksell (1934).   The most extensive modern statement is that of Chamberlin (1933).

TABLE 7.2

Producer A	Producer B	
	Low price	High price
Low price	0 \\ 0	-5 \\ 10
High price	10 \\ -5	5 \\ 5

mode of behavior of the producers and assume that they will be price adjusters rather than quantity adjusters, there still remains some uncertainty about the outcome. The alternatives may be contrasted very effectively in terms of game theory. Assume there are two producers, A and B, each with a pair of strategies at his disposal: (1) to name a high price for his product, (2) to name a low price for his product. Say the utility payoffs are as shown in Table 7.2, where the entry in the upper right hand corner of a box is the return to producer B for the intersection of two strategies and the lower entry is the return to producer A for the intersection of these strategies. For example, if A chooses the low price and B chooses the high price, A's reward is 10, and B receives -5. This is a variant of the prisoner's dilemma game.* In strict game-theory terms, the solution is for each producer to choose the low price, yielding the Bertrand result. This follows because the low-price strategy dominates the high-price strategy; regardless of what B does, A makes more by choosing the low price. If B chooses the low price, A would prefer 0 to -5, so the low price is the best choice; if B chooses the high price, A would prefer 10 to 5, so again the low price is the best choice. The logic of game theory dictates that each

---

* The prisoner's dilemma game is attributed to A. W. Tucker [Luce and Raiffa (1957)].

should choose the low price and earn zero. Yet if they each behaved "irrationally" and adopted the dominated strategy, they would enjoy a return of 5 each—the Pareto solution in this case.

The Bertrand Model

Let us construct an oligopoly model that is similar to the setting designed by Cournot, except that we shall let price be the decision variable. Say the demand function is of the form

$$Q = a - bP \qquad P \leq \frac{a}{b}$$

where Q is the aggregate output of the oligopolistic group, which is determined by the selection of P, the ruling price in the market. The ruling price is the lowest price quoted by any of the producers. If one producer quotes the lowest price, he gets all the sales, Q. If L producers tie for the lowest price quotation, their expected share of the market is Q/L, for the product is perfectly homogeneous. The parameters a and b represent, respectively, the quantity axis intercept of the demand function and the slope of the demand function. Let us assume that each participant has a fixed cost F which is incurred on any bid; further, if his price quotation is higher than that of any of his rivals so that he sells nothing, he incurs an additional cost of E for the transaction. The cost E may be considered a penalty for submitting an unsuccessful bid.

Bertrand assumed that each producer would try to maximize his own profits, taking the price quotation of his opponent as given data, not affected by his own decision. In our terminology Bertrand assumed that all participants would behave as *simple maximizers*. The objective of the simple maximizer is his own profit, π_1. In the Bertrand setting we define this variable as

$$\pi_1 = \frac{aP_1 - bP_1^2}{L} - F \qquad \text{if } P_1 \leq P_j \, (j = 2, \ldots, N) \quad (7.15)$$

where P_1 is the price quoted by producer 1 and $L - 1$ other producers.   Otherwise

$$\pi_1 = -F - E \qquad \text{if } P_1 > P_k$$

where P_k is the minimum of P_j ($j = 2, \ldots, N$).

To maximize π_1, it is necessary to adopt a strategy which ensures, first, that $P_1 \leq P_j$; second, that $L = 1$; finally, given the first two conditions, that $P_1 = \dfrac{1}{2}\dfrac{a}{b}$.* These three conditions are not likely to be compatible: if a producer adopts a price of $\dfrac{1}{2}\dfrac{a}{b}$, the monopoly price, it is most unlikely that all of his rivals will charge higher prices.   The third requirement is apt to be sacrificed to achieve the first two conditions: To guarantee that he will have the unique low price in the market, the simple maximizer will tend to act as a price cutter.†   This is the Bertrand prediction.

The Condition of Incomplete Information

To induce all bargaining types to behave as simple maximizers, it would be necessary to design a setting in which the profits of the other participants seemed to be invariant with respect to the price choice of a particular producer.   Then, whether the participants were *simple maximizers* (objective: π_1), *cooperators* (objective: increased joint profits), or *rivalists* (objective: to make more than the others), all would try to maximize the unique variable π_1.

---

* $d\pi_1/dP_1 = a - 2bP_1 = 0$; $d^2\pi_1/dP^2 = -2b < 0$; $P_1 = \dfrac{1}{2}\dfrac{a}{b}$.   The amount a/b is the demand curve's price axis intercept; the price $\dfrac{1}{2}\dfrac{a}{b}$ is the price a monopoly would charge.

† The simple maximizer will try to name a price P_0 which is just under the lowest price P_1 quoted by an opponent, provided $P_1 \leq \dfrac{1}{2}\dfrac{a}{b}$.   This is because the profit when $L = 1$ is greater than when $L > 1$ as P_0 approaches $P_1 (L = 1, 2, \ldots, N)$:

$$\frac{aP_0 - bP_0^2}{1} - F < \frac{aP_1 - bP_1^2}{2} - F.$$

This would follow because the other participants' profits, $\sum_{j=2}^{N} \pi_j$, would be regarded as a constant by the participant under consideration.   As in the quantity adjuster model, the closest experimental replication we can make of the implied Bertrand conditions is to provide the subjects with incomplete information.   This condition prevents the subject from knowing *what* effect his action has on the fortunes of his counterparts and may lead him to assume that his action has *no* effect on $\sum_{j=2}^{N} \pi_j$.   Again, for experiments under the condition of incomplete information, we would expect a tendency for negotiated contracts to approximate the equilibrium solution (the Bertrand solution) and to display relatively little dispersion around that solution.   In this case, the equilibrium solution is the lowest feasible price bid available to the subjects.

The Condition of Complete Information

If the subjects can identify a relation between their own price choice and the profits of their counterparts, then it is more likely that the various bargaining types and signals will exercise an influence on the oligopoly outcome.   This is less true for price adjuster models than for quantity adjuster models because:

1.   The nature of the relation between the decision variable and the other participants' profits is easier to imagine in the price variation model under incomplete information.
2.   The rivalistic type will follow the same strategy as the simple maximizer in the price variation model (provided price is nonnegative).   That is, if he desires to make more than his opponent, he must ensure that $P_1 < P_k$, which implies $L = 1$; the rivalistic type also must behave as a price cutter.

The Paretian Optimal Solution

Complete information does enable the cooperative participants to follow a different strategy, however.   The objective of the

cooperative bargainer is to increase joint profits. At the limit
his objective might be considered the maximization of joint
profits. The objective variable is defined as

$$\pi_1 + \sum_{j=2}^{N} \pi_j = aP - bP^2 - NF - (N - L)E. \qquad (7.16)$$

For this function to be a maximum it is necessary to:

1. Set L equal to N, so that no participant incurs the penalty E
    for having a high price.
2. Choose P so that the first derivative of (7.16) with respect
    to P is zero, and the second derivative is negative. Thus
    the cooperative player tries to *match* the lowest price in the
    market to meet requirement number 1 above (provided that
    price is not greater than the monopoly price). If he can
    choose which price that is, he will pick

$$\frac{d\left(\pi_1 + \sum_{j=2}^{N} \pi_j\right)}{dP} = a - 2bP = 0$$

$$P = \frac{1}{2}\frac{a}{b}. \qquad (7.17)$$

The cooperative solution is for *each* participant to name the
monopoly price; this action maximizes joint profits and places
the group in a Paretian optimal position. The expected profit
of each participant would be $1/N \left(\sum_{j=1}^{N} \pi_j\right)$, since the product is
homogeneous; the probability of any given customer going to
any given producer is $1/N$.

In summary, the *cooperative* subject will try to match the
lowest price set by his opponents; the *simple maximizer* and the
rivalistic subject will try to cut under the prices set by the opponents. The ability of the cooperative participant to match the
lowest price quoted by his competitors depends in part upon his

knowledge of the past pattern of price bids by the opponents. Consider, for example, the problem confronting two cooperative duopolists who have no knowledge of the likely price bid of the other or even of which price will maximize their joint profits. They are as likely to engage in what appears to be price cutting as two rivalistic participants. Indeed, the two cooperators may end up at the Bertrand price by such a process simply because the Bertrand price, as we have structured the situation, forms the lower limit of price cuts. Therefore it is the one price that suggests itself to each of the participants as a bid that may not cause a penalty to be imposed upon anyone for having a higher price. This would not be a problem for the cooperators if they could communicate in some fashion, either by a pattern of bidding (if they can inform their counterpart of their bids) or by any other means. Also, cooperation would be possible from the outset if they had enough information to identify that price which would yield the maximum joint profits.

The amount of information available to the participants will be quite relevant to the outcome for the cooperative subjects. This is not true for the simple maximizers and the rivalists: they are likely to seek a successively dominating price strategy, with the Bertrand price as the limit, under either information condition. Thus, information will to a limited extent be a relevant experimental condition.

The Condition of Number of Participants

Another significant experimental condition is N, the number of participants in an oligopoly. If it would be difficult for cooperative duopolists to establish a tacit agreement under incomplete information, it would be much more difficult for three cooperators to come to some sort of agreement in the absence of communication channels. Further, the presence of only one participant who behaves as a simple maximizer or rivalist is enough to ensure the Bertrand result, under either information condition. Indeed, the convergence to the Bertrand price should be substantially faster with three participants than it was with two.

We would anticipate the Bertrand solution in the instance of three producers for every situation except that of three cooperators possessing complete information.

Derivation of Predictions under Various Experimental Conditions

Table 7.3 presents the two states of the two experimental variables, information and the number of participants, and the effect of these states on the predicted outcome for various possible combinations of bargaining types. The Bertrand solution is predicted for every combination except those consisting exclusively of cooperators under complete information.

TABLE 7.3   Possible Oligopolistic Combinations of Bargaining Types and Related Predictions

Number of bargainers	Possible combinations of bargaining types or signals	Predicted price (P)	
		Incomplete information	*Complete information*
$N = 2$	CC	$P = B$	$P > B$
	CM	$P = B$	$P = B$
	CR	$P = B$	$P = B$
	MM	$P = B$	$P = B$
	MR	$P = B$	$P = B$
	RR	$P = B$	$P = B$
$N = 3$	CCC	$P = B$	$P > B$
	CCM	$P = B$	$P = B$
	CCR	$P = B$	$P = B$
	CMM	$P = B$	$P = B$
	CMR	$P = B$	$P = B$
	CRR	$P = B$	$P = B$
	MMM	$P = B$	$P = B$
	MMR	$P = B$	$P = B$
	MRR	$P = B$	$P = B$
	RRR	$P = B$	$P = B$

Key: C = cooperative
M = simple maximizer
R = rivalistic
B = the Bertrand price

SUMMARY

Bargaining behavior in oligopoly depends on whether the bargainers are quantity adjusters or price adjusters, i.e., depends on the nature of the decision open to them.   Bargaining behavior also depends on the information available to the bargainer and on the number of opponents with whom he is faced in the marketplace.   Finally, bargaining behavior depends on the individual's objective and signaling style, that is, whether he is a simple maximizer, a rivalist, or a cooperator.   In Tables 7.1 and 7.3 we have summarized predictions of adjustments that bargainers will reach depending on each of the factors just mentioned.   We conducted a series of quantity adjuster and price adjuster experiments to test these predictions.   These experiments shared a number of features, and these shared features are described in Chapter 8, which follows.   The results of the quantity adjuster experiments are then reported in Chapter 9, while those of the price adjuster experiments are reported in Chapter 10.

Experimental Procedures

In order to test the hypotheses presented in Chapter 7, we conducted two series of experiments, one in which the bargainers were quantity adjusters and one in which they were price adjusters. Each experiment simulated a market situation involving either two sellers (duopoly) or three sellers (triopoly), and each was designed to test one or more different hypotheses. Although each experiment had certain distinctive controls, distinctive procedures related to the various independent and dependent variables, and so forth, the common features of most of the experiments loom larger than the differences among them.

113

Therefore, the first sections of this chapter describe those procedures common to all of the experiments to be reported, and later sections present particular studies and the procedures distinctive to them.

SUBJECTS

In all, 291 individual subjects participated in 10 different oligopoly experiments, serving in 124 bargaining groups. All subjects were male students at The Pennsylvania State University. Each experimental session was conducted with different subjects; no subject participated in more than one session. Further, none of the subjects in the oligopoly studies had participated in any of the bilateral monopoly experiments.

At the time the subjects were recruited, they were given no information about the nature of the experiments. The students were told that if they volunteered, they could make some money by participating in a research project, but they were given no indication of the amount of money that could be earned; they were assured there would be no noxious stimuli.

Most of the subjects (265 of the 291) were juniors and seniors enrolled in sections of an all-university Reserve Officers Training Corps. The procedures and randomization methods relating to these subjects are described first; the procedures for the remaining 26 non-ROTC subjects are presented in a subsequent section of this chapter.

RANDOMIZATION

One purpose of the experimental procedures was to randomize the effects of certain variables which were not of interest to us at the present stage of research. Since comparisons were desired between the results of different experiments, the randomization method used gave all subjects an equal opportunity of being selected for any experiment. This was accomplished by securing the names of a large number of students willing to participate and then randomizing these names into conditions before the initial experiment, using a table of random numbers.

A total of 279 ROTC students volunteered to participate in the research project. All of the 279 subjects who volunteered to take part were notified one week ahead of the night they were scheduled to appear. A total of 265 of these subjects appeared on schedule and were run in their assigned experiment. This constitutes 95 per cent overall attendance. The attendance for every experiment exceeded 90 per cent.

Before the subjects arrived at an experimental session, they were randomized into pairs for the duopoly experiments and into triplets for the triopoly experiments. These groups represented the various bargaining teams.

PROCEDURES

An experimental session began with the subjects coming to an assigned room, where they were met individually by the experimenter. As each subject arrived, he was given a number corresponding to the order of his arrival. This number assigned him to one of the instruction rooms. Once in the assigned room, the subject exchanged the initial number for a second one, randomly drawn. The second number identified the subject in the experiment, and grouped him with one other subject (in the case of duopoly) or two other subjects (in the case of triopoly). This exchange of numbers made sure that the order in which the various subjects arrived did not determine their identifying numbers in the experiment and that the subjects in one room were not aware of the numbers identifying subjects in any other room. Bargaining rivals always received instructions in separate rooms.

In their respective instruction rooms, subjects were given a printed set of instructions, a payoff matrix, and a profit sheet.*

---

* Instructions, payoff matrices, and profit sheets for each experiment are displayed in the appendixes.

The instructions were read to the subjects, and each had his own copy of them for use throughout the experimental session.

After hearing the instructions read, the subjects were given the opportunity to ask questions. Most of the questions centered on interpreting and using the profit tables. Specific examples were presented to clarify the use of the tables. The fact that any profit the subject earned would become his personal property was emphasized. The sellers were instructed to remain seated once in their cubicles and to maintain silence throughout the entire session.

The period of instruction lasted about 20 minutes. The subjects were then taken individually into a large room containing separate cubicles, partitioned by 6-foot walls, each furnished with a desk and chair. Once in his assigned cubicle, a subject could not see anyone except the research personnel, nor could he be seen by anyone but them.

After all the subjects were in their assigned cubicles, a general announcement was made calling for the bargaining to begin. The negotiations consisted of a series of written transactions concerning the quantity (or price) of a fictitious product to be sold by each seller. As a result of each transaction, and depending upon the quantities (or prices) selected for that transaction, each seller earned a profit or sustained a loss. This profit or loss was shown in the body of the profit table furnished each participant and served to provide incentive and assure seriousness among the subjects. At the end of the session, a cash payoff was made of the total amount each subject earned during the transactions. At that time, each subject was asked not to discuss the experiment with anyone, in order to prevent bias in subsequent research. Analysis of the results and interviews with the subjects of the various experimental sessions indicated that the subjects probably had kept this trust.

On each transaction, the subject would record his choice on the profit sheet provided for this purpose. An assistant would then record these choices on a record sheet and, after all participants had made their choices, inform the subject of his profit or loss for that transaction.   Each subject was always informed of his profit or loss before he was required to make his next bid of the series. At one point in the planning stage of the experiment, we considered paying the subject at the end of each transaction; but we rejected this because of the time it would consume.

The first three transactions, called practice trials, were provided to let the subjects become accustomed to the use of the profit table; the profit from these trials was not included in determining the cash payoff.   After the practice trials, the session consisted of a predetermined number of transactions:* 22 for the quantity variation experiments, 15 for the price variation experiments.   The subjects were not told how many transactions would take place, but knew that there would be a "large number."   Before the final transaction, a general announcement informed all the subjects that the next bid would be their last one.

* The number of transactions necessary to approximate stabilized behavior was determined before the initial experiment, on the basis of pilot studies. Such a decision is always a compromise: Some groups are still in the learning stage and require additional transactions to stabilize; others appear to learn faster, identify a mutually acceptable solution early, and, if the experiment continues too long, they may become bored and turn to unusual choice patterns for amusement.   The choice of the number of trials must be a compromise between these forces.

The fact that the subjects were not informed of the number of transactions involved in the experiment and that one of the regular transactions was used as the relevant statistic suggests that subjects might still be attempting to communicate on the relevant transaction.   That is, subjects might be exchanging rivalistic or cooperative signals on that transaction as a means of getting to some other objective—say the maximization of individual profit.   However, it is the value of a decision that is important for economic analysis, not the motive behind the act.   Two players, motivated by self-interest, might choose rivalistic strategies as appropriate vehicles for reaching their objective; their behavior and the economic adjustment they produce will not differ from that of two rivalists intent upon beating each other (except perhaps in end effects, but even this is by no means certain).   Thus the combination of various types of signalers has as much significance for our analysis as the combination of various bargaining types.   Indeed, it is difficult to separate the two factors in an individual case; we can see some distinction, however, when a situation tends to induce a substantial increase in one type of signal.

Following the final transaction, the subjects totaled their profits and compared their totals with those calculated by the assistant. A receipt was signed for the amount paid, and the subject was released unless it was felt that a personal interview was necessary. Those subjects whose bids were unusual were interviewed for insight into the rationale behind these bids. To avoid any possible contact between bargaining rivals, all members of a particular bargaining group were dismissed individually.

Procedures Specific to Particular Studies

Six of the ten studies to be reported dealt with the quantity adjuster condition, while four dealt with the price adjuster condition. A total of 130 of the 265 ROTC students participated in the quantity variation experiments, 64 (32 groups) participating as duopolists and 66 (22 groups) as triopolists; 135 took part in the experiments on price variation, 72 (36 groups)* as duopolists, and 63 (21 groups) as triopolists.

Approximately one-half of the groups in each of these oligopoly situations negotiated under incomplete-information conditions, and one-half negotiated under complete-information conditions. Under *incomplete information* each subject knew what his own payoff would be for any particular combinations of bids; he did not know what profit his rival (or rivals) would make. Under complete information he knew the profits accruing to his rivals as well as the profits assigned to him.

Quantity Adjuster Models

Two profit tables were used for the experiments on quantity variation: one for complete information (see Appendix IX), and one for incomplete information (see Appendix VII). Both profit tables were based on the same demand curve, and each offered

* Two price variation bargaining groups, each consisting of two subjects, were dropped from the study at the time the sessions in which they participated were being conducted when it became evident that one subject in each group did not understand the instructions or grasp the meaning of the profit table. Thus, data are reported for 68 subjects in 34 bargaining groups under price variation duopoly.

identical quantity choices.* The only difference between the matrices was that each entry in the body of the incomplete-information table contained only the profit to the seller making the choice, while each entry in the complete-information table showed the profit to both the seller *and* his competition. All profits shown in these tables were in hundredths of a cent.

Thus, subjects participating in the *duopoly* studies, when told of their rival's quantity choice, could determine their own profit for the transaction and, under complete information, could also

* The profits in the payoff tables were rounded off in half-cent amounts, and not always consistently. The reasons for this were as follows: (1) We were afraid that such a large table of four-digit numbers would be confusing to naïve subjects and require protracted learning periods. (2) Since the numbers represent such small sums (hundredths of a cent), the motivation might not be sufficient for long learning periods. (3) There were constraints on the amount of the payoff, not only in terms of research budget, but also because we wanted to compare the results with those of other experiments involving modest payments. (4) We thought such rounding would help the subject keep a record of his profits (and those of his rival under complete information). (5) Our experiments on discriminability indicated that small differences in payoffs around critical values contributed to dispersion around those solutions. The last consideration led us to round the payoffs in such a way that there was at least a half-cent difference around each of the predicted profits: the cooperative (Pareto), the Cournot, and the competitive. Alternatively, one could say we tried to make each alternative solution equally prominent. For example, the joint payoff in the Table in Appendix IX is 36 cents only for the Pareto predictions of individual choices of 15 (duopoly) and 10 (triopoly). For other combinations of aggregate output of 30, the joint profit is 35.5 cents.

This choice had some unfortunate consequences: (1) When we decided to conduct experiments 11 and 12, we found that there was not a unique rivalistic solution, as required by the theory, and that the Pareto solutions were too distinctive for the cooperative version. This required the new tables presented in Appendix XI. (2) In simplifying the tables to make them easier for naïve subjects to interpret, we also made it harder to make adjustments toward an equilibrium solution such as Cournot's. For example, a quantity choice of 25 is equally good against opposing outputs from 8 to 17; alternatively, if the opponent produces 17, a player makes his maximum profit of 18 cents by any quantity choice from 18 to 25. This characteristic undoubtedly is one reason for dispersion in the experiments. A replication with improved tables is reported in Chapter 11.

determine their rival's profit. Subjects participating in the triopoly studies, under incomplete information, were told only the sum of their rivals' choices, as this was the only information they needed to determine their own profits. Under complete information, however, each subject in a triopoly was given both rivals' quantity choices, so he could determine both of their profits. Care was taken to see that after each transaction the subject's profit sheet correctly contained all three quantity choices and all three profits.

Each seller could select any of the quantities (8 to 32) listed across the top of the table; the quantities (8 to 64) listed down the left margin of the table represented the possible choices of his competition.

Single-shot Transactions

Two additional duopoly experiments, involving a total of 26 subjects (13 pairs), were conducted in conjunction with the above quantity variation experiments. Although these experiments did not draw their subjects from the same ROTC population, the randomization procedures preliminary to the actual negotiations were essentially the same as those described above. That is, subjects were randomized into two conditions (rivalistic and cooperative) and into bargaining pairs, and order of arrival was controlled by randomization.

Instead of a series of transactions, however, the bargaining session for each of these experiments consisted of 10 practice trials plus *one* regular transaction. The profit table furnished to each subject (see Appendix XI) was a double-entry (complete-information) table, with profits represented in hundredths of a cent.

Price Adjuster Models

The subjects in the price adjuster experiments competed for profits on each transaction by means of the price chosen for the fictitious product they were selling. If the price a particular seller chose was the *low* price in the market (either duopoly or triopoly), then he received all the sales in that market, and, consequently, all the profit. If his price was *tied* for low, with either one or two other persons, then these sellers shared the associated profits equally. If, however, the seller's price bid was neither low or tied for low, then he would not gain any of the market profits and would lose his fixed costs plus a penalty (a total of 25 cents) on that bid.

Each seller was given a profit table which showed the 10 prices from which he could choose; associated with each price on the table was the profit or loss the seller would earn if his price were low, tied for low, or high. Price choices on each profit table ranged from 0.5 to 5.0, the interval between choices being 0.5. The profits corresponding to each price choice were derived from a linear demand curve and from a constant cost function (to be presented later), while the losses for each bid were fixed at a total of 25 cents.

For motivation each subject was given an initial capital of \$2.50 and was assured that this money plus any that he earned during the session would be his to keep. Losses were subtracted from the total amount of money (including the \$2.50 stake) that the subject earned.

Under *incomplete-information* conditions, the sellers were told whether they were bidding against two or three other persons, but they were not given any information concerning the revenue or cost structure of their rivals. All they were told was that they would choose a price and, depending upon the prices chosen by their competition, would receive a profit or loss. Thus, for each transaction, the seller would know his own bid and the resulting profit or loss, but he would not be informed of his opponents' price choice or profit.

The subjects run under *complete information* were told that their competition had a profit table identical to their own. In addition, after each transaction the assistant told each subject what price the rivals had bid and made sure that each subject had recorded his own price choice and the resulting profit as well as the price choices of his competition. Thus, before making his next price offer of the series, each seller had full knowledge of what price his competition had chosen previously and the profits he (or they) had made.

DISCUSSION OF THE PROCEDURES

One purpose of the experimental procedures was to minimize interpersonal reactions between subjects. The bargainers were physically separated and communicated only through an intermediary, using bids of prescribed form. Subjects did not know the identities of their bargaining rivals. The negotiations were conducted in silence, to preclude the possibility that a subject might identify his opponent by recognizing his voice. Moreover, the members of any oligopoly were given instructions in separate rooms, so that bargaining rivals could not see each other during the instruction period. At the conclusion of a session, payoffs were made individually, and each subject left the session alone.

This procedure eliminates certain variables which may well be important in bargaining—variables concerned with interpersonal perceptions, prejudices, incompatibilities, sympathies, etc. We believe that such variables should be either systematically studied or controlled in experimentation on bargaining. It cannot be assumed that such variables may simply be neglected. We have chosen to control these variables in our present research program; they may be manipulated and studied systematically in future studies.

Another purpose of our experimental procedures was to randomize the effects of certain variables which were not of interest at the present stage of the research. Randomization procedures were used to cancel any possible effects of order of arrival of subjects, for example, since those who came early might differ from latecomers in strength of motivation to participate, utility of money, compulsiveness, etc. These are variables which may well be significant in bargaining, but which could not be studied systematically at this time. Randomization procedures were also used to control for those preferences which may draw particular bargainers into negotiations with each other. Most important, randomization was used in assigning subjects to the various treatment conditions, so that statistical comparisons of behavior in these conditions would be assisted.

In the two chapters which follow, the hypotheses which underlie the various experimental sessions will be presented together with the results of the experiments. Chapter 9 deals with studies in which quantity is the decision variable—studies designed to test quantity adjuster models. Chapter 10 deals with studies in which price is the decision variable and in which the price adjuster models are tested. Chapter 11, the final chapter, is an overview, giving some additional results and attempting an integration and appraisal of the theoretical and experimental work presented in the book, for both bilateral monopoly and oligopoly.

CHAPTER 9

Experimental Tests of the Quantity Adjuster Models

The theoretical models reviewed in Chapter 7 offer three distinct solutions for the oligopoly bargaining situation under conditions of quantity variation. Let

A = price axis intercept of the average revenue function
B = slope (negative) of the average revenue function
N = number of bargainers in the oligopoly
q_i = quantity output of the ith bargainer (firm)
Q = aggregate quantity output of the N bargainers (firms)

The solutions yielded by the three models are:

1. The Cournot solution: Each bargainer (firm) assumes that the quantity choices of the other bargainers are invariant with respect to changes in his own quantity choices. The Cournot model yields the prediction that the quantity output of each bargainer will be

$$q_i = \frac{1}{N+1} \frac{A}{B} \qquad (9.1)$$

and the aggregate Cournot quantity is

$$Q = \frac{N}{N+1} \frac{A}{B}. \qquad (9.2)$$

It follows from this solution that as N increases, the aggregate quantity (9.2) *increases* but the quantity output of the individual bargainers (9.1) *decreases*.

2. The Paretian optimal solution: Each bargainer chooses a quantity output such that the aggregate output is always that which maximizes joint profits. (For convenience this will be referred to as the Pareto solution.) The Paretian optimal model yields the prediction that the quantity output of each bargainer will be

$$q_i = \frac{1}{2} \frac{A}{B} - \sum_{\substack{j=1 \\ j \neq i}}^{N} q_j \qquad (9.3)$$

and the aggregate Paretian optimal quantity is the monopoly output

$$Q = \frac{1}{2} \frac{A}{B}. \qquad (9.4)$$

3. The competitive solution: Each bargainer chooses a quantity output such that the aggregate output yields zero profits to each of the oligopolists. The competitive solution implies that under equal cost conditions the representative participant would have an output of

$$q_i = \frac{1}{N} \frac{A}{B}. \qquad (9.5)$$

The aggregate output under the competitive solution is

$$Q = \frac{A}{B}. \qquad (9.6)$$

The theoretical discussion in Chapter 7 suggested that none of these three economic models offers a general solution to the oligopoly bargaining situation. It was shown that a behavioral model of oligopolistic bargaining must incorporate certain psychological variables. From the formulation presented in Chapter 7, it may be seen that the predicted solution in each case of oligopolistic bargaining is affected by three variables (see Table 8.1):

1. *Amount of information* available to the bargainers
2. *Number of bargainers in the oligopolistic structure*
3. *Composition of bargaining or signaling types* in the oligopolistic structure

The behavioral model yields certain interesting testable hypotheses. It offers distinctly different predictions for oligopolistic bargainers under incomplete information than for oligopolistic bargainers under complete information. Under *incomplete information*, a bargainer knows only his own profit resulting from any particular set of quantity choices; he has no indication of the amounts of the profits accruing to his opponents. Under *complete information*, a bargainer knows not only his own profits resulting from a set of quantity choices but also the profits to his opponents resulting from their quantity choices.

For oligopolists under conditions of incomplete information, regardless of what bargaining types they may represent, the theory yields the Cournot solution (Equations 9.1 and 9.2). It is of interest to note that according to the theory presented in Chapter 7, the Cournot solution is appropriate for bargainers under incomplete information for various sizes of N and regardless of the bargaining types or signals (rivalistic, cooperative, and/or simple maximizers) employed by the participants.

For oligopolists under conditions of complete information, the behavioral model does not yield predictions as invariant as those for incomplete information. We suggest that the solution to oligopolistic bargaining under complete information is a function both of the number of participants in the oligopolistic structure and of the composition of bargaining types or signals employed by the negotiators. The predictions from the model for complete information are reviewed later in this chapter, where the relevant experimental data are presented.

The first section of this chapter presents the experiments which were designed to study oligopolistic bargaining under incomplete information: to test predictions (9.1) and (9.2), and to test the Cournot hypothesis that as N increases, the aggregate quantity increases but the individual quantity decreases.

Operational Definitions

In all the experiments to be reported, the parameters were $A = 2.4$ cents and $B = 0.04$ cent.

With these parameters, the Cournot solution for $N = 2$ is $Q = 40$, and for $N = 3$ it is $Q = 45$.

Both the Pareto solution and the competitive solution are invariant with respect to the number of bargainers in the oligopoly N. The Pareto solution is $Q = 30$, and the competitive solution is $Q = 60$.

BARGAINING UNDER INCOMPLETE INFORMATION

Two experiments were conducted in which subjects negotiated as quantity adjusters under incomplete information. That is, for each transaction they knew only their own profits for any quantity choice. In the first of these, the oligopoly was formed by two bargainers, and in the second it was formed by three.

Experiment 7: Duopoly

Introduction. The first experiment in the oligopoly series, experiment 7, concerns bargaining in a duopoly by quantity adjusters. It provides a test of the hypothesis that under incom-

plete information duopolists will negotiate transactions supporting the Cournot solution rather than either the Pareto or the
competitive solutions.

Subjects and Procedure. Thirty-two male undergraduates
(16 bargaining pairs) participated in experiment 7. Each subject was given a printed set of instructions, a profit record sheet,
and a profit table showing the payoffs to him (and only to him)
for any quantity chosen by him and his opponent. These
materials are shown in Appendix VII, with the exception of the
instructions, which are presented here:

Instructions to Seller A

The National Science Foundation, the Ford Foundation, and the
Office of Naval Research have provided funds for the conduct of
research regarding economic decisions. If you follow instructions
carefully and make appropriate decisions, you may earn an appreciable amount of money. *You may keep all the money that you earn.*
You cannot lose your own money, but poor choices will result in
small or no profit to you.

You will be paired at random with one other person. You will
not see this person or speak with him at any time. You will never
know the identity of your competition, called seller B, nor will he
be aware of yours.

Imagine that you and seller B are the sole producers of some
standardized commodity. You and he will engage in a series of
transactions by means of written bids, the bids on each transaction
representing the quantity of the commodity produced for that
transaction. You must bid on each transaction.

You will be furnished with a table which shows the various levels
of profit or loss you can attain. The quantities you may produce
are listed across the top of the table, while the quantities produced by
seller B are listed down the left hand margin. Your profits are
represented within the body of the table by the intersection of the
quantity produced by you and the quantity produced by seller B.
For example, on a given transaction you might select a quantity of 24;
you would receive one of the profits in the 24th column. If seller B
had selected a quantity of 28, then your profit would be at the intersection of column 24 (your bid) and row 28 (his bid). The profit

shown at this point is 750, or 7.50 cents. Decimal points have been omitted for simplicity, but may always be considered to be located two places in from the right.

The process is started by each player selecting and recording a quantity on the yellow sheet provided for that purpose. You may select any quantity across the top of the table, and then record it. An experimental assistant will then inform you of the quantity chosen by seller B, and the amount of profit or loss you made on that transaction. After each transaction your yellow sheet should show your quantity bid, seller B's quantity bid, and your profit or loss from that transaction.

The process is repeated over and over. You may select the same quantity each time; you do not have to do so, however. Decisions will ordinarily be made every few minutes, but extra time will be granted when necessary.

In order for you to become accustomed to using the profit table, the first 3 bids will be for practice, and will involve no profit or loss. At the end of the session we will add up your profit and loss column and give you the resulting amount of money. This will be done in separate counting rooms, so you will not see the person with whom you have been bidding.

Are there any questions?

As was explained in Chapter 8, subjects were assigned to pairs at random, and possible influences of order of arrival to the experimental session were controlled by randomization. The two members of each pair were kept apart and were given instructions in different rooms. After the instruction period was completed, each subject was escorted individually to his assigned cubicle, where he was isolated from all but the experimenters. No communication was permitted between the participants, except for the written quantity bids between two members of a pair.

In all, 25 transactions were conducted. The first 3 were practice trials, and the next 22 were the regular trials—those having monetary payoffs. Before regular transaction 22, a general announcement was made indicating that the next transaction was to be the final one.

TABLE 9.1   Quantity Choices on Transaction 21 of
Experiment 7, Duopoly under Incomplete Information

Group	q_1	q_1 supports	q_2	q_2 supports	Q	Q supports
1	16	C	20	M	36	M
2	18	M	20	M	38	M
3	19	M	19	M	38	M
4	20	M	20	M	40	M
5	20	M	20	M	40	M
6	20	M	20	M	40	M
7	20	M	20	M	40	M
8	15	C	25	M, R	40	M
9	18	M	23	M	41	M
10	19	M	22	M	41	M
11	19	M	22	M	41	M
12	23	M	20	M	43	M
13	18	M	25	M, R	43	M
14	25	M, R	20	M	45	M
15	31	R	20	M	51	R
16	27	R	25	M, R	52	R
Mean	20.5	M	21.3	M	41.8	M
Median	19.5	M	20.0	M	40.5	M

Key: C = Pareto (cooperative) solution
M = Cournot (maximizing) solution
R = competitive (rivalistic) solution

Results.   Transaction 21 was taken to represent the relevant statistic.* It was the final regular transaction prior to the announcement that the forthcoming transaction was the final one. The purpose of this announcement was to elicit any possible end-play behavior on the twenty-second trial. The transactions negotiated by the pairs on transaction 21 are presented in Table 9.1. Complete protocols of data for all bargaining pairs on all transactions are presented in Appendix VII.

* The number of transactions to be conducted in this experiment was determined in advance on the basis of pilot data, and the decision to use transaction 21 to represent relevant behavior was also made in advance. Inspection of the data indicates that there is little difference among the average results of transactions 19, 20, and 21.

The hypothesis under test is that the Cournot solution ($q_1 = q_2 = 20$; $Q = 40$) will be supported rather than the Paretian optimal solution ($q_1 = q_2 = 15$; $Q = 30$) or the competitive solution ($q_1 = q_2 = 30$; $Q = 60$). An observation is said to support a particular hypothesis if it is closer to the magnitude derived from that hypothesis than to the others. Thus an individual output of 19 is said to support the Cournot hypothesis because it is closer to the predicted Cournot production than to the alternatives. An observation midway between two predictions is counted as one-half unit of support for each. Data are analyzed separately for the subjects assigned at random to the roles of first seller and second seller.

Of the 16 first sellers, 11.5 chose outputs closer to the individual Cournot quantity. According to the binomial test, this result is significantly different from chance expectation at $p < .11$. Of the 16 second sellers, 14.5 chose outputs closer to the Cournot quantity. According to the binomial test, this result is significantly different from chance expectation at $p < .002$. Of the aggregate quantities (for each duopoly, the sum of the individual quantities), 14 of the 16 observations supported the Cournot model. According to the binomial test, this result is significantly different from chance expectation at $p < .002$. From these results, it is concluded that the results of this experiment favor the Cournot model.

Further evidence in favor of this conclusion may be drawn from the mean and median values. The mean output for the first sellers is 20.5, the median 19.5. These deviate by only .5 units from the Cournot value. The mean output for the second sellers is 21.3, which is closer to the Cournot value than to the Pareto or competitive predictions. The median output is the Cournot value 20. The mean aggregate output is 41.8, compared to the Cournot prediction of 40; the median aggregate output is 40.5. It would appear that quantity adjuster duopolists behave in accordance with the Cournot predictions under conditions of incomplete information.

Experiment 8: Triopoly

Introduction.   In the eighth experiment, bargaining groups consisted of three individuals, whereas in experiment 7 they consisted of two.   Experiment 8 was conducted to test the Cournot solution for $N = 3$.   The other hypothesis under test was that as N increases the aggregate quantity increases but the individual quantities decrease.   Specifically, the hypotheses were:

H_1:   Transaction 21 by triopolists under incomplete information will show a greater tendency toward the Cournot solution than toward either the Pareto or the competitive solutions.

H_2:   As N increases, oligopoly bargaining will yield an increased aggregate quantity Q, but the individual quantities q_i will decrease.

One may note that the second hypothesis is not entirely dependent on the first.   It is possible for data to support H_2 while providing little or no support for H_1.   It is also possible for data to support H_1 while providing little support for H_2.

Subjects and Procedure.   The first hypothesis was tested with data from the eighth experiment, in which 33 male undergraduates participated in 11 bargaining groups.   None of these men had participated in any previous bargaining studies.

The second hypothesis, H_2, was tested with data from both the seventh and the eighth experimental sessions.   Thus 65 subjects yielded data used in the test of H_2, 32 serving in bargaining groups of 2, and 33 serving in bargaining groups of 3.   The fact that subjects were assigned at random to experiments 7 and 8, from a common overall pool of subjects, permitted a direct statistical comparison between the two sessions.

Each of the subjects was given an appropriate set of instructions, a profit record sheet, and a profit table exhibiting the payoffs to him (and only to him) for any quantity chosen by him and his opponent (or opponents).   The materials for the duopolistic bargainers (experiment 7) are displayed in Appendix

VII; those for the triopolistic bargainers (experiment 8), in Appendix VIII.

The procedures of the experiment are explained in Chapter 8. Subjects were randomized into conditions (duopoly or triopoly) and were randomly assigned to bargaining groups.

Both experiment 7 and experiment 8 consisted of 25 transactions. The 25 transactions consisted of 3 practice trials and 22 regular transactions, the difference being that the regular transactions involved a real monetary payoff. Prior to regular transaction 22, a general announcement was made indicating that the forthcoming transaction would be the last. The purpose of the announcement was to induce end effects.

Results. The contracts negotiated by the triopolistic groups on transaction 21 are presented in Table 9.2. Complete protocols for all triopolists on all transactions are exhibited in Appendix VIII.

TABLE 9.2 Quantity Choices on Transaction 21 of Experiment 8, Triopoly under Incomplete Information

Group	q_1	q_1 supports	q_2	q_2 supports	q_3	q_3 supports	Q	Q supports
17	15	M	10	C	15	M	40	M
18	8	C	10	C	25	R	43	M
19	14	M	15	M	17	M	46	M
20	15	M	16	M	15	M	46	M
21	15	M	15	M	16	M	46	M
22	12	C	15	M	20	R	47	M
23	16	M	16	M	16	M	48	M
24	15	M	21	R	14	M	50	M
25	16	M	15	M	20	R	51	M
26	19	R	19	R	15	M	53	R
27	20	R	20	R	19	R	59	R
Mean	15.0	M	15.6	M	17.5	M	48.1	M
Median	15.0	M	15.0	M	16.0	M	47.0	M

Key: C = Pareto (cooperative) solution
M = Cournot (maximizing) solution
R = competitive (rivalistic) solution

The first hypothesis is that the final transactions by triopolists under incomplete information will show a greater tendency toward the Cournot solution ($q_1 = q_2 = q_3 = 15$; $Q = 45$) than toward either the Pareto solution ($q_1 = q_2 = q_3 = 10$; $Q = 30$) or the competitive solution ($q_1 = q_2 = q_3 = 20$; $Q = 60$).

Of those subjects assigned the role of first sellers, 7 out of 11 chose quantities closer to the Cournot prediction; of the second sellers, 6 out of 11; of the third sellers 7 out of 11.

While these proportions are individually not impressive against the null hypothesis, the Cournot solution is supported by the majority of the bargainers in each of the three roles. Further, over twice as many observations support the Cournot solution as support the favored alternative solution: 20 observations support the Cournot solution, while 9 support the competitive solution. (The remaining 4 support the Pareto solution.) Finally, the mean and median quantity choices of sellers in each of the three roles are in every instance closer to the Cournot solution, varying substantially from the alternative predictions.

More important to the economic theory than the individual quantities q_i is the aggregate quantity Q. The Cournot prediction is that this value will be $Q = 45$. In 9 of the 11 triopolies, the aggregate output is closer to this value than to either of the alternative predictions. According to the binomial test, this result is significantly different from chance expectation at $p < .035$. The median and mean aggregates are also closer to the Cournot solution than to its alternatives.

The consistent implication is that the Cournot model yields better predictions for quantity adjuster triopolists under incomplete information than does either alternative theory.

There appears to be more variation in the individual choices under triopoly than under duopoly. Interestingly enough, this too may be consistent with the dynamic Cournot model. In a recent series of articles in *The Review of Economic Studies*, Theocharis (1960), Fisher (1961), and McManus and Quant (1961) indicate that simple Cournot quantity adjusters will converge on the Cournot prediction for $N = 2$; they will oscillate around

136   Oligopoly

TABLE 9.3   Quantities on Transaction 21 in Experiments 7 and 8

Condition	$\bar{q}_1$	$\bar{q}_2$	$\bar{q}_3$	$\bar{q}_i$	$\bar{Q}$
Duopoly: $N = 2$ (experiment 7)	20.5	21.3		20.9	41.8
Triopoly: $N = 3$ (experiment 8)	15.0	15.6	17.5	16.0	48.1

the Cournot prediction for $N = 3$; they will produce explosively alternating outputs for $N > 3$.

The second hypothesis is that as N increases from 2 to 3, oligopolistic bargaining will yield an increased aggregate quantity but the individual quantities will be smaller. Data relevant to this hypothesis were yielded by experiment 7 and 8 and are presented in Tables 9.1 and 9.2. In Table 9.3 a summary of the data pertinent to the hypothesis is exhibited.

The mean aggregate quantity $\bar{Q}$ was larger in experiment 8 than in experiment 7. Under triopoly $\bar{Q} = 48.1$, whereas under duopoly $\bar{Q} = 41.8$. This confirms the Cournot prediction. The difference between the two sets of aggregate quantities is significant at $p < .001$ ($t = 3.44$, $df = 25$).

On the other hand, the average individual quantity output was smaller in experiment 8 than in experiment 7. Under triopoly $\bar{q}_i = 16.0$, whereas under duopoly $\bar{q}_i = 20.9$. This also confirms the Cournot prediction. The difference between the two sets of individual quantities is significant at $p < .0001$ ($t = 5.92$, $df = 53$).

Both hypotheses H_1 and H_2 were supported by the data. It seems clear that under incomplete information, oligopolistic bargaining behavior under conditions of quantity variation will tend to support the Cournot solution. With respect to H_2, it is of interest to note that only two subjects in the duopoly session (one in group 1 and one in group 8) had quantities as low as the average of the individual quantities in the triopoly session. To the same point, only two groups in the duopoly session (groups 15 and 16) had aggregate quantities as high as the average aggregate quantity in the triopoly session.

Discussion.   From the two experiments we have reported, it may be concluded that oligopolists bargaining under incomplete information as quantity adjusters show a tendency toward the Cournot solution regardless of the number of participants in the oligopoly and regardless of individual bargaining characteristics (rivalistic, cooperative, and/or simple maximizing) represented in the oligopoly.   Additional discussion of these data appears in Chapter 11, where an integrated analysis of all the findings is presented.

BARGAINING UNDER COMPLETE INFORMATION

The first section of this chapter was devoted to experimental studies of oligopoly behavior by quantity adjusters under conditions of incomplete information.   These studies supported the theoretical formulation presented in Chapter 7 concerning such bargaining.   It would appear that when the individual bargainer cannot identify the effect that changes in his own quantity output may have on the profits of his competitors, he acts as if he is treating those profits as a constant and is concentrating on maximizing his own net payoff.   That is, under incomplete information the oligopolist acts as if he were a simple maximizer and sends signals accordingly.   The condition of incomplete information reduces the effectiveness of rivalistic or cooperative signals, for the bargainer has no knowledge of the effects of his own bids on his opponents' profits.   That is, it is difficult to function as a rivalist or a cooperator because these roles require communication beyond the level consistent with incomplete information.

For the condition of *complete* information, on the other hand, the theoretical formulation does not yield predictions as invariant as those for incomplete information.   When each participant can identify the relation between his quantity choice and the profits accruing to his rival (or rivals), the solution to oligopolistic bargaining is a function of both the number of bargainers in the oligopolistic structure and the particular combination of bargaining characteristics or signaling proclivities represented by the participants.

If all the members of a given oligopoly are cooperative, i.e., if each signals as if he were trying to increase joint profits, the result expected under the theoretical formulation (at the limit) is the Pareto solution:

$$Q = \frac{1}{2}\frac{A}{B}. \tag{9.4}$$

If all the participants in a given oligopoly are simple maximizers, i.e., if each is behaving as if he were trying simply to maximize his own profit without regard to the profits accruing to his rivals, the result is expected to be the Cournot solution:

$$Q = \frac{N}{N+1}\frac{A}{B}. \tag{9.2}$$

If all the participants in a given oligopoly are of the rivalistic type, i.e., if each is signaling as if he were striving to increase the difference between his profits and those of his rivals, the individual output is expected to be (at the limit)

$$q_i = \frac{1}{2}\frac{A}{B}. \tag{9.7}$$

This is the quantity a monopoly would select; the aggregate output is expected to be the rivalistic output

$$Q = \frac{N}{2}\frac{A}{B}. \tag{9.8}$$

If the oligopolistic structure consists of a mixed combination of the bargaining types or signals, the results are expected to fall between the extremes just stated.   Table 7.1 presents all possible combinations of bargaining types for $N = 2$ and $N = 3$ and gives the limiting theoretical prediction associated with each combination for the condition of complete information.

Two experiments were conducted in which bargainers negotiated as quantity adjusters in an oligopolistic market, doing so under complete information.

With the exception of the amount of information available to the bargainers, the conditions of experiments 9 and 10 were strictly comparable to the conditions of experiments 7 and 8. In all four experiments, the parameters are $A = 2.4$ cents and $B = 0.04$ cent. Thus $A/B = 60$. Furthermore, as has been noted, subjects were assigned at random from a common pool to one of the four sessions. The purpose of this randomization procedure was to assist statistical comparisons between these four experiments.

Our principal hypotheses concerning experiments 9 and 10 had to do with differences we expected to observe between contracts negotiated in those experiments and contracts negotiated in experiments 7 and 8. For clarity in the presentation of our results, we shall proceed here to report our procedures and our findings in experiments 9 and 10. In the section which follows, hypotheses are stated concerning the differences to be expected as a result of the change in the information available to the bargainers, and the relevant comparisons are reported.

Experiment 9: Triopoly

Subjects and Procedure. For a study of quantity adjuster bargaining by triopolists under complete information, 33 male undergraduates served as subjects. They were assigned on a random basis to 11 groups.

The instructions given to the subjects are presented in Appendix IX. Also presented there is the profit table, a double-entry table showing the profits both to the subject and to his opponents for any set of quantity choices.

A total of 25 transactions were executed by each bargaining group. The first three were practice trials. For the 22 regular transactions a real monetary payoff was employed. Prior to regular transaction 22, an announcement was made indicating that the next transaction would be the final one. The purpose of this announcement was to induce end effects, if any.

TABLE 9.4   Quantity Choices on Transaction 21 of
Experiment 9, Triopoly under Complete Information

Group	q_1	q_1 supports	q_2	q_2 supports	q_3	q_3 supports	Q	Q supports
28	10	C	10	C	20	R	40	M
29	15	M	14	M	15	M	44	M
30	15	M	16	M	15	M	46	M
31	15	M	12	C	20	R	47	M
32	15	M	16	M	20	R	51	M
33	17	M	30	R	15	M	62	R
34	20	R	15	M	23	R	58	R
35	19	R	20	R	20	R	59	R
36	17	M	20	R	22	R	59	R
37	20	R	15	M	28	R	63	R
38	17	M	28	R	25	R	70	R
Mean	16.4	M	17.8	R	20.3	R	54.5	R
Median	17	M	16	M	20	R	58	R

Key: C = Pareto (cooperative) solution
M = Cournot (maximizing) solution
R = competitive (rivalistic) solution

Results.   The contracts negotiated on the twenty-first regular transaction are shown in Table 9.4.   No clear central tendency is revealed in these data; this is in accord with the theoretical discussion in Chapter 7.   It may be noted that less than one-half of the individual values of q_i support the Cournot solution: 15 values support that solution, an equal number support the competitive solution, and the remaining 3 support the Pareto solution.   With respect to the aggregate output Q, the observations are also split, about half favoring the Cournot solution and half favoring the competitive solution.   The means and medians exhibit a similar tendency.

Experiment 10: Duopoly

Subjects and Procedure.   For the experimental study of bargaining by quantity adjusters in a situation of duopoly with complete information, 32 male undergraduates served as subjects.   They were assigned on a random basis to 16 bargaining pairs.

The instructions given these subjects are displayed in Appendix X.   Their double-entry profit table is also shown there.

As in the other sessions of bargaining by quantity adjusters, there were 3 practice trials and then 22 regular transactions in experiment 10, with an announcement identifying transaction 22.
Results.   The quantity choices of each bargainer on transaction 21 are shown in Table 9.5.   As would be predicted by the theory, there is no clear trend in these results.   Although the plurality of the q_i values are closer to the Cournot (maximizing) solution than to either of its alternatives, the majority in fact favor one

TABLE 9.5   Quantity Choices on Transaction 21 of Experiment 10, Duopoly under Complete Information

Group	q_1	q_1 supports	q_2	q_2 supports	Q	Q supports
39	17	C	8	C	25	C
40	15	C	15	C	30	C
41	15	C	15	C	30	C
42	19	M	13	C	32	C
43	25	M, R	8	C	33	C
44	15	C	23	M	38	M
45	19	M	20	M	39	M
46	20	M	20	M	40	M
47	15	C	25	M, R	40	M
48	20	M	24	M	44	M
49	25	M, R	20	M	45	M
50	26	R	23	M	49	M
51	30	R	20	M	50	M, R
52	27	R	28	R	55	R
53	30	R	29	R	59	R
54	30	R	30	R	60	R
Mean	21.8	M	20.1	M	41.8	M
Median	20	M	20	M	40	M

Key: C = Pareto (cooperative) solution
M = Cournot (maximizing) solution
R = competitive (rivalistic) solution

of these: 11 of the q_i values favor the Cournot solution; 3 are equally favorable to the Cournot and the competitive solutions; 8 favor the competitive solution; and 10 favor the Pareto (or cooperative) solution. There is similar lack of unanimity in the aggregate outputs negotiated by the duopolists. Of the 16, 7 values of Q favor the Cournot solution; 1 is equally favorable to the Cournot or the competitive solutions; 3 favor the competitive solution; and 5 favor the Pareto (or cooperative) solution.

Since the Cournot solution is intermediate between the Paretian optimal solution and the competitive solution, the mean and median values tend to favor the Cournot solution. As the frequency counts (just reported) indicate, however, these indexes of central tendency are not to be interpreted as meaning that the Cournot solution is the predominant one reached by the various bargainers.

THE EFFECT OF AMOUNT OF INFORMATION

Introduction

Economic theories concerning oligopoly behavior under conditions of quantity variation do not usually include explicit statements about the amount of information available to the oligopolists, but the derivation of most solutions assumes complete information. According to the hypothesis offered here, oligopolists bargaining under complete information may be expected to exhibit considerable variability in the solutions they reach. The expected variability arises because in each case the solution is derived, at least in part, as a function of the composition of the bargaining types or signalers making up the oligopoly. For bargainers under incomplete information, in contrast, the solutions predicted are the same—the Cournot solution. Thus, the major implication of the hypothesis is that oligopolistic transactions negotiated under complete information will be more variable than oligopolistic transactions negotiated under incomplete information.

To test this hypothesis concerning the effect of amount of information, two comparisons were made, one between transactions of triopolists negotiating under complete and incomplete information, and one (a replication) between transactions of duopolists negotiating under complete and incomplete information. These comparisons are meaningful because all the other relevant variables were controlled: Subjects were randomized into information conditions (complete and incomplete); subjects were randomized into groups of different sizes (triopolies and duopolies); the payoff function was the same for all groups; the number of trials was the same for all groups, etc.

The general hypothesis concerns the difference in *variability* (dispersion) of the transactions between conditions of complete and incomplete information. The hypothesis concerns variability rather than central tendency or typical values of transactions because, according to the theory under test, the typical value of oligopolistic transactions under complete information cannot be specified without prior knowledge of the particular combination of bargaining types making up the oligopoly or the signals they employ in their negotiations. Specifically, the hypotheses were:

H_1: Transaction 21 by triopolists under complete information will exhibit greater variability than will transaction 21 by triopolists under incomplete information.

H_2: Transaction 21 by duopolists under complete information will exhibit greater variability than will transaction 21 by duopolists under incomplete information.

Variability of Triopolists as a Function of Amount of Information

The first hypothesis was tested by comparing the results of experiment 8 with the results of experiment 9. This comparison, then, considers the bargaining behavior of 66 male undergraduates serving in 22 bargaining groups, 3 to a group. Eleven of these groups negotiated under incomplete information, and eleven negotiated under complete information. The fact that the 66 subjects were assigned at random to the two sessions (information conditions) and to the various bargaining groups or triopolies assists a direct statistical comparison between experiments 8 and 9.

The instructions to the subjects under incomplete information are displayed in Appendix VIII, along with the single-entry profit table used by those subjects. The instructions to the subjects under complete information are displayed in Appendix IX, along with their double-entry profit table.

Whereas a triopolist under incomplete information knew only his own profit for each possible quantity choice, a triopolist under complete information knew both the profit to himself and the profit to his opponents for each possible quantity choice.

The data used in testing H_1 are shown in Table 9.6. These are the aggregate quantities Q resulting from transaction 21 by triopolists in experiment 8 (incomplete information) and experiment 9 (complete information). Complete protocols exhibiting all transactions and payoffs for these subjects are presented in Appendixes VIII and IX.

The hypothesis is that final transactions by triopolists under complete information will exhibit greater variability than will final transactions by triopolists under incomplete information. To facilitate inspection of the data in Table 9.6, the aggregate quantities are arranged in approximately ascending order for

TABLE 9.6 Aggregate Quantities on Transaction 21 for Triopolists under Incomplete and Complete Information

Group	Incomplete information	Group	Complete information
17	40	28	40
18	43	29	44
19	46	30	46
20	46	31	47
21	46	32	51
22	47	33	62
23	48	34	58
24	50	35	59
25	51	36	59
26	53	37	63
27	59	38	70

TABLE 9.7   Standard Deviations of Q for Each Transaction by Triopolists under Two Conditions of Information

Transaction	Incomplete information (experiment 8)	Complete information (experiment 9)
1	6.22	6.79
2	6.14	5.68
3	4.21	5.26
4	8.72	9.02
5	8.77	8.09
6	7.29	10.42
7	3.69	9.04
8	8.31	8.18
9	8.29	7.52
10	4.77	6.85
11	7.60	6.54
12	6.19	4.70
13	8.72	5.37
14	6.56	8.12
15	7.73	3.60
16	3.77	6.85
17	5.37	6.67
18	4.49	5.04
19	3.37	8.25
20	5.42	8.99
21	4.87	8.96
22	3.82	7.45

each condition.   The data were tested by the Siegel-Tukey procedure [Siegel and Tukey (1960)], a nonparametric test for differences in variability.   Under this test, the null hypothesis of equal variability under the two information conditions may be rejected at the $p < .06$ level of significance.   As predicted, greater variability was exhibited by the equilibrium transactions under complete information than those under incomplete information.

These results are based on a single transaction, number 21. Additional support for the hypothesis may be found in comparisons of variability on each of the other regular transactions.   Table 9.7 presents the standard deviations of the aggregate quantities Q for each of the 22 regular transactions under both complete and incomplete information by triopolists. The reader will observe that the standard deviations are larger, in general, for the complete-information condition than for the incomplete-information condition. This is true for about two-thirds of the 22 triopolistic transactions, including all of the 7 final transactions.

Variability of Duopolists as a Function of Amount of Information

Two hypotheses were formulated concerning the effect of varying amounts of information on negotiations of quantity adjusters. The first concerned triopolists and was confirmed by a comparison of the data from experiments 8 and 9, as we have just reported.

The second hypothesis was that transaction 21 by duopolists under complete information will exhibit greater variability than will transaction 21 by duopolists under incomplete information.

This hypothesis was tested by comparing the results of experiment 10 with the results of experiment 7. Under consideration in this comparison are 64 undergraduate male subjects serving in 32 bargaining pairs. One-half of these pairs negotiated under complete information (experiment 10). The other half negotiated under incomplete information (experiment 7).

Experiments 7 and 10 are strictly comparable except with respect to the independent variable under consideration—amount of information. Subjects were assigned at random from a common pool to the two experiments. Further, subjects were assigned randomly to the roles of first seller or second seller. The profit tables used by all subjects were based on the same parameters.

Duopolists under incomplete information were given the instructions and profit table presented in Appendix VII, while those under complete information were given the instructions and profit table presented in Appendix X. Whereas a duopolist under incomplete information knew only his own profit for each possible quantity choice, a duopolist under complete information knew both the profit to himself and the profit to his opponent for each possible quantity choice.

The reader will recognize that the comparison under discussion is an analogue, or a replication, of the comparison just reported concerning the effect of varying amounts of information on triopolistic bargaining. It differs in that here our concern is with bargaining groups of $N = 2$, whereas in the previous comparison our concern was with bargaining groups of $N = 3$.

The data employed in the test of H_2 are presented in Table 9.8.

Complete protocols for these subjects, exhibiting all transactions and payoffs, are presented in Appendix VII for the subjects under incomplete information and in Appendix X for those under complete information.

The data were tested by the Siegel-Tukey procedure, and application of this test for differences in variability to the data in Table 9.8 permits rejection of the null hypothesis of equal variability at the $p < .005$ level of significance. As predicted, transaction 21 of duopolists under complete information exhibited

TABLE 9.8   Aggregate Quantities on Transaction 21 for Duopolists under Incomplete and Complete Information

Group	Incomplete information	Group	Complete information
1	36	39	25
2	38	40	30
3	38	41	30
4	40	42	32
5	40	43	33
6	40	44	38
7	40	45	39
8	40	46	40
9	41	47	40
10	41	48	44
11	41	49	45
12	43	50	49
13	43	51	50
14	45	52	55
15	51	53	59
16	52	54	60

TABLE 9.9   Standard Deviations of Q for Each Transaction by
Duopolists under Two Conditions of Information

Transaction	Incomplete information (experiment 7)	Complete information (experiment 10)
1	6.96	7.24
2	5.04	9.06
3	5.70	8.86
4	5.98	8.22
5	5.61	7.65
6	7.01	8.16
7	4.46	8.93
8	6.52	9.82
9	5.01	8.39
10	2.65	10.90
11	3.85	10.51
12	4.62	9.84
13	5.64	9.12
14	3.49	9.28
15	4.48	9.80
16	3.61	10.27
17	2.67	8.36
18	3.72	7.59
19	5.85	8.48
20	5.89	7.47
21	4.20	10.30
22	3.35	7.88

greater variability than was exhibited under incomplete
information.

As was the case for triopolistic bargaining, additional support
for the hypothesis about the effects of varying information is
found in the case of duopoly when attention is given to the entire
course of the bargaining. Table 9.9 presents the standard deviation of the aggregate quantity Q for each of the 22 duopolistic
transactions under both complete and incomplete information.
The reader will note that for all 22 transactions the standard
deviations are larger under complete information than under
incomplete information.

Discussion

The data of experiments 7 to 10 support the general hypothesis that bargaining by oligopolists under complete information leads to more diverse outcomes than does such bargaining under incomplete information.   This is true not only for the final transactions, but also in general for the entire course of the bargaining. The data support this prediction for bargaining groups of both two and three.

It is of interest that the standard deviations for the incomplete-information experiments (see Tables 9.7 and 9.9) are, in general, consistent with the stability propositions of dynamic Cournot bidding.   The most damaging exceptions to this proposition are the large standard deviations for duopoly under incomplete information on transactions 19 and 20.

Table 9.6 shows that the range of Q, the aggregate output, for triopolists under incomplete information is 19, while that for triopolists under complete information is 30.   For duopolists, as Table 9.8 shows, the range for Q under incomplete information is 16, while under complete information it is 35.

It is revealing to note that for both incompletely informed groups, 23 of the 27 observations of aggregate output were closer to the Cournot solution than to either the Paretian optimal or the competitive solutions.   That is, for incompletely informed bargainers there is clearly a central tendency toward one solution. On the other hand, for the subjects under complete information there is no clear central tendency revealed in the data (Tables 9.4 and 9.5), and this is in accord with the approach presented in Chapter 7.

The results of the four experiments with quantity adjusters are summarized in Table 9.10.   Under conditions of incomplete information, more choices in each experiment supported the Cournot prediction than all alternative predictions combined. Under complete-information conditions more choices in each experiment favored alternative predictions than favored the Cournot values.

Examination of the standard deviations of the aggregate quan-

TABLE 9.10   Frequency with Which Three Alternative Solutions Were Supported on Transaction 21 in Four Sessions of Bargaining by Quantity Adjusters

Solution	Experimental session							
	7: duopoly, incomplete information		*8: triopoly, incomplete information*		*9: triopoly, complete information*		*10: duopoly, complete information*	
	q_i	Q	q_i	Q	q_i	Q	q_i	Q
Pareto	2	0	4	0	3	0	10	5
Cournot	26	14	20	9	15	5	12.5	7.5
Competitive	4	2	9	2	15	6	9.5	3.5

tities in each transaction (presented in Tables 9.7 and 9.9) also supports the notion that completely informed bargainers are more variable. In general the standard deviations of choices are ordered as follows: $D(C) > T(C) > T(I) > D(I)$, where

D = duopoly
T = triopoly
I = incomplete information
C = complete information

The implication is that complete information is a more important experimental condition than the number of bargainers, in explaining dispersion of data. Indeed, the effect of the number of bargainers on variability is not consistent. Under complete information the duopoly relation gives rise to more dispersion than does the triopoly relation, perhaps as a result of the relative ease of forming a cooperative coalition with two players in contrast with three; the result of this is a widening of the range from the Cournot adjustment. Under incomplete information, triopoly is more variable, perhaps as a result of the stability properties of the Cournot model [Theocharis (1960)].

It seems clear that bargaining by oligopolists under complete information may lead to results falling all along the distribution of possible outcomes. The theory presented in Chapter 7 predicts dispersion as a function of the combination of the bargaining types and signals represented in the oligopolistic structures. Through random assignment of subjects to groups, we expected to obtain a large variety of these combinations and thus to observe the variability which was evident.

LEVEL OF ASPIRATION

The data from the four experiments with quantity adjusters provided an opportunity to test the hypotheses from level-of-aspiration theory. They were developed and tested in conjunction with the experiment on bilateral monopoly under price leadership (see Chapter 6).

The assumption underlying the first hypothesis we tested is that bargainers tend to establish a level of aspiration associated with an even division of profits [Siegel and Fouraker (1960)]. A subject who aspires to receive his "fair share" of profits, according to this assumption, will be frustrated if he receives less than an even division. His response to this frustration will be to search for some means to relieve the frustration [Simon (1957)]. In the bargaining situation of quantity adjusters, the most appropriate means to ensure a fair split on future transactions is to send a rivalistic signal. In the situation of quantity adjustment oligopoly, a rivalistic signal takes the form of an increase in output. Since the level of profits is directly related to amount of production in these experiments, we predict that if a subject's output (and therefore profit) is the smallest in his group on trial i, on the following trial he will increase his output. That is, where q_i is the quantity choice of a player on the ith trial and q_{ir} is the quantity choice of his rival (or rivals) on the same trial, the rivalistic (R) hypothesis is as follows: if $q_i < q_{ir}$, then $q_{i+1} > q_i$.

A related hypothesis would be that if a player had the largest output (and therefore the largest profit) on a given transaction, he would tend to reduce his output on the next transaction: if

TABLE 9.11   Number of Transactions For and Against the Rivalistic Hypothesis in Four Experiments on Quantity Variation

	Experiment			
	7: duopoly, incomplete information	*8: triopoly, incomplete information*	*9: triopoly, complete information*	*10: duopoly, complete information*
Observations for hypothesis	164.0	129.5	144.0	160.5
Observations against hypothesis	100.0	59.5	43.0	81.5
Ratio of above	1.64	2.18	3.35	1.97
Number of bargaining groups	16	11	11	16
Number of bargaining groups providing more observations for than against the hypothesis (ties count one-half)	13.5	11	11	15

$q_i > q_{ir}$, then $q_{i+1} < q_i$. This cooperative (S) hypothesis does not have the same support from level-of-aspiration theory that the rivalistic hypothesis enjoys, so we would anticipate somewhat weaker support for it in our data.

To test the rivalistic and the cooperative hypotheses, each of the 21 regular transactions in experiments 7 to 10 was examined. (The relevant data are presented in Appendixes VII to X.) If an observation was neither for nor against the hypotheses, e.g., if a player offered the same production on several transactions and his choices were either low or high values, then it was counted as one-half an observation for the appropriate hypothesis and one-half an observation against it. If two or more subjects offered the same quantity choices on a transaction, so that there was no unique high or low bid, no observation was recorded. The results are summarized in Table 9.11 and Table 9.12.

In every experiment the direction of change from one transaction to the next was, on balance, in the direction predicted by the two hypotheses.

We may take the ratio of observations for an hypothesis to observations against it as a rough measure of the strength of the hypothesis. These ratios are displayed in Tables 9.11 and 9.12. Comparison of these ratios reveals that the rivalistic hypothesis is generally stronger than the cooperative hypothesis. For example, for triopolistic bargaining under complete information, the ratio for the rivalistic hypothesis is 3.35, whereas the ratio for the cooperative hypothesis is 2.70. For three of the four circumstances where everything is the same except the hypotheses under test, the ratio is higher for the rivalistic than for the cooperative hypothesis. The exception is duopolistic bargaining under complete information (experiment 10).

Examination of the ratios also reveals that both the rivalistic and the cooperative hypotheses are stronger under complete

TABLE 9.12   Number of Transactions For and Against the Cooperative Hypothesis in Four Experiments on Quantity Variation

	Experiment			
	7: duopoly, incomplete information	*8: triopoly, incomplete information*	*9: triopoly, complete information*	*10: duopoly, complete information*
Observations for hypothesis	152.0	118.0	141.5	164.5
Observations against hypothesis	112.0	73.0	52.5	77.5
Ratio of above	1.36	1.62	2.70	2.12
Number of bargaining groups	16	11	11	16
Number of bargaining groups providing more observations for than against the hypothesis (ties count one-half)	13.5	10	11	15.5

information than under incomplete information. For example, for the cooperative hypothesis the ratio for duopolists is 1.36 under incomplete information, but 2.12 under complete information. Four such comparisons may be made where all states except information are comparable; in each case stronger confirmation for the hypotheses is obtained for bargainers under complete information.

A third conclusion emerges from examination of the ratios. The hypotheses found stronger support in the triopoly experiments than they did in the duopoly experiments. For example, the ratio of observations favoring the rivalistic hypothesis to those opposing it was 3.35 for triopolists under complete information, while it was 1.97 for duopolists under complete information. Again, the conclusion holds in all four instances in which a meaningful comparison may be made.

We conclude that the quantity adjuster negotiations provide a remarkably orderly pattern of relations with regard to the signaling behavior of the participants. When on a given transaction an oligopolist's output was smaller than that of his rival (or rivals), on the following trial he tended to increase his output. We call this a rivalistic signal. On the other hand, when on a given transaction an oligopolist's output was larger than that of his rival, he tended to reduce his output on the next transaction, i.e., send a cooperative signal. These two tendencies were more marked for completely informed bargainers than for incompletely informed bargainers and more marked for triopolists than for duopolists.

INDUCED BARGAINING STRATEGIES

It was demonstrated in the previous section that when each participant in oligopolistic bargaining can identify the relation between his quantity choice and the profits accruing to his rivals, highly variable results emerge. In a sense, the distribution of results was trimodal: some completely informed groups supported the Paretian optimal model, some the Cournot model, and some the competitive model. Such results are consistent with the theoretical formulation in Chapter 7. The combination of the bargaining and signaling types in the various oligopolistic structures in the experiments depended upon random assignment of subjects to groups. Thus variable results were expected.

The fact that variability was observed when it was expected, however, can hardly be taken as a strong demonstration that variability was observed for the expected reasons. That is, there may be other reasons for the variability of the observed contracts oligopolists reached when negotiating as quantity adjusters under complete information. For example, an increase in the amount of information available to them might have confused them, and this confusion might account for the variable results.

One approach to demonstrating that the variability reflected diverse bargaining strategies would be to attempt to identify in advance which subjects are disposed to be rivalists and which are disposed to be cooperative. Some test for cooperativeness and competitiveness, for example, might be employed to categorize the subjects. We would then predict that the strategies adopted by the subjects in bargaining would be consonant with their predispositions as measured.

We rejected this approach, partly out of an a priori preference for the experimental rather than the psychometric approach, partly because of the difficulty of constructing a sufficiently reliable test for classifying subjects in bargaining types. We suspect, in fact, that some of our single-shot experiments are better than any psychometric approach for such classification.

The alternative approach would be to alter the experimental situation in some way which might induce the subject to adopt a particular strategy, either rivalistic or cooperative. This approach, experimental manipulation, was the one we employed.

The presumption is that the cooperative bargainer is one who derives satisfaction from increasing joint profits. This characteristic favors the Pareto solution.

If we could manipulate the payoff structure so that we were reasonably certain that a strategy leading to increasing joint profits would be attractive to the subjects, would they be sufficiently perceptive to identify and arrive at the Pareto solution? If they could not, our behavioral hypothesis would suffer, and we would have to look elsewhere for an explanation of the increased variability in experiments 9 and 10. On the other hand, if we could induce the Pareto optimal solution *via* artifically imposed preference for cooperative signals and attitudes, we could conclude that such preference might in general be one reason that some bargainers reach Pareto solutions.

Similarly, the rivalistic bargainer is one who derives satisfaction from making more profit than his rival (or rivals). Because this is satisfying to him, he employs a rivalistic strategy and thus tends toward a given contract: for duopoly, the competitive output. By manipulating the payoff structure so that beating the opponents becomes an attractive goal for all subjects, would we be able to create rivalists? That is, given a good reason for employing a rivalistic strategy, can undergraduate men bargainers identify and follow that strategy?

If cooperative and rivalistic behavior cannot be induced by suitable manipulation of the payoff structure, our hypothesis that the variability observed in experiments 9 and 10 reflects the dispersion of the subjects with respect to preferred strategies would be damaged.

Two experiments were conducted in which we attempted to induce bargainers to reach solutions at the Pareto and competitive contracts, by manipulating the motivational structure. Experiment 11 was an effort to induce cooperative bargaining; experiment 12 was an effort to induce rivalistic bargaining.

The two experiments were identical in all respects other than the payoff structure. Subjects were assigned at random to the two experiments. In both experiments they bargained in duopolies. The parameters were $A = 24$ cents and $B = 0.4$ cent. Thus, the Paretian optimal solution is $Q = 30$, with the maximum joint payoff for a transaction being \$3.60. The competitive solution, on the other hand, is $Q = 60$, with zero profit going to each bargainer.

These experiments differed from those already reported in that they were single-shot experiments. Only one transaction involved a monetary payoff; all others were practice trials.

Experiment 11: Induced Cooperation

Experiment 11 was conducted to test the hypothesis that bargainers could be induced to negotiate cooperatively, i.e., to attempt to maximize joint profits. The prediction was that they would arrive at the strategy of choosing quantities q_i such that $Q = 30$, the Pareto solution.

Subjects and Procedures. The subjects were 12 undergraduate men, recruited from the same student population as were those in the quantity adjuster experiments already reported. However, they were not drawn from the same common pool that served all the other regular experiments. These men were taken from a common pool of 26 names used in experiments 11 and 12. On a random basis they were paired in six duopolies.

The usual procedures were employed to assure that order of arrival to the session did not influence a subject's role in the experiment.

The instructions given the subjects (displayed in Appendix XI) pointed out that there would be but one transaction with a real monetary payoff in the experiment. This would be preceded by 10 practice trials; these would not involve any payoffs or losses.

The subjects were told that if on the one real transaction they succeeded in arriving at a contract whose *joint* profit exceeded $3.55, then an additional $8.00 would be given to them—$4.00 to each member of a successful duopoly. The purpose of this payoff, of course, was to induce cooperative behavior, as defined earlier. The 10 practice trials gave the subjects an opportunity to send cooperative signals to each other and thus to establish mutual confidence as a setting for their giving cooperative bids on the one transaction that "counted."

The profit table used by the subjects, a double-entry table giving complete information, is displayed in Appendix XI.

158 Oligopoly

TABLE 9.13   Quantity Choices Made by Subjects in Experiment 11

Group	q_1	q_2	Q
55	15	15	30
56	15	15	30
57	15	15	30
58	15	15	30
59	15	15	30
60	8	22	30

Results. The quantity choices made by the duopolists in experiment 11 are shown in Table 9.13. As the table shows, all duopoly groups supported the hypothesis that these bargainers would arrive at the Paretian optimal quantity $Q = 30$.

Complete protocols, showing choices on both the 10 practice trials and the 1 real payoff transaction, are presented in Appendix XI.

The results of experiment 11 are discussed below, following the presentation of experiment 12.

Experiment 12: Induced Rivalry

An experiment similar in most ways to Experiment 11 was conducted to test the hypothesis that subjects could be induced to adopt a rivalistic strategy, as in experiment 11 they had been induced to adopt a cooperative one. The prediction was that they could be induced to attempt to maximize the difference between their own and their opponents' profits and thus would arrive at the strategy of choosing quantities q_i such that $Q = 60$, the competitive solution for $N = 2$.

Subjects and Procedures. The subjects in experiment 12 were drawn at random from the same pool of 26 subjects from which the subjects of experiment 11 were drawn. None had participated in any other bargaining study. Seven groups of duopolists (14 subjects) served in experiment 12; all were undergraduate men.

The double-entry profit table used in experiment 12 was the

same as the one used in experiment 11; it is displayed in Appendix XI.

The usual controls through randomization were employed to negate any possible effects of order of arrival. Assignment of subjects to bargaining pairs was on a random basis.

In experiment 12, as in experiment 11, subjects were told that there would be but a single real transaction, preceded by 10 practice trials. The method of inducing rivalry was to inform the subjects that an additional $8 would be paid to the bargainer in each pair who succeeded in making the larger profit (or the smaller loss) on the one real-payoff transaction. These subjects were told that only if their two profits were equal on that transaction would they split the extra $8 equally. The instructions are displayed in Appendix XII.

Results. The quantity choices made by the duopolists in experiment 12 are shown in Table 9.14. The reader will observe that 6 of the 7 groups arrived at the aggregate rivalistic quantity $Q = 60$, and 13 of the 14 individual bargainers chose the individual output predicted by the rivalistic model $q_i = 30$.

Complete protocols, showing choices on both the practice trials and the one real-payoff transaction are presented in Appendix XII.

The results of experiment 12 provide support for the hypothesis that through the appropriate use of payoffs subjects can be induced to adopt a rivalistic strategy, i.e., to attempt to maximize

TABLE 9.14   Quantity Choices Made by Subjects in Experiment 12

Group	q_1	q_2	Q
61	30	30	60
62	30	30	60
63	30	30	60
64	30	30	60
65	30	30	60
66	30	30	60
67	28	30	58

the difference between their own and their opponents' profits, and thus the duopoly can be induced to arrive at the competitive solution.

Discussion

These two experiments together demonstrate that the objectives subjects adopt depend on the payoff structure of the experiment. With appropriate bonus payoffs, subjects can be induced, almost without exception, to adopt either a cooperative or a rivalistic strategy. We conclude, then, that given cooperative motivation, subjects can identify and follow Pareto strategies; given rivalistic motivation, subjects can negotiate appropriate rivalistic solutions.

Of particular interest are the signals employed by the bargainers in the two experiments. The signals here were the bids made on the 10 practice trials. These signals were not reinforced by any monetary payoff—subjects were clearly informed that only the eleventh trial would involve a real payoff—but they were probably offered with serious interest in communicating, in view of the large payoff forthcoming on the single trial.

As would be expected, cooperative signals dominate the practice bidding in experiment 11. The parties needed to communicate their willingness to cooperate, establishing an implicit commitment to produce the joint output which yields an $8 bonus. In the first five groups (groups 55 to 59), each player at one time or another signaled his willingness to take one-half (or less) of the maximum joint profits. Each of these pairs negotiated an equal division of the Pareto profits on their real-payoff transaction. In contrast, in one group (pair 60), the Pareto optimal contract was negotiated, but with an unequal division of profits (see Table 9.13). From the outset, one player in this pair gave simple maximizing signals; he did not vary from this strategy throughout the practice trials. The other player made an accommodation to this position by making 10 cooperative offers in succession. By the seventh practice trial, this man was committed to an output of 8 against his partner's output of 22. This was the final contract.

TABLE 9.15   Signals Employed on Practice Trials in Experiments 11 and 12

Group	Experiment 11 Signal type			Group	Experiment 12 Signal type		
	C	M	R		C	M	R
55	18	2		61	10	10	
56	10	10		62	2	7.5	10.5
57	15	4	1	63	9	8	3
58	20			64	8	7.5	4.5
59	15	1.5	3.5	65	5	8.5	6.5
60	10	10		66	12	6.5	1.5
				67	12	6	2
Total	88	27.5	4.5		58	54	28
Per cent	73.3	22.9	3.8		41.4	38.6	20.0

Key: C = cooperative signal
M = maximizing signal
R = rivalistic signal

Table 9.15 shows the frequency with which signals of each type were employed in the practice trials in experiments 11 and 12. The reader will note that almost three-fourths of all signals given in experiment 11 were cooperative signals. Most of the others were maximizing signals; slightly less than 4 per cent in all were rivalistic.

In experiment 12, the practice bids served a different function. The purpose of a rivalist's communications is to set his opponent up for a double cross. The practice trials provide an opportunity for the rivalist to trap his opponent on the real-payoff trial. Our subjects rose to the challenge.

Consider pair 61, for example. Each bargainer gave a series of simple maximizing and cooperative bids on the practice trials. On the one transaction that counted, however, each double-crossed, selecting the dominating output of 30 units. The two bargainers in pair 61 were not unusual; end play like theirs characterized all but one subject.   Of the 14 subjects, 13 did not quote the dominant rivalistic output (30) on a single one of their practice trials; there was only one subject (in pair 65) who signaled his choice on the last four practice trials, and held to it on the real-payoff transaction.   Yet all but one of the 14 subjects named the rivalistic output of 30 on the trial that counted.

There was only one victim of this rapacity; he was in pair 67. After the session he protested that he had been "taken" by a double crosser.   His opponent had given 10 lesser bids in practice and then on the real-payoff trial he quoted the dominant amount of 30, bringing a profit of \$8.25 to himself.   The victim made 20 cents, having gone from a bid of 16 on the final practice trial to a bid of 28 on the payoff trial.   Even so, the adjustment of this pair was closer to the rivalistic prediction than to any alternative under consideration.

The bids made by the subjects of experiment 12 in their practice trials are classified in Table 9.15.   The reader will observe that four-fifths of the practice bids were either cooperative or maximizing, whereas on the payoff trial every bid was rivalistic, as we have shown (Table 9.14).

We have no reason to believe that the subjects in experiment 12 differ in any significant way from any of the subjects in the other quantity adjuster experiments, and we know for fact that they differ only according to the chance of the draw from those in experiment 11.

SOURCES OF VARIABILITY IN BARGAINING

All the variation in the quantity adjuster experiments cannot be explained in terms of the arguments presented above.   Two additional factors might be considered:

1. The subjects are naïve and might get confused by the complexity of the decision situation or bored by the small payoff over a series of transactions.   We did find, in the bilateral monopoly experiments, that mature subjects tended to converge on predicted solutions more readily than student subjects; further, by

increasing the discriminability around critical points in the bilateral monopoly experiments, we induced shifts toward the predicted values. We collected similar data in these experiments. After transaction 21, subjects were informed the next trial would be their last, inducing end effects; they were then informed there would be one more trial, involving triple payoffs. In those experiments with a predicted central tendency for observations (the incomplete-information experiments 7 and 8), our expectation was that the choices on transaction 23 would move toward the predicted amounts. Of the sixteen duopoly groups in experiment 7, ten changed their aggregate output; eight of these changes were toward the Cournot prediction. Of the eleven triopoly groups in experiment 8, six changed their aggregate output toward the Cournot prediction; two groups altered their choices in the opposite direction. Again it would appear that increasing the discriminability of the payoffs tended to shift observations toward the predicted values [cf. Fouraker, Shubik, and Siegel (1961)].

2. The rounding-off of the payoff table may have made it difficult to approach the Cournot equilibrium value, since there are often many optimum responses for any given decision of the rival. After these experiments, we conducted some pilot studies for an experiment regarding the stability properties of the Cournot model. We used the same parameters and instructions that were employed in experiments 7 and 8, but corrected the payoff tables to 4 places. The results for four duopolists were (amounts are individual quantity choices in the twenty-first transaction): (20, 21), (24, 22), (26, 23), and (19, 21); for four triopolists the results were: (13, 16, 15), (15, 25, 13), (17, 18, 8), (20, 13, 16). Again the general results support the Cournot predictions of (20, 20) for duopoly and (15, 15, 15) for triopoly. There is at least as much dispersion as in experiments 7 and 8. (The average deviation of individual choices from the Cournot amounts is greater in both duopoly and triopoly pilot studies; the average deviation per aggregate output is greater for the pilot duopoly, less for the pilot triopoly; the mean in the pilot duopoly

is further from the Cournot prediction than the mean in experiment 7; the mean for the pilot triopoly is nearer the Cournot value than the comparable mean in experiment 8.) It is not clear from the pilot studies that the rounding procedure we employed in the quantity adjuster tables contributed to variation around the Cournot values. Indeed the difference in the results of experiments 7 and 8 and the comparable pilot studies appears negligible. (The difference in the individual sample means is insignificant, $.40 > p > .30$ for duopoly; $.90 > p > .80$ for triopoly.) The table and a complete set of data are presented in Appendix XVII.

We also conducted some pilot studies regarding motivation techniques in the quantity adjuster context. Four groups of incomplete-information duopolists, with the same parameters and instructions as used in experiment 7, but with payoff tables corrected to 4 places, were informed as follows: (1) The subject who made the most money during the evening, in comparison with all other subjects involved in the experiment (and there seemed to be 20 or more subjects) would receive a bonus of $8. (2) The subject who made the second highest amount during the experiment would receive a bonus of $5. (3) The third place subject would receive a $2 bonus. The results on the twenty-first transaction were (20, 20), (24, 17), (20, 20), and (19, 19).* This is a closer approximation to the Cournot prediction than was obtained in either the pilot replication of experiment 7 or in experiment 7. It would appear that this form of motivation might reduce dispersion considerably.

Five additional transactions were conducted at the end of the triopoly pilot study, with a comparable bonus arrangement for first-, second-, and third-place men on the special set of five

---

* One pair of duopolists was mixed, consisting of one subject with regular instructions, as in experiment 7, and one subject with the special instructions regarding the bonus. The mix-up occurred in part because the apparently superstitious subject who received chip number 13 upon arrival at the laboratory managed to disappear before his group reached the instruction room. The mixed pair came to a twenty-first transaction of (19, 19).

transactions alone; the mean individual choices on the last five transactions were near the Cournot predictions: (15.4, 19.0, 14.4), (15.0, 16.8, 12.4), (16.2, 16.2, 12.2), (15.0, 15.8, 15.0). The dispersion of the transactions also was reduced, as compared with the twenty-first trial of the pilot and the data of experiment 8.

It would appear that special motivation, in the form of a bonus for the top few subjects, can reduce dispersion around predicted equilibrium solutions under conditions of incomplete information.

CONCLUSIONS

Seven experiments were conducted with oligopolists negotiating as quantity adjusters. The results may be summarized as follows:

1. When duopolists negotiate under incomplete information, they tend to arrive at contracts at the Cournot solution.
2. When triopolists negotiate under incomplete information, they tend also to arrive at contracts at the Cournot solution, although in this instance there is somewhat greater dispersion of observations around the expected adjustment. This may reflect the stability properties of simple Cournot adjustment under dynamic conditions [Theocharis (1960)].
3. When oligopolists negotiate under complete information, their contracts are considerably more diverse than those of oligopolists negotiating under incomplete information. The tendency toward diversity is more characteristic of duopoly than of triopoly. This result was consistent with the prediction that complete information would provide a setting in which interpersonal differences in bargaining predisposition would be revealed, and in which subjects would attempt to communicate by means of nonmaximizing decisions.
4. Through appropriate manipulation of the payoffs, subjects under complete information were induced to adopt either cooperative or rivalistic strategies. This finding—that the extreme observations in experiments 9 and 10 can be dupli-

cated consistently through manipulation of the payoff structure as in experiments 11 and 12—suggests that in fact the
subjects in experiments 9 and 10 may be variously motivated
and this diversity in motivation may account for the dispersion observed.
5.   The bids made by the subjects may be viewed as signals, or as
attempts to communicate, and an analysis of the bids as
signals and in terms of the level-of-aspiration hypothesis
yields remarkably orderly results.

CHAPTER 10

Experimental Tests of the
Price Adjuster Models

The theoretical models reviewed in Chapter 7 offer two distinct
solutions for the oligopoly bargaining situation under conditions
of price variation.   Where

a = quantity axis intercept of the demand function
b = slope (negative) of the demand function
P = ruling (lowest) price in the market
N = number of competitors in the oligopolistic structure

the solutions yielded by the two models are:

167

1. The Bertrand solution: Each bargainer (firm) assumes that the price choices of the other bargainers are invariant with respect to changes in his own price choices. The objective of a "Bertrand bargainer" is to maximize his own profit π_1. He is led to choose his price such that

$$p_1 < p_j \qquad j = 2, \ldots, N. \tag{10.1}$$

2. The Pareto optimal solution (once more referred to as the Pareto solution, for convenience): Each bargainer chooses that price which maximizes joint profits. The Pareto model yields the prediction that

$$P = \frac{1}{2}\frac{a}{b}. \tag{10.2}$$

In the theoretical discussion in Chapter 7, it was suggested that the Bertrand solution has strong equilibrium characteristics and may be expected to hold in the great majority of cases of oligopoly bargaining under conditions of price variation. This is especially true as the number of bargainers in the oligopoly increases.

The strength of the prediction of the Bertrand solution becomes clear when oligopolistic bargaining is viewed in the light of certain relevant psychological variables. As is shown in Chapter 7, the presence in an oligopoly of but one bargainer with either the simple maximizing or the rivalistic objective ensures the Bertrand solution. This is so because both the simple maximizer and the rivalistic bargainer, in their attempts at securing a unique low price, tend to act as price cutters. With even one price cutter in the oligopoly, the ruling (lowest) price in the market tends inexorably to the Bertrand price.

Under random assignment of bargainers to oligopolistic groups, as N increases, the possibility of having no simple maximizing or rivalistic bargainers in the oligopolistic groups decreases. (That is, the possibility of having an oligopoly completely constituted of cooperative bargainers decreases.) Thus as N increases, the Bertrand solution becomes more and more likely.

The amount of information available to the bargainers is a

relevant variable in the price variation situation.   However, the amount of information may be expected to be less influential for price adjuster models than it appeared to be for quantity adjuster models, since under either information condition (complete or incomplete) the presence of but one participant behaving as a simple maximizer or as a rivalistic bargainer is sufficient to ensure the Bertrand result.

This chapter presents the experiments designed to study oligopolistic bargaining under conditions of price variation.   The two independent variables discussed above—number of bargainers and amount of information available to bargainers—were manipulated to take on two states each: $N = 2$ and $N = 3$, and complete and incomplete information.

Parameters and Operational Definitions

In the experimental sessions, we let $a = 56$ cents and $b = 8$ cents.   The oligopolists were confronted with the linear demand curve $Q = 56 - 8P$, where Q represents the quantity that consumers will take in response to the lowest quoted price P.   Each participant incurred a fixed cost of 13 cents for each bid.   Moreover, when his price bid exceeded that of any of his rivals he incurred an additional cost of 12 cents.   Thus, the penalty for offering a higher price for any given transaction was a loss of 25 cents.   (See the profit table in Appendix XIII.)   If the subject offered a price bid which was lower than any other or tied for low with others, his profit was [from (7.15)]

$$\pi = \frac{56P - 8P^2}{L} - 13$$

where P = low price bid

L = number of participants in the oligopolistic group who bid P.

For example, if both members of a duopoly bid a price of 2.0 on the same transaction, their individual profits would be

$$\pi = \frac{\$1.12 - \$0.32}{2} - \$0.13$$

$$= \$0.27.$$

If one lowered his price to 1.5 on the next transaction, while the other held firm at 2.0, the low price bidder would earn

$$\pi = \frac{\$0.84 - \$0.18}{1} - \$0.13$$
$$= \$0.53$$

while his rival would lose $0.25 on the transaction.

Ten discrete price choices were made available to the subjects in their profit tables. (See, for example, the profit table in Appendix XIII.) These choices ranged from 0.5 cent to 5.0 cents, in increments of 0.5 cent. The Pareto (joint maximizing) price is 3.5 cents. The Bertrand price is 0.5 cent.

Procedures in the Price Adjuster Sessions

In all the experiments reported in this chapter, the general procedures detailed in Chapter 8 were followed. Subjects were randomized into information conditions and also into duopoly and triopoly conditions. Within each condition, subjects were assigned to bargaining groups at random. In addition, order of arrival to the experimental session was controlled by randomization procedures. For all experiments, the members of any given bargaining group were kept apart during the instruction period and were given instructions in different rooms. After the instruction period, each subject was escorted individually to his assigned cubicle, where he was isolated from all but the experimenters. No communication was permitted between the participants except for the written price bids, the form of which was specified.

No subject participated in more than one experimental session, and none of the subjects had participated in any earlier bargaining studies.

In each of the price adjuster experiments, 18 transactions were conducted. The first 3 were practice trials, and the next 15 were the regular transactions—those involving monetary payoffs or losses. Before the final regular transaction, a general announcement was made indicating that the next transaction was to be the final one.

The transaction immediately preceding this announcement, i.e., the fourteenth regular transaction, was assumed to be the relevant statistic; this is consistent with our practice in other experiments. Coming prior to the announcement, the fourteenth transaction was not contaminated by any end-effect behavior. The number of transactions to be conducted in the experimental sessions was determined in advance of the studies, on the basis of pilot-study data. Similarly, the decision to take the fourteenth transaction as an operational definition of a solution was made in advance of the studies. (It may be noted that inspection of the data indicates that there was little difference between the results of transaction 14 and those of transactions 11 to 13.)

The profit table used by each subject showed the profit to him for any price chosen by him that was lower than his competitors' and also the profit to him for any price that was tied for lowest with his competitors'. The table also showed that he suffered a loss of 25 cents when his price choice was not the lowest. The profit table used by duopolists is exhibited in Appendix XIII, and the table used by triopolists is exhibited in Appendix XIV.

BARGAINING UNDER INCOMPLETE INFORMATION

Introduction

Two experiments were conducted in which subjects negotiated as price adjusters under incomplete information. The two experiments, numbers 13 and 14, differed in the size of the bargaining groups. They were alike in all other relevant respects, and the subjects of the two were assigned at random to the two sessions from a common pool, so that statistical comparisons between the experiments were assisted.

Experiment 13: Duopoly

Introduction. In the initial experiment on price variation, experiment 13, bargainers negotiated in duopolies. The experiment was planned to provide a test of the hypothesis that under incomplete information duopolists will negotiate transactions supporting the Bertrand solution rather than the Pareto solution. **Subjects and Procedure.** The subjects in experiment 13 were 34 male undergraduates, comprising 17 groups of duopolists. Each subject was given a printed set of instructions, a profit record sheet to use in recording the progress of the negotiations, and a profit table. These materials are shown in Appendix XIII, with the exception of the instructions, which are reproduced here:

Instructions to Seller A

The National Science Foundation, the Ford Foundation, and The Office of Naval Research have provided funds for the conduct of research regarding economic decisions. If you follow instructions carefully and make appropriate decisions, you may earn an appreciable amount of money.

We will give you $2.50 of capital to start with. *You may keep this money plus all that you earn during the session.* It is possible to end the session with considerably more than $2.50. However, you can lose part or all of the $2.50 you are given if your decisions are not made carefully, but you cannot lose more than that amount. The session will be stopped, if, at any time, you should happen to lose all of your earnings as well as the $2.50 of capital.

You will be paired at random with another person. *You will not see this person or speak with him at any time.* You will never know the identity of this other person, called Seller B, nor will he be aware of yours.

You and your anonymous counterpart will engage in a series of transactions by means of written bids. Imagine that you and he are engaged in selling some standardized commodity. *You must bid on each transaction.* The bids are in terms of the price you will charge for the commodity for that transaction. If your price bid for a given transaction is lower than Seller B's price bid, you will earn some amount of money. If your bid is higher than his, you will lose money on that transaction. If you both should bid the same price, you will not lose money, but you may not gain any either.

You will be furnished with a table showing the various levels of profit or loss you can attain. The figures within the table are the profits that you will receive depending on the price set by you and your counterpart. For example, on a given transaction you might select a price of 2.0; you would receive one of the profits in the fourth row, depending upon the price selected by Seller B for that transaction. Say that he had selected a price higher than 2.0 on that transaction; then you would receive a profit of 67¢. If he had selected the same price as you on that transaction, you would have received a profit of 27¢. Had your counterpart selected a price lower than your bid of 2.0, then you would have lost 25¢ on the transaction.

The process is started by each player selecting and recording a price on the yellow sheet provided for that purpose. You may select any price on the left-hand side of the table, and then record it. An experimental assistant will then inform you of the amount of profit or loss you made on that transaction. After each transaction your yellow sheet should show both your price bid and your profit from that transaction.

The process is repeated over and over. You may select the same price each time; you do not have to do so, however. You will be given a few minutes for each decision. You will have three practice trials so that you may become accustomed to using the profit table.

For each transaction you will record the price selected as well as the profit or loss resulting from your decision. At the end of the session we will add up your profit column and give you that amount of money, or take back any losses you incurred, up to the $2.50 you received initially. This will be done in separate counting rooms, so you will not see the person with whom you have been bidding.

Are there any questions?

On each transaction, the two members of each duopoly stated their bids independently and simultaneously. After the transaction, a subject was informed only whether he had chosen the lower price, had tied with his opponent in the price choice, or had chosen the higher price. Since this was an incomplete-information experiment, a subject was not informed of the actual price choice of his competitor, nor was he given any information about the amount of his competitor's profit or loss.

Results.   The data from transaction 14 which provide a test of
the hypothesis are presented in Table 10.1.   Complete protocols
for the session for all bargaining pairs and all transactions are
presented in Appendix XIII.

The hypothesis under test is that the Bertrand solution
($P = 0.5$) will obtain rather than the Pareto solution ($P = 3.5$).
The ruling price in each duopoly was nearer the Bertrand prediction than the Pareto prediction.   This provides significant support for the Bertrand model against the Pareto model ($p < .001$,
binomial test).   In six of the pairs both sellers named a price of
0.5; in four other groups one seller named 0.5 and the other
selected 1.0; the eleventh group had a price of 0.5 and 1.5.   Of
the six groups that named higher ruling prices, five had a low

TABLE 10.1   Ruling Prices on Transaction 14 by Duopolists under
Incomplete Information

(Experiment 13)

Group	Ruling price	Supports
1	0.5	R
2	0.5	R
3	0.5	R
4	0.5	R
5	0.5	R
6	0.5	R
7	0.5	R
8	0.5	R
9	0.5	R
10	0.5	R
11	0.5	R
12	1.0	R
13	1.0	R
14	1.0	R
15	1.0	R
16	1.0	R
17	1.5	R

Key: R = Bertrand solution
C = Pareto solution

price of 1; there was only one pair in which both players named identical prices above 0.5 (pair 12, with two bids of 1). The mean ruling price is .706; the mean of all prices on the fourteenth transaction is .912. Both values are closer to the Bertrand prediction than they are to the Pareto prediction.

In this experiment, as in the previous studies, the condition of incomplete information strongly favors the equilibrium solution, in this case the Bertrand solution. Additional discussion of these data appears in Chapter 11.

Experiment 14: Triopoly

Introduction.   In the initial theoretical formulation (Chapter 7), it was suggested that as the number of bargainers in an oligopoly (N) is increased, the Bertrand solution will be reinforced and become an even stronger equilibrium. In experiment 13, oligopoly groups consisted of two individuals. In the experiment to be reported here, the conditions were comparable and the oligopoly groups consisted of three individuals. The experiment with triopolists was conducted to test the Bertrand prediction for $N = 3$. A second purpose was to compare the results for duopolists and triopolists. Specifically, the hypotheses were:

H_1:   Price bids on transaction 14 by triopolists under incomplete information will show a greater tendency toward the Bertrand solution ($P = 0.5$) than toward the Pareto solution ($P = 3.5$).

H_2:   As N increases, oligopolies under incomplete information will show an increased tendency to the Bertrand solution. That is, triopolists will show a greater tendency (and faster approach) to the Bertrand solution than will duopolists.

One may note that the second hypothesis is independent of the first; it is entirely possible for data to support H_1 while providing no support for H_2.

Subjects and Procedure.   The first hypothesis was tested with data from experiment 14, in which 33 male undergraduates bargained under price variation in 11 bargaining triopolies.

The second hypothesis was tested with data from both experiment 13 and experiment 14. Thus, 67 subjects served in the experiments testing H_2, 34 of them serving in bargaining groups of 2 (17 groups of duopolists) and 33 of them serving in bargaining groups of 3 (11 groups of triopolists). The fact that subjects were assigned at random from a common pool to experiments 13 and 14 assisted a direct statistical comparison between the results of the two sessions.

Each subject was given an appropriate set of instructions, a profit record sheet, and a profit table. For the duopolists, these materials are in Appendix XIII; for the triopolists these materials are in Appendix XIV.

The procedures have already been presented, briefly at the beginning of this chapter, more fully in Chapter 8. On each transaction, subjects were informed only whether they had chosen the lowest price, had tied for low, or had chosen a higher price. Subjects were not informed of the actual price choice or the amount of the profits or losses of their competitor (or competitors).

Results. The data for transaction 14 by the triopolists are presented in Table 10.2. Complete protocols for all triopolists, showing all transactions and their profits and losses, are presented in Appendix XIV.

The first hypothesis, H_1, is that triopolists under incomplete information will show a greater tendency to the Bertrand solution ($P = 0.5$) than to the Pareto solution ($P = 3.5$). As Table 10.2 indicates, all groups of triopolists chose ruling prices on the equilibrium transaction at precisely the Bertrand solution, 0.5. The evidence therefore supports H_1 ($p < .001$, binomial test).

The second hypothesis, H_2, is that as N increases from duopoly to triopoly, oligopolists under incomplete information will show a greater tendency (and faster approach) to the Bertrand solution. Data relevant to this hypothesis were secured in experiments 13 and 14 and are presented here in Tables 10.1 and 10.2. In Table 10.3 a summary of the data pertinent to the hypothesis is presented. The mean ruling price for triopolists is precisely the

TABLE 10.2   Ruling Prices on Transaction 14 by Triopolists under
Incomplete Information
(Experiment 14)

Group	Ruling price	Supports
18	0.5	R
19	0.5	R
20	0.5	R
21	0.5	R
22	0.5	R
23	0.5	R
24	0.5	R
25	0.5	R
26	0.5	R
27	0.5	R
28	0.5	R

Key: R = Bertrand solution
     C = Pareto solution

Bertrand solution, $P = 0.5$, whereas the mean ruling price for
duopolists is $P = 0.706$.   Although the difference is small, it is
nonetheless significant because of the slight variability in the
data ($t = 2.20$, $df = 26$, $p < .025$).

To represent the relative speed of approach to equilibrium, we
consider the ruling price bids on each of the 14 regular transactions.   These data are presented in Table 10.4 for duopolists
under incomplete information, and in Table 10.5 for triopolists
under incomplete information.   The entries in the body of each

TABLE 10.3   Mean Ruling
Prices on Transaction 14 by
Duopolists and Triopolists under
Incomplete Information

Condition	Mean ruling price
Duopoly	0.706
Triopoly	0.500

table are frequencies: They represent the number of groups which negotiated that ruling price for that specific transaction.

The data in Table 10.4 indicate that the duopolists gradually shifted toward the Bertrand price of 0.5 as the transactions progressed. In contrast, the data in Table 10.5 indicate that the triopolists moved abruptly and rapidly to the Bertrand price. By the third transaction, 10 of the 11 groups of triopolists chose ruling prices precisely on the Bertrand price of 0.5. On the next 11 transactions (numbers 4 to 14) in only 3 instances did 1 group reach any price but the competitive one; in the other 118 instances the ruling price was 0.5.

Further evidence in support of this conclusion is obtained when all price bids on the fourteenth transaction are considered. In seven of the eleven triopoly groups, each player bid the Bertrand price; in three other groups, two players bid 0.5. Of the five price bids above the Bertrand prediction, four were bids of 1. The mean of all price bids on the fourteenth transaction was 0.606, a close approximation of the Bertrand value.

It would appear that price variation oligopoly under incom-

TABLE 10.4   Frequency of Various Individual Ruling Prices for the 14 Regular Transactions by Duopolists under Incomplete Information (Experiment 13)

Price	Transaction number														Sum	Per cent
	1	*2*	*3*	*4*	*5*	*6*	*7*	*8*	*9*	*10*	*11*	*12*	*13*	*14*		
5.0																
4.5																
4.0																
3.5												1			1	.4
3.0											1		1		2	.8
2.5	1	1					1			1					4	1.7
2.0	2	1	2				1		1	1					8	3.4
1.5	6	3	4	6	5	3	2	4	4	2	3	1		1	44	18.5
1.0	1	7	4	5	4	8	5	4	4	4	5	7	7	5	71	29.8
0.5	7	5	7	6	8	6	8	9	8	9	8	8	9	11	108	45.4

TABLE 10.5   Frequency of Various Individual Ruling Prices for the 14 Regular Transactions by Triopolists under Incomplete Information (Experiment 14)

Price	Transaction number														Sum	Per cent
	1	2	3	4	5	6	7	8	9	10	11	12	13	14		
5.0																
4.5																
4.0																
3.5																
3.0																
2.5																
2.0																
1.5			1												1	.6
1.0	7	4				1	1				1				14	9.1
0.5	4	7	10	11	11	10	10	11	11	11	10	11	11	11	139	90.3

plete information is a conflict structure that is not conducive to cooperative signaling; this tendency is quite marked when the number of players increases from two to three.

BARGAINING UNDER COMPLETE INFORMATION

Introduction

In the theory presented in Chapter 7, it was suggested that when oligopolistic bargainers can identify a relationship between their own choices and the profits of their competitors, then it is more likely that the various bargaining signals and characteristics—cooperation, simple maximizing, and rivalry—will exercise an influence on the oligopoly transactions and outcome.   This is perhaps less true for oligopolists under conditions of price variation than we have found it to be under conditions of quantity variation.   As the argument in Chapter 7 demonstrates, both simple maximizers and rivalists tend to behave as price cutters, and with just a single price cutter in the group the bargainers will be driven to the Bertrand solution.

Complete information does enable the cooperative participants to follow a different strategy. The cooperative bargainer with information regarding his counterparts' price choices may try to match the price set by his opponents rather than to undercut it. Such cooperative behavior, feasible only under complete information, may lead to ruling prices above the Bertrand price.

In the two studies already reported in this chapter, all oligopolistic groups were under incomplete information, knowing neither the price choices of their competitors nor the profits or losses accruing to them. We have seen that under these circumstances the experimental results strongly support the predicted Bertrand solution.

For the condition of complete information, on the other hand, the theoretical formulation does not yield predictions as invariant as those for incomplete information.

If all the members of a given oligopoly are cooperators, i.e., if each is behaving as if he were trying to increase the profits of all, then the result expected at the limit is the Paretian optimal solution:

$$P = \frac{1}{2}\frac{a}{b}. \tag{10.2}$$

The cooperative bargainer will try to match the lowest price set by his competitors rather than undercut it and therefore may "teach" an uncooperative opponent the advantage of such a strategy. In the case of an oligopoly containing a cooperative bargainer, then, it may be expected that the result will lie in the region between the Bertrand solution and the Pareto solution.

Two experiments were conducted in which oligopolists bargained as price adjusters under complete information. The two differed only in the size of the bargaining groups: In experiment 15, groups of three negotiated, whereas in experiment 16 groups of two negotiated.

Experiment 15: Triopoly

Subjects and Procedure. The triopolists who negotiated as price adjusters under complete information were 30 male undergraduates, assigned at random to 10 triopolies.

The instructions and profit table presented to these subjects are displayed in Appendix XV. Each subject was told that his competitors had the same profit table he had. Further, after each transaction each subject was told of the price choices of his two competitors. The subject could also keep a record of the price choices and profits and losses of his competitors.

Results. The ruling prices on the final transaction of the triopolists under complete information are shown in Table 10.6. Complete protocols showing all transactions and payoffs for these subjects are presented in Appendix XV.

It will be observed that the ruling price was in every instance the Bertrand price: 0.5. This result is significant at $p < .001$ (binomial test) against the null hypothesis that observations are equally likely to support the Pareto price.

TABLE 10.6 Ruling Prices on Transaction 14 by Triopolists under Complete Information

(Experiment 15)

Group	Ruling price	Supports
29	0.5	R
30	0.5	R
31	0.5	R
32	0.5	R
33	0.5	R
34	0.5	R
35	0.5	R
36	0.5	R
37	0.5	R
38	0.5	R

Key: R = Bertrand solution
     C = Pareto solution

TABLE 10.7 Frequency of Various Individual Ruling Prices for the 14 Regular Transactions by Triopolists under Complete Information (Experiment 15)

Price	Transaction number														Sum	Per cent
	1	*2*	*3*	*4*	*5*	*6*	*7*	*8*	*9*	*10*	*11*	*12*	*13*	*14*		
5.0																
4.5																
4.0																
3.5																
3.0																
2.5																
2.0	1														1	.7
1.5	2	2		1			1								6	4.3
1.0	3	3	3	1	2	2	1	1		2		1			19	13.6
0.5	4	5	7	8	8	8	9	8	10	8	10	9	10	10	114	81.4

The ruling price bids on each of the 14 regular transactions by the triopolists under complete information are shown in Table 10.7.

Experiment 16: Duopoly

Subjects and Procedure. In the fourth experiment in the price adjuster series, 34 male undergraduates served in 17 duopolies, negotiating under complete information.

As in experiment 15, a subject in experiment 16 was told that his competitor had the same profit table that he had. In addition, after each transaction the subject was notified of the price choice of his competitor on that transaction. The subject could also keep a record of the price choices and profits and losses of his competitor.

Results. The ruling prices on the equilibrium transaction of the duopolists under complete information are shown in Table 10.8. Complete protocols showing all transactions and payoffs for these subjects are presented in Appendix XVI.

Of the 17 groups, 6 arrived at the Bertrand solution as the ruling price on the equilibrium transaction. Of the 11 duopolies which arrived at ruling prices higher than the Bertrand solution, 3 arrived at a price of 1.0, 4 at a price of 2.0, 2 at a price of 3.0, and 2 at a price of 3.5. Any price below 2.0 is closer to the Bertrand solution than to its rival, so 9 of the 17 groups may be said to have supported the Bertrand solution. The price of 2.0 is intermediate, so the four groups which arrived at that price support the two solutions equally. Four groups arrived at ruling prices closer to the Pareto solution than to its rival. We conclude that 11 of the 17 observations support the Bertrand solution. This result is not significant against the null hypothesis $(p < .17)$.

TABLE 10.8   Ruling Prices on Transaction 14 by Duopolists under Complete Information
(Experiment 16

Group	Ruling price	Supports
39	0.5	R
40	0.5	R
41	0.5	R
42	0.5	R
43	0.5	R
44	0.5	R
45	1.0	R
46	1.0	R
47	1.0	R
48	2.0	R, C
49	2.0	R, C
50	2.0	R, C
51	2.0	R, C
52	3.0	C
53	3.0	C
54	3.5	C
55	3.5	C

Key: R = Bertrand solution
     C = Pareto solution

TABLE 10.9   Frequency of Various Individual Ruling Prices for the 14
Regular Transactions by Duopolists under Complete Information
(Experiment 16)

Price	Transaction number														Sum	Per cent
	1	2	3	4	5	6	7	8	9	10	11	12	13	14		
5.0																
4.5																
4.0																
3.5	2	2	3	2	2	2	2	3	4	2	2	2	2	2	32	13.4
3.0	1	2	1	2	2	1	4	3	2	3	2	1	2	2	28	11.8
2.5		3	1	1		2			1			1	1		10	4.2
2.0	4	4	4	2	5	3	1	1	1	2	3	4	2	4	40	16.8
1.5	6	6	5	7	1	1	3	2	1	1	2	2	3		42	17.6
1.0	4		3		3	4	3	2	3	4	2	2	2	3	33	13.9
0.5				3	4	4	4	6	5	5	6	5	5	6	53	22.3

The ruling price on each of the 14 regular transactions by the
completely informed duopolists is shown in Table 10.9.

Discussion

Experiments 15 and 16 were conducted to provide a contrast
with their counterpart sessions under incomplete information and
thus to highlight the effect of amount of information on price
adjuster negotiations.   Discussion of the results of the two
experiments will be deferred until the relevant comparisons concerning amount of information are made.

THE EFFECT OF AMOUNT OF INFORMATION

Introduction

Because of the possibility of cooperation when bargainers have
complete information, oligopolists under complete information
may be expected to exhibit more variability in the solutions they
reach than do oligopolists under incomplete information.

In order to test this hypothesis concerning the effect of amount of information, two comparisons were made, one between transactions of duopolists negotiating under complete and under incomplete information, and one between transactions of triopolists negotiating under the same two conditions. These comparisons are meaningful because all other relevant variables were controlled: Subjects were randomized into information conditions and into triopolies and duopolies; the payoff function was the same for all groups; the number of trials was the same for all groups, etc.

The general hypothesis concerns the difference in variability (dispersion) of the transactions. The central tendency or typical value of transactions under complete information is not the topic of the hypothesis because according to the theory under test the typical value cannot be specified without prior knowledge of the particular combination of bargaining types or signaling tendencies characterizing the group (or groups). The hypotheses were:

H_1:   Ruling prices reached by duopolists on the fourteenth transaction under complete information will exhibit greater variability than will those under incomplete information.

H_2:   Ruling prices reached by triopolists on the fourteenth transaction under complete information will exhibit greater variability than will those under incomplete information.

Variability of Duopolists as a Function of Amount of Information

The first hypothesis concerning the effect of amount of information was tested with data from 68 male undergraduates serving in 34 bargaining groups of duopolists. Of these, 34 subjects (17 groups) served in experiment 16, which was conducted under conditions of complete information. The data of experiment 16 were compared with those of experiment 13, in which 34 subjects (17 groups) were observed under conditions of incomplete information.

The duopolist under incomplete information knew nothing

about the profit table of his competitor. At hand, he had only his own profit table (presented in Appendix XIII). After each transaction, the bargainer was told only whether he had chosen the low price, had tied for low, or had chosen a higher price than his rival. He was not told about the level of his competitor's price choice—only how it compared with his own. Nor was he told about the profit or loss to his competitor on any transaction.

The duopolist under complete information, on the other hand, was told that his competitor had the same profit table that he had (presented in Appendix XVI). Moreover, after each transaction he was told of the price choice his competitor had made. He could keep a record of the price choices and profits and losses of his competitor.

The ruling prices negotiated by duopolists under incomplete information are displayed in Table 10.1. Those negotiated by duopolists under complete information are displayed in Table 10.8.

The hypothesis for which these data provide a test is H_1: Ruling prices reached by duopolists under complete information will be more variable than those reached by duopolists under incomplete information. The data in Tables 10.1 and 10.8 were analyzed for differences in variability by the Siegel-Tukey test [Siegel and Tukey (1960)]. By this test, the null hypothesis of equal variability may be rejected at the $p < .04$ level of significance ($z = 1.78$, corrected for ties) in favor of H_1. Further, all observations in experiment 13 favored the Bertrand theory; only 11 of the 17 observations in experiment 16 favored the Bertrand price.

It should be noted that the probability of rejecting the null hypothesis is reduced by restrictions on the possible range of the data and by differences in central tendency (here, in average ruling price) when this test is used [Siegel and Tukey (1960, p. 434)]. The fact that in spite of these hazards the data permit rejection of the null hypothesis in this instance must be attributed to the power of the hypothesis. Siegel and Tukey point out that in the presence of differences between means "rejection of the

TABLE 10.10   Frequency with Which Various Ruling Prices Were
Reached by Duopolists under Complete and Incomplete Information

Ruling price	17 duopolies under incomplete information (experiment 13)	17 duopolies under complete information (experiment 16)
5.0		
4.5		
4.0		
3.5		2
3.0		2
2.5		
2.0		4
1.5	1	
1.0	5	3
0.5	11	6

null hypothesis can almost certainly be attributed to differences in variability."

For descriptive purposes, the data concerning variability on the equilibrium transaction are summarized in Table 10.10. The frequency with which duopolists reached various ruling prices under the two information conditions is shown. Table 10.10 highlights the greater variability of the ruling prices reached by duopolists under complete information.

If we turn our attention from transaction 14 to the entire course of the bargaining—all transactions—then additional support may be seen for the general hypothesis that oligopoly bargaining under complete information leads to more variable results than does such bargaining under incomplete information.

It is revealing to compare the two tables showing the frequency with which various ruling prices were reached on each of the 14 transactions by duopolists (Table 10.4 for incompletely informed duopolists and Table 10.9 for completely informed duopolists). Duopolistic bargainers with complete information exhibit considerably more variability than do their incompletely informed counterparts, and many fewer are driven to the Ber-

TABLE 10.11   Per Cent of All Transactions Negotiated at Various Individual Ruling Prices by Duopolists under Two Conditions of Information

Ruling price	Duopolies under incomplete information	Duopolies under complete information
5.0		
4.5		
4.0		
3.5	.4	13.4
3.0	.8	11.8
2.5	1.7	4.2
2.0	3.4	16.8
1.5	18.5	17.6
1.0	29.8	13.9
0.5	45.4	22.3

trand price.   In neither case did a single transaction occur above the Pareto price (3.5), but under complete information there were many more transactions at, and close to, that level.

The percentage of transactions occurring at each ruling price is summarized in Table 10.11; the data are taken from Tables 10.4 and 10.9.

In sum, both the data for the fourteenth transaction, as summarized in Table 10.10, and the data for all 14 transactions, as summarized in Table 10.11, support the hypothesis that duopolistic bargaining by price adjusters is more variable under complete information than under incomplete information.   The mean values of ruling price bids on the fourteenth transaction under complete information for duopolists was 1.59, whereas under incomplete information the mean was 0.71.

Variability of Triopolists as a Function of Amount of Information

The analysis of variability in price bids as a function of amount of information available to the bargainers may be replicated for triopolistic bargainers.   The hypothesis under test here is H_2: Ruling prices reached by triopolists on the fourteenth transaction under complete information will exhibit greater variability than will those under incomplete information.

The second hypothesis was tested with data from 63 male undergraduates serving in 21 bargaining groups of triopolists. Of these, 30 subjects (10 groups of triopolists) served in experiment 15, which was conducted under conditions of complete information. The data of this session were compared with those of experiment 14, in which 33 subjects (11 groups of triopolists) were observed under conditions of incomplete information.

The triopolist under incomplete information knew nothing about the profits to his competitors on any of the 14 transactions. After each transaction, he was not told what his rivals had bid; but he was told whether his own bid was the low price, had tied for low, or was higher than the others. The triopolist under complete information, in contrast, was told that his competitors had the same profit table he had, and after each transaction he was told the price choices his competitors had made.

Triopolists under incomplete information were given the instructions and profit table presented in Appendix XIV, while those under complete information were given those presented in Appendix XV.

As has been mentioned, subjects were assigned to the four price adjuster bargaining sessions from a common pool, so direct comparisons between sessions are assisted. The randomization procedures and other techniques are reported in Chapter 8.

Results. The ruling prices on the fourteenth transaction by incompletely informed triopolists are shown in Table 10.2. Comparable data for their completely informed counterparts are shown in Table 10.6. Complete protocols showing all transactions and payoffs for these subjects are presented in Appendixes XIV and XV.

The reader will note immediately that there is no difference in variability between the two sessions. Whether completely or incompletely informed, all triopolists arrived at a ruling price of 0.5 on the equilibrium transaction. It would seem that the size of the bargaining group is the decisive influence on the ruling

TABLE 10.12   Per Cent of All Transactions Negotiated at Various
Individual Ruling Prices by Triopolists under Two Conditions of
Information

Ruling price	Triopolies under incomplete information	Triopolies under complete information
5.0		
4.5		
4.0		
3.5		
3.0		
2.5		
2.0		.7
1.5	.6	4.3
1.0	9.1	13.6
0.5	90.3	81.4

prices.   The increase in N from 2 to 3 cancels out any possible
effect of differences in the information conditions.

Also of interest is the comparison between the ruling prices
throughout the course of the negotiations.   It is revealing to
compare the two tables showing the frequency with which various
ruling prices were reached on each of the 14 transactions by
triopolists (Table 10.5 for incompletely informed triopolists and
Table 10.7 for completely informed triopolists).   The percentages
which summarize one characteristic of those tables are presented
in Table 10.12.

Although the overwhelming tendency is for ruling prices to fall
at the Bertrand point in both instances, there is nonetheless
somewhat more variability under complete information than
under incomplete: 81.4 per cent of the ruling prices are at the
competitive point under complete information, while 90.3 per
cent are at that point under incomplete information.   Further,
under complete information 5 per cent of the ruling prices are
1.5 or higher, whereas under incomplete information less than
1 per cent are as high.   Regardless of information condition, in
no case did any triopoly reach a ruling price near the Pareto point.

The mean of all price bids on transaction 14 by triopolists under complete information was .817.   This value exceeds its counterpart for triopolists under incomplete information, which is .606.

Insofar as there is any difference in variability between triopolists negotiating under contrasting information conditions, the difference is in the direction predicted by H_2.   That is, greater variability is exhibited by completely informed triopolists. Much more impressive than the variability, of course, is the uniformity of the results, the invariance of the observations.

Discussion

If it is true, as we have suggested, that both the number of bargainers and the amount of information at their disposal are relevant to the bargaining outcome, with N being the more decisive variable, then it should be expected that duopoly groups will in general show more variability than triopoly groups and that within both conditions of N, completely informed subjects will show more variability than incompletely informed subjects. That is, the hypothesis is suggested that the variability of ruling prices on all transactions will be ordered as follows:

$$H_3: \quad D(C) > D(I) > T(C) > T(I)$$

where D = duopoly
T = triopoly
I = incomplete information
C = complete information

A test of this hypothesis may be provided by analysis of the standard deviations of the ruling prices for each of the fourteen transactions under both information conditions for both duopolists and triopolists.   These data are presented in Table 10.13.

The reader will observe that in general the standard deviations are larger for the complete-information condition than for the incomplete-information condition.   In fact, for duopolists the standard deviations are larger on every one of the fourteen transactions for the completely informed bargainers than they are for

TABLE 10.13   Standard Deviations of P for Each Transaction under Two Conditions of Information

Transaction	Triopoly		Duopoly	
	Incomplete information	Complete information	Incomplete information	Complete information
1	.240	.500	.640	.785
2	.240	.391	.549	.687
3	.287	.229	.528	.848
4	.000	.320	.420	.936
5	.000	.200	.428	1.01
6	.144	.200	.353	1.01
7	.144	.150	.581	1.11
8	.000	.320	.412	1.20
9	.000	.000	.482	1.22
10	.000	.200	.591	1.11
11	.144	.000	.629	1.07
12	.000	.150	.705	1.01
13	.000	.000	.588	1.06
14	.000	.000	.300	1.09

their incompletely informed counterparts. For triopolists, the standard deviations are larger for the completely informed groups for about two-thirds of the fourteen transactions. (Approximately the same result held for quantity variation data.)

A statistical test of H_3 is provided by a Jonckheere test on the data in Table 10.13. This test [Jonckheere (1954)] is a nonparametric test against ordered alternatives for k independent groups. The data are ordered as expected under the hypothesis,[*] and this trend is significant against the null hypothesis at $p < .0001$ ($z = 6.62$).

* By way of contrast, the quantity variation data were ordered, in general, $D(C) > T(C) > T(I) > D(I)$, which suggests that the information condition is more important in that setting than the number of participants (see Table 9.8).

We may conclude that the amount of information available to duopolists is a significant determinant of the ruling price they will negotiate, but that its significance is reduced as the size of the oligopoly increases. Of the two variables which were treated as independent variables in the four price adjuster experiments— size of oligopoly and amount of information—it would appear that the first, size of the oligopoly, is the more important one in determining the adjustments bargainers reach.

LEVEL OF ASPIRATION

On the basis of a bilateral monopoly experiment, two hypotheses were stated in Chapter 6 regarding signaling behavior. These hypotheses—the R hypothesis concerning rivalistic signals, and the S hypothesis concerning cooperative signals—were tested with the quantity adjuster data in Chapter 9. Our purpose here is to construct and test similar hypotheses for the price variation data.

The R hypothesis assumes that bargainers will set their levels of aspiration at equal profit contracts. If one bargainer makes less than the other on a transaction, he will be frustrated and send a rivalistic signal on the next transaction, i.e., lower his price. In the price variation setting, since price and profit are inversely related, the R hypothesis may be stated: if $P_i > P_{ir}$, then $P_{i+1} < P_i$, where P_i is a player's price bid on the ith transaction, P_{ir} is his rival's bid on that transaction, and P_{i+1} is the player's bid on the next transaction. The prediction is that if a player's price is high (and therefore his profit low) on a given transaction, he will lower his price on the next transaction (a rivalistic signal).

The S hypothesis is that if a player has the low price on a transaction (and therefore gains high profits), he will raise his price on the next transaction (a cooperative signal). That is, if $P_i < P_{ir}$, then $P_{i+1} > P_i$.

The R hypothesis is derived from level-of-aspiration considerations; the S hypothesis is not. Therefore the general expectation has been that the R hypothesis would find stronger experimental support than the S hypothesis. This was the case for bilateral monopoly and quantity adjuster oligopoly.

To test the R and S hypotheses with the price adjuster data, we examined each of the 14 regular transactions in experiments 13 to 16, counting how many supported and how many opposed each hypothesis. If an observation was neither for nor against the hypothesis, e.g., if a player offered the same price for several transactions and that price was either high or low, then such an observation was counted as one-half for and one-half against the appropriate proposition.

The results for the R hypothesis are shown in Table 10.14. The ratio of observations for the hypothesis to observations against the hypothesis is reported as an approximate index of the strength of the hypothesis for that experimental condition.

TABLE 10.14 Number of Transactions For and Against the Rivalistic Hypothesis in Four Experiments on Price Variation

	Duopoly under incomplete information (experiment 13)	Triopoly under incomplete information (experiment 14)	Triopoly under complete information (experiment 15)	Duopoly under complete information (experiment 16)
Observations for hypothesis	114.5	61.5	69.5	107.5
Observations against hypothesis	20.5	9.5	13.5	23.5
Ratio of above	5.59	6.47	5.15	4.57
Number of bargaining groups	17	11	10	17
Number of bargaining groups providing more observations for than against the hypothesis (ties count one-half)	13.5	11	11	15

TABLE 10.15   Number of Transactions For and Against the
Cooperative Hypothesis in Four Experiments on Price Variation

	Duopoly under incomplete information (experiment 13)	Triopoly under incomplete information (experiment 14)	Triopoly under complete information (experiment 15)	Duopoly under complete information (experiment 16)
Observations for hypothesis	93.5	20.5	36.0	90.5
Observations against hypothesis	41.5	10.5	17.0	40.5
Ratio of above	2.25	1.95	2.12	2.23
Number of bargaining groups	17	11	10	17
Number of bargaining groups providing more observations for than against the hypothesis (ties count one-half)	15.5	8	8.5	13.5

The results for the S hypothesis are shown in Table 10.15.
Again, the hypothesis is supported in each of the four experiments.

Because subjects were assigned at random from a common pool
to the four experimental sessions, we may make direct comparisons across sessions.

In the comparison between the R hypothesis and the S hypothesis, the R hypothesis would appear to be stronger in all four
experiments.   This conclusion emerges from a comparison of the
various ratios of observations for and against each hypothesis.
For example, for duopolists under incomplete information (experiment 13), the ratio for the R hypothesis was 5.59, while that for
the S hypothesis was 2.25.   Similar comparisons for each experiment reveal that the R hypothesis ratio is larger in each instance.
This result is consistent with our analysis in other bargaining
experiments and with level-of-aspiration theory.

196   Oligopoly

COMPARISON BETWEEN QUANTITY VARIATION AND PRICE VARIATION

The reader will recognize that the analysis of rivalistic and cooperative signals just presented is directly comparable to the analysis of such signals in the quantity adjuster experiments reported in Chapter 9. It is of interest now to compare the results for the R hypothesis and the S hypothesis for two forms of oligopolistic bargaining: quantity adjustment and price adjustment. That is, the ratios which are indexes of the strength of the R and S hypothesis in the price adjuster experiments may be compared with their opposite numbers, the ratios from the quantity adjuster experiments.

The difference in the nature of the conflict situation, between quantity variation and price variation oligopoly, leads us to expect price adjusters to rely more heavily on signaling. In quantity variation, the player with the smaller output choice on a given trial made less money than his rivals, but the difference was relatively slight. In price variation, in contrast, the player with the high price bid suffered substantially. Rather than making a small profit, he lost money. Further, his opponent made a larger profit on the transaction than he might have in a comparable quantity adjustment situation. Because the price variation experiments magnified profit differences for unmatched decisions, they placed a premium on signaling and communica-

TABLE 10.16   Support for the Rivalist Signaling Hypothesis in Quantity Variation and Price Variation Oligopoly Experiments

	Incomplete information		Complete information	
	Duopolists (experiments 7 and 13)	Triopolists (experiments 8 and 14)	Duopolists (experiments 10 and 16)	Triopolists (experiments 9 and 15)
Price adjusters	5.59	6.47	4.57	5.15
Quantity adjusters	1.64	2.18	1.97	3.35

TABLE 10.17   Support for the Cooperative Signaling Hypothesis in Quantity Variation and Price Variation Oligopoly Experiments

	Incomplete information		Complete information	
	Duopolists (experiments 7 and 13)	Triopolists (experiments 8 and 14)	Duopolists (experiments 10 and 16)	Triopolists (experiments 9 and 15)
Price adjusters	2.25	1.95	2.23	2.12
Quantity adjusters	1.36	1.62	2.12	2.70

tion. For this reason we would expect the communication hypotheses to find stronger support in the price variation experiments than in the quantity variation experiments.

Table 10.16 summarizes the relevant data for the R hypothesis. The table is based on certain data in Tables 9.11 and 10.14. The ratio of observations for the R hypothesis to those against it is shown for the eight principal oligopoly experiments. The reader will note that in every case the comparison between these ratios for price adjusters and for quantity adjusters confirms the expectation. Price adjusters are much more likely than are quantity adjusters to send rivalist signals on a given transaction if on the previous transaction they were frustrated. This generalization holds true for both duopolists and triopolists; and it holds true for incompletely informed bargainers as well as for completely informed bargainers.

Table 10.17 summarizes the data for the S hypothesis. It abstracts the relevant data from Tables 9.12 and 10.15. In three of the four comparisons, cooperative signaling is more characteristic of price adjusters than of quantity adjusters; the exception is provided by completely informed triopolists.

The signaling hypotheses appear to hold quite consistently in both quantity adjuster and price adjuster conflict situations. Further, the strength of support for the hypotheses apparently forms a stable and reasonable relationship: In general it is likely that a frustrated subject will send a rivalistic signal, if he signals at all; it is somewhat less likely that a satisfied subject will send a cooperative signal. These proclivities are stronger under price variation conditions than they are under quantity variation conditions.

END EFFECTS

Thus far in this chapter we have been concerned with data from the first 14 of the 15 transactions in the price variation sessions. The final transaction, number 15, was preceded by an announcement indicating that it was to be the last. The purpose of this announcement was to produce end effects. Changes in ruling price from transaction 14 to transaction 15 are displayed in Table 10.18. In general, these end effects are small but consistent. For groups close to or at the Bertrand solution on their fourteenth trials, i.e., groups at the point of low profit or no profit, there was a slight tendency to take a "last chance" gamble on the final trial, seeking higher profits. For groups at or close to the Pareto solution, some double-crossing was observed on the final

TABLE 10.18   End Effects: Ruling Prices on Transactions 14 and 15 in Oligopoly Bargaining under Two Conditions of Information

Price	Incomplete information				Complete information			
	Duopoly		*Triopoly*		*Duopoly*		*Triopoly*	
	14	*15*	*14*	*15*	*14*	*15*	*14*	*15*
5.0								
4.5								
4.0								
3.5					2			
3.0					2			
2.5						1		
2.0		2		1	4	3		
1.5	1	2				4		
1.0	5	4			3	3		1
0.5	11	9	11	10	6	6	10	9

transaction. For examples, see protocols 52 to 55 in Appendix XVI. In groups 54 and 55, which were transacting at the Pareto solution and sharing maximum joint profits throughout the entire fourteen transactions, *both* participants in each duopoly double-crossed on the fifteenth transaction.

SUMMARY AND CONCLUSIONS

In four different experiments, a total of 55 groups of subjects bargained for monetary payoffs in simulated oligopoly situations under conditions of price variation. The transactions of the groups support the following conclusions:

1. Bargainers under incomplete information tend to negotiate transactions at the Bertrand price.
2. As the number of bargainers in the oligopolistic structure increases, oligopolies under incomplete information show a stronger tendency, and faster approach, to the Bertrand price.
3. As the amount of relevant information available to the bargainers increases, duopolies decrease their tendency to the Bertrand competitive price.
4. Duopoly groups under complete information exhibit more variability of outcomes than do duopoly groups under incomplete information.
5. The variability of results for duopolies under complete information seems to be because of the incidence of cooperative signals from bargainers who, in their attempt to reach a result on the Paretian optima, refuse to undercut their competitor's price choice.
6. As the number of bargainers in the oligopolistic structure increases, irrespective of the information condition, oligopolies show an increased tendency to the Bertrand price.

These conclusions, as well as additional results concerning oligopoly bargaining under conditions of price variation, will be discussed further in Chapter 11.

PART FOUR

Conclusion

Overview

Our purpose in this book was to use the experimental method in the analysis of some traditional economic situations. We hoped to learn more about the theory being considered, about the experimental methodology, and about the resolution of human conflict.

THE THEORY

We started this sequence of experiments with a consideration of price leadership bilateral monopoly. The traditional solution for this situation is associated with Bowley. The Bowley solution has game-theory equilibrium properties: Assuming the players are motivated solely by their own profits, the Bowley price is the optimum choice for the seller, and the Bowley quantity is the optimum choice for the buyer, given the seller's price. This adjustment does not maximize joint profits, however. The joint maximizing solution is the alternative solution associated with Pareto. We found, over six experiments, that Bowley's prediction was a useful one. However, by manipulating the experimental conditions (amount of information, form of bidding, and location of the equal-profit contract), we could induce the Pareto solution for an appreciable number of subjects. The sixth experiment was a replication of experiments 3 and 5, using, as subjects, mature people affiliated with a large business concern rather than college students. The results were consistent with those for students with respect to support for the Bowley or the Pareto predictions.

We concluded that incomplete-information conditions were favorable to the solution based on an assumption of simple maximizing behavior (the Bowley solution in this case). This was consistent with our previous experimental results (where the Fellner predictions for equal-strength bilateral monopoly were supported, and Fouraker's 1957 predictions for the same situation were not). The result was employed as a prediction for the oligopoly studies, where the proposition found further support.

As a corollary, complete-information conditions apparently encouraged a variety of nonsimple maximizing behavior. We classified such behavior as: rivalistic (a decision which reduces a player's profits, but generally reduces his opponent's profits by a larger margin); cooperative (a decision which reduces a player's profits, but generally increases his opponent's profits even more); and simple maximizing (an optimal individual decision). In general, rivalistic behavior reduced joint profits, cooperative behavior increased joint profits, and simple maximizing behavior led to equilibrium solutions. A rivalistic decision could reflect two distinct motivations: (1) that the player derives satisfaction from reducing the profits of his opponent; typically, he wants to beat his rival by making more profit than the rival, and (2) that the player wishes to send a punitive bid, as a signal that he is dissatisfied with the past responses of his opponent and wants him to alter his decisions in a manner that benefits the signaler. That is, he may be motivated solely by his own profits and employ the rivalistic signal as a means of increasing those profits.

It would be very difficult to distinguish between such motives in the instance of a rivalistic decision in a repeated-play game; indeed, both motivations might be operative in the subject at one time or another during the experiment. We did not attempt to make such distinctions. The same considerations apply to cooperative behavior.

The significance of such a classification is that it is activated by complete information, producing more varied results than those associated with simple maximizing behavior. This prediction was made for the quantity adjuster and price adjuster oligopoly experiments and found continued support: The incomplete-information experiments produced data consistent with the equilibrium models (Cournot for quantity adjusters, Bertrand for price adjusters); complete information tended to increase the dispersion of the observations in both the quantity adjuster and the price adjuster experiments.

Some of the dispersion in the experiments might be explained by (1) the lack of discriminability in the payoff tables, which were large and complex (compared to those used in most decision-making experiments); (2) the small size of the individual payoffs and the small difference between an optimal choice and a random choice; and (3) the naïveté of the subjects. We feel that such dispersion could be reduced by better tables (certainly ours could be improved), larger payoffs (or some alternative form of increased motivation), and more knowledgeable subjects. These conclusions follow from the special trials at the end of most of the experiments (which shed light on the discriminability question), from replications of the experiments with mature subjects and larger payoffs, from pilot work with different tables and form of motivation, and from the work of others (see below).

All of the variation in observed decisions could not be explained by these considerations, however. We felt that much of this behavior was consistent with a theory from psychology: the level-of-aspiration model. We had imputed a relationship between level of aspiration and bargaining behavior in our initial work on equal-strength bilateral monopoly; the continued relevance of this relationship suggests that it may be a fruitful hypothesis in future investigations of bargaining and group decision processes.

THE METHODOLOGY

One might argue that the gulf between our experimental procedure and the full blown richness of empirical conflict situations is too great and that the conclusions derived in the laboratory have no relevance to the policies which must be made in practice. After all, we are employing student decision makers in a radically simplified situation; economic conflict in the *real* world generally takes place among gargantuan organizations with varying historical backgrounds and current postures. The entrepreneur in a *real* situation may be concerned about the financial structure of the organization or about public opinion as reflected in the actions of, for example, the Justice Department; he may be worried about potential competitors or product obsolescence. Indeed, the list of possible critical variables is without end. Thus it *is* dangerous to go blithely from a study such as this to prediction or policy formation in business. However, this gap results more from the shortcomings of the theory than it does from innate deficiencies of the experimental method. Most economic theory presupposes individual actors with relatively simple objectives; if these assumptions lead to grievously incorrect conclusions, we must construct better economic models. Perhaps economic conflict among organizations leads to substantially different results than the same sort of conflict among individuals;

if so, we need an organizational model as an initial component for our theory.

In any case we cannot cope directly with the complexity of the actual phenomenon: There seem to be too many facts and relations for a brain, even a mechanical one, to treat in an orderly fashion. Abstraction and model building are necessary to reduce the problem to manageable proportions. The experimental method can contribute to the process of identifying critical variables and the nature of their roles in conflict situations. Thus, if the behavior of mature, experienced business executives in an economic conflict situation were significantly different from that of college students, we would have identified a new critical variable in the phenomenon. Such a variable could be incorporated in the appropriate economic model.

The experimental method has produced fairly consistent results within the context of our own study. Further, our results seem reasonably consistent with those obtained by independent investigators who have employed controlled experimentation in the study of similar situations. For examples, refer to the quantity adjuster oligopoly experiments conducted by Shubik (1962), Stern (1960, 1962), Hoggatt (1959), and Sauermann and Selten (1960); the prisoners' dilemma games at Ohio State [Loomis (1959), Lutzker (1959), Marlowe, Minas, Scodel, and Rawson (1960)]; the game-conflict experiments of Willis and Hale (1960) and Willis and Joseph (1959) at Carnegie Institute of Technology and Deutsch (1960) at Bell Telephone Laboratories; the learning experiments (using game situations) by Atkinson and Suppes (1958); the price bidding experiments of Chamberlin (1948), Smith (1962), and Feeney; the experiments by mathematicians relative to game-theory propositions [Flood (1954), Aumann and Maschler (1961), Kalisch, Milnor, Nash, and Nering (1954)]. Rapoport and Orwant (1962) provide a review of such research. Our work is not uniformly consistent with all these studies, but differences can be attributed to variations in the design of the experiments in most instances.

There has been a substantial increase recently in the use of controlled experimentation to study conflict situations.   This has occurred at a variety of universities and in several disciplines. The psychologists and sociologists, following Lewin, have made extensive use of experiments to study group behavior and group conflict.   Lewin said (1948, p. 71): "I am persuaded that it is possible to undertake experiments in sociology which have as much right to be called scientific experiments as those in physics and chemistry." Economists have less of an experimental tradition, but they have a wider variety of intricate and related hypotheses about human behavior than the other social scientists have.   Some distinguished investigators are optimistic about the use of experimentation in discriminating among such propositions.*   Mathematicians have turned to the laboratory to test conjectures about game theory.

This juncture of interest among several disciplines is encouraging; further, game theory has provided a common structure for many of the experiments, so the results are comparable, and the investigators can communicate across disciplines.   Hopefully our understanding of human conflict and its resolution will experience the same pattern of growth that characterized other experimental sciences.

FUTURE WORK

The following five propositions might be regarded as a summary of the experimental results reported in this book.   Alternatively, they may be considered as general hypotheses about human conflict.   It would be instructive to see whether they are applicable in noneconomic situations.   In considering the propositions, one

---

* For example, from O. Morgenstern (1954, p. 486): "On the contrary, I do believe that there exist great opportunities for direct experiments now and in the future.   I am thinking of the actual, *physical* experiment, i.e., one in which physical reality is being subjected to desired conditions, as distinguished from the so-called 'thought-experiment.'"

From the same source (p. 512): "The frequently encountered opinion that direct experiments (apart from the experimental character of the measure-

might think of Pareto optimal solutions as appropriate resolutions of conflict; they maximize the mutual benefit of the disputing parties; but they may not always be desirable from the viewpoint of the larger community.

H_1: Pareto optimal conflict resolutions are most likely where (1) there is a prominent Pareto optimal solution, (2) there is complete information so the prominent solution is recognizable by the contesting parties, (3) each party has veto power; that is, the final solution must be mutually acceptable, and (4) there are only two parties involved.

H_2: Lack of information favors an equilibrium solution, where each participant seeks the best individual strategy, given the behavior of the other participants. This condition tends to dampen communication, although there is a tendency toward rivalistic behavior as the number of participants increases. Even if appropriate Pareto optimal goals exist in such a situation, there is no efficient way of reaching them because they cannot be mutually recognized.

H_3: An increase in information does not necessarily improve relations among the participants; it may cause them to identify contradictory goals and establish incompatible levels of aspiration. This may cause intense rivalistic behavior before the dispute can be resolved. This can be avoided if (1) the present adjustment of the participants is not Pareto optimal, and (2) it is possible to communicate in such a way that the position of each participant is improved in the movement toward the Pareto optima.

H_4: Cooperative nonequilibrium solutions are much more likely with two antagonists than with three or more. Increases

---

ments involved in passive observations) for all practical purposes are impossible, cannot be maintained. On the contrary, the possibilities are numerous and depend to a large extent merely on the (monetary) means to be utilized."

Or again (p. 518): "Experiments of this kind may advance economics more surely as a theoretical discipline than those dealing with aggregates."

in the number of participants lead to more rivalry, especially if the penalty for following a nondominant strategy is increased.

H_5: The level-of-aspiration concept may have some explanatory and predictive value for group decisions and N person games.   If so, it may be useful in constructing an organizational model for the study of conflict within and among organizations.

Bibliography

Atkinson, R. C., and P. Suppes. 1958. An analysis of two-person game situations in terms of statistical learning theory. *Journal of Experimental Psychology*, 55, 369–378.

Aumann, R. J., and M. Maschler. 1961. The bargaining set for cooperative games. Princeton: Econometric research program. *Research Memorandum* 34.

Bertrand, J. 1883. Review of Cournot, "Recherches." *Journal des Savants*, 503.

Bishop, R. L. 1960. Duopoly: Collusion or warfare? *American Economic Review*, 50, 933–961.

Bowley, A. L. 1928. On bilateral monopoly. *The Economic Journal*, 38, 651–659.

Chamberlin, E. H. 1933. *The theory of monopolistic competition: A reorientation of the theory of value.* Cambridge: Harvard University Press.

Chamberlin, E. H. 1948. An experimental imperfect market. *Journal of Political Economy*, 56, 95–108.

Cournot, A. 1897. *Recherches sur les principes mathématiques de la théorie des richesses.* Paris. English translation: *Researches into the mathematical principles of the theory of wealth.* New York: Macmillan.

Deutsch, M. 1949. An experimental study of the effects of cooperation and competition upon group process. *Human Relations*, 2, 199–232.

Deutsch, M. 1960. The effect of motivational orientation upon trust and suspicion. *Human Relations*, 13, 123–140.

Fellner, W. 1947. Price and wages under bilateral monopoly. *The Quarterly Journal of Economics*, 61, 503–532.

Fellner, W. 1949. *Competition among the few.* New York: Knopf.

Fisher, F. M. 1961. The stability of the Cournot oligopoly solution: The effects of speeds of adjustment and increased marginal costs. *Review of Economic Studies*, 28, 125–135.

211

212   Bibliography

Fisher, I. 1898. Cournot and mathematical economics. *Quarterly Journal of Economics*, 12, 119–138.

Flood, M. M. 1954. Game-learning theory and some decision-making experiments. In R. M. Thrall, C. H. Coombs, and R. L. Davis (eds.), *Decision processes*. New York: Wiley, 139–158.

Flood, M. M. 1958. Some experimental games. *Management Science*, 5, 5–26.

Fouraker, L. E. 1957. Professor Fellner's bilateral monopoly theory. *The Southern Economic Journal*, 24, 182–189.

Fouraker, L. E., M. Shubik, and S. Siegel. 1961. Oligopoly bargaining: The quantity adjuster models. *Research Bulletin* 20, The Pennsylvania State University, Department of Psychology.

Hoggatt, A. C. 1959. An experimental game. *Behavioral Science*, 4, 192–203.

Jews liturgy and ritual sabbath prayers. 1960. *Sabbath and festival prayer book*. New York: Behrman.

Jonckheere, A. R. 1954. A test of significance for the relation between m rankings and k ranked categories. *British Journal of Statistical Psychology*, 7 (2), 93–100.

Kalisch, G., J. W. Milnor, J. F. Nash, and E. D. Nering. 1954. Some experimental n-person games. In R. M. Thrall, C. H. Coombs, and R. L. Davis (eds.), *Decision processes*. New York: Wiley, 301–328.

Lewin, K. 1948. *Resolving social conflict*. New York: Harper.

Loomis, J. L. 1959. Communication, the development of trust, and cooperative behavior. *Human Relations*, 12, 305–315.

Luce, R. D., and H. Raiffa. 1957. *Games and decisions*. New York: Wiley.

Lutzker, D. R. 1959. Internationalism, sex role, and amount of information as variables in a two-person, non-zero-sum game. Dissertation. Ohio State University.

McManus, M., and R. Quant. 1961. Comments on the stability of the Cournot oligopoly model. *Review of Economic Studies*, 28, 136–139.

Minas, J. S., A. Scodel, D. Marlowe, and H. Rawson. 1960. Some descriptive aspects of two-person non-zero-sum games. *Journal of Conflict Resolution*, 4, 193–197.

Moore, H. L. 1906. Paradoxes of competition. *Quarterly Journal of Economics*, 20, 211–230.

Morgenstern, O. 1954. *Economic activity analysis*. New York: Wiley.

Murdoch, D. C. 1957. *Linear algebra for undergraduates*. New York: Wiley.

Pareto, V. 1909. *Manuel d'économie politique*. Paris: M. Giard.

Pigou, A. 1932. *The economics of welfare*. London: Macmillan.

Rapoport, A., and C. Orwant. 1962. Experimental games: A review. *Behavioral Science*, 7, 1–37.

Sauermann, H., and R. Selten. 1960. An experiment in oligopoly. *General Systems*, Vol. V. Ann Arbor: Society for General Systems Research.

Schelling, T. C. 1957. Bargaining, communication and limited war. *Journal of Conflict Resolution*, 1, 19–36.

Schneider, E. 1952. *Pricing and equilibrium*. New York: Macmillan.

Schumpeter, J. 1928. The instability of capitalism. *Economic Journal*, 38, 361–386.

Shubik, M. 1959. *Strategy and market structure: Competition, oligopoly, and the theory of games*. New York: Wiley.

Shubik, M. 1961. Some experimental non-zero-sum games with lack of information about the rules. Cowles Foundation Discussion Paper No. 105.

Siegel, S. 1956. *Nonparametric statistics for the behavioral sciences*. New York: McGraw-Hill.

Siegel, S. 1957. Level of aspiration and decision making. *Psychological Review*, 64, 253–262.

Siegel, S., and L. E. Fouraker. 1960. *Bargaining and group decision making: Experiments in bilateral monopoly*. New York: McGraw-Hill.

Siegel, S., and D. L. Harnett. 1961. Bargaining, information, and the use of threat. *Research Bulletin* 21, The Pennsylvania State University, Department of Psychology.

Siegel, S. and J. W. Tukey. 1960. A nonparametric sum of ranks procedure for relative spread in unpaired samples. *Journal of the American Statistical Association*, 55, 429–455.

214   Bibliography

Simon, H. 1957. *Models of man.* New York: Wiley.
Smith, V. L. 1962. An experimental study of competitive market behavior. *Journal of Political Economy,* 70, 111–137.
Stern, D. H. 1960. Bargaining experiments: An exploratory study. Dissertation. Princeton University.
Suppes, P., and R. C. Atkinson. 1960. *Markov learning models for multiperson interactions.* Stanford: Stanford University Press.
Theocharis, R. D. 1960. On the stability of the Cournot solution on the oligopoly problem. *Review of Economic Studies,* 27, 133–134.
von Neumann, J., and O. Morgenstern. 1947. *Theory of games and economic behavior* (2d ed.). Princeton: Princeton University Press.
von Stackleberg, H. 1934. *Markform und Gleichgewicht.* Berlin: J. Springer.
Wicksell, K. 1934. *Lectures on political economy.* Vol. I. London: Routledge.
Willis, R. H., and J. F. Hale. 1960. Dyadic interaction as a function of amount of feedback and instructional orientation. Carnegie Institute of Technology (mimeograph).
Willis, R. H., and M. L. Joseph. 1959. Bargaining behavior I: "Prominence" as a predictor of the outcome of games of agreement. *Conflict Resolution,* 3, 102–113.
Young, A. A. 1925. Review of Bowley's "Mathematical groundwork of economics." *Journal of the American Statistical Association,* 20, 133–135.
Zeuthen, F. 1930. *Problems of monopoly and economic warfare.* London: Routledge.

Appendix I

EXPERIMENT 1

BILATERAL MONOPOLY

CSE_b Condition (Complete Information, Single Bid, Equal-split Payoff at Bowley Point):

Complete Results for Subjects
Profit Table
(Instructions Reproduced in Chapter 4)

EXPERIMENT 1   Results of CSE_b Experiment

Pair	Seller's price bid	Buyer's quantity bid	Seller's profit	Buyer's profit
1	11	7	\$3.62	\$3.70
2	9	10	4.44	4.44
3	9	10	4.44	4.44
4	9	10	4.44	4.44
5	9	10	4.44	4.44
6	9	10	4.44	4.44
7	9	10	4.44	4.44
8	9	11	4.82	4.42
9	9	11	4.82	4.42
10	7	12	4.20	5.32

Profit Table, CSE_b

Price		0	1	2	3	4	5	6	7	8	9	10	11	12	13	14	15	16	17	18
1	B	0	3.14	3.80	4.42	5.00	5.54	6.04	6.50	6.92	7.30	7.64	7.94	8.20	8.42	8.60	8.74	8.84	8.90	8.92
	S	0	-1.10	-.68	-.30	.04	.34	.60	.82	1.00	1.14	1.24	1.30	1.32	1.30	1.24	1.14	1.00	.82	.60
2	B	0	3.10	3.72	4.30	4.84	5.34	5.80	6.22	6.60	6.94	7.24	7.50	7.72	7.90	8.04	8.14	8.20	8.22	8.20
	S	0	-1.06	-.60	-.18	.20	.54	.84	1.10	1.32	1.50	1.64	1.74	1.80	1.82	1.80	1.74	1.64	1.50	1.32
3	B	0	3.06	3.64	4.18	4.68	5.14	5.56	5.94	6.28	6.58	6.84	7.06	7.24	7.38	7.48	7.54	7.56	7.54	7.48
	S	0	-1.02	-.52	-.06	.36	.74	1.08	1.38	1.64	1.86	2.04	2.18	2.28	2.34	2.36	2.34	2.28	2.18	2.04
4	B	0	3.02	3.56	4.06	4.52	4.94	5.32	5.66	5.96	6.22	6.44	6.62	6.76	6.86	6.92	6.94	6.92	6.86	6.76
	S	0	-.98	-.44	.06	.52	.94	1.32	1.66	1.96	2.22	2.44	2.62	2.76	2.86	2.92	2.94	2.92	2.86	2.76
5	B	0	2.98	3.48	3.94	4.36	4.74	5.08	5.38	5.64	5.86	6.04	6.18	6.28	6.34	6.36	6.34	6.28	6.18	6.04
	S	0	-.94	-.36	.18	.68	1.14	1.56	1.94	2.28	2.58	2.84	3.06	3.24	3.38	3.48	3.54	3.56	3.54	3.48
6	B	0	2.94	3.40	3.82	4.20	4.54	4.84	5.10	5.32	5.50	5.64	5.74	5.80	5.82	5.80	5.74	5.64	5.50	5.32
	S	0	-.90	-.28	.30	.84	1.34	1.80	2.22	2.60	2.94	3.24	3.50	3.72	3.90	4.04	4.14	4.20	4.22	4.20
7	B	0	2.90	3.32	3.70	4.04	4.34	4.60	4.82	5.00	5.14	5.24	5.30	5.32	5.30	5.24	5.14	5.00	4.82	4.60
	S	0	-.86	-.20	.42	1.00	1.54	2.04	2.50	2.92	3.30	3.64	3.94	4.20	4.42	4.60	4.74	4.84	4.90	4.92
8	B	0	2.86	3.24	3.58	3.88	4.14	4.36	4.54	4.68	4.78	4.84	4.86	4.84	4.78	4.68	4.54	4.36	4.14	3.88
	S	0	-.82	-.12	.54	1.16	1.74	2.28	2.78	3.24	3.66	4.04	4.38	4.68	4.94	5.16	5.34	5.48	5.58	5.64
9	B	0	2.82	3.16	3.46	3.72	3.94	4.12	4.26	4.36	4.42	4.44	4.42	4.36	4.26	4.12	3.94	3.72	3.46	3.16
	S	0	-.78	-.04	.66	1.32	1.94	2.52	3.06	3.56	4.02	4.44	4.82	5.16	5.46	5.72	5.94	6.12	6.26	6.36
10	B	0	2.78	3.08	3.34	3.56	3.74	3.88	3.98	4.04	4.06	4.04	3.98	3.88	3.74	3.56	3.34	3.08	2.78	2.44
	S	0	-.74	.04	.78	1.48	2.14	2.76	3.34	3.88	4.38	4.84	5.26	5.64	5.98	6.28	6.54	6.76	6.94	7.08

Quantity

Profit Table, CSE_b (Continued)

Quantity

Price		0	1	2	3	4	5	6	7	8	9	10	11	12	13	14	15	16	17	18
11	B	0	2.74	3.00	3.22	3.40	3.54	3.64	3.70	3.72	3.70	3.64	3.54	3.40	3.22	3.00	2.74	2.44	2.10	1.72
	S	0	-.70	.12	.90	1.64	2.34	3.00	3.62	4.20	4.74	5.24	5.70	6.12	6.50	6.84	7.14	7.40	7.62	7.80
12	B	0	2.70	2.92	3.10	3.24	3.34	3.40	3.42	3.40	3.34	3.24	3.10	2.92	2.70	2.44	2.14	1.80	1.42	1.00
	S	0	-.66	.20	1.02	1.80	2.54	3.24	3.90	4.52	5.10	5.64	6.14	6.60	7.02	7.40	7.74	8.04	8.30	8.52
13	B	0	2.66	2.84	2.98	3.08	3.14	3.16	3.14	3.08	2.98	2.84	2.66	2.44	2.18	1.88	1.54	1.16	.74	.28
	S	0	-.62	.28	1.14	1.96	2.74	3.48	4.18	4.84	5.46	6.04	6.58	7.08	7.54	7.96	8.34	8.68	8.98	9.24
14	B	0	2.62	2.76	2.86	2.92	2.94	2.92	2.86	2.76	2.62	2.44	2.22	1.96	1.66	1.32	.94	.52	.06	-.44
	S	0	-.58	.36	1.26	2.12	2.94	3.72	4.46	5.16	5.82	6.44	7.02	7.56	8.06	8.52	8.94	9.32	9.68	9.96
15	B	0	2.58	2.68	2.74	2.76	2.74	2.68	2.58	2.44	2.26	2.04	1.78	1.48	1.14	.76	.34	-.12	-.62	-1.16
	S	0	-.54	.44	1.38	2.28	3.14	3.96	4.74	5.48	6.18	6.84	7.46	8.04	8.58	9.08	9.54	9.96	10.34	10.68
16	B	0	2.54	2.60	2.62	2.60	2.54	2.44	2.30	2.12	1.90	1.64	1.34	1.00	.62	.20	-.26	-.76	-1.30	-1.88
	S	0	-.50	.52	1.50	2.44	3.34	4.20	5.02	5.80	6.54	7.24	7.90	8.52	9.10	9.64	10.14	10.60	11.02	11.40

Key: B = Profit to buyer
S = Profit to seller

Appendix II

EXPERIMENT 2

BILATERAL MONOPOLY

CSE_p Condition (Complete Information, Single Bid, Equal-split Payoff on Paretian Optima):

> Instructions
> Complete Results for Subjects
> Profit Table

Instructions

The National Science Foundation and the Ford Foundation have provided funds for the conduct of research regarding economic decisions. If you follow instructions carefully and make an appropriate decision, you will earn an appreciable amount of money. *You may keep all the money you earn.* You cannot lose your own money, but a poor choice can result in small or no profit to you.

You will be paired, at random, with another person. You will not see this person or speak with him at any time. You will never know the identity of your opponent, nor will he be aware of yours.

You and your anonymous partner will engage in a single transaction by means of a written bid. Imagine that you and he are exchanging some commodity. One of you will be selected (at random) to act as the seller of this commodity, the other will act as the buyer. You must deal only with your unknown counterpart and he must deal only with you.

You will be furnished with a table showing the various levels of profit you can attain. Prices are listed on the left-hand side of the table, quantities across the top. The upper figure in each box of the body of the table represents the profit the *buyer* will receive, depending upon the price and quantity selected. The lower figure in each box represents the profit the *seller* receives for the associated price and quantity choices. For example, at a price of

218

7 and a quantity of 2, the buyer's profit is $1.32 and the seller's profit is $1.80.   All figures in the body of the table are in dollars.

The *seller* will start the transaction by quoting a price.   He may select any one of the prices on the left-hand side of the table.   The price he has selected will be recorded by an experimental assistant on a yellow sheet provided for that purpose.

The yellow sheet then is taken by the assistant to the *buyer*.   He sees the price which has been established for the transaction.   In the light of this information he selects the quantity to be exchanged at this price.   He may choose any of the quantities across the top of the table.   In other words, the seller chooses the price line, the buyer chooses the quantity column. The box where these choices intersect indicates the amount of profit you receive for the transaction, the upper figure being the buyer's profit, the lower figure being the seller's profit.

After the buyer has made his quantity choice the seller will be informed of the decision and both buyer and seller will be paid the amount of money (profit) indicated in the table.   This will be done in separate counting rooms so you will not see the person with whom you have been bidding.

Are there any questions?

EXPERIMENT 2   Results of CSE_p Experiment

Pair	Seller's price bid	Buyer's quantity bid	Seller's profit	Buyer's profit
11	9	7	$5.06	$2.26
12	9	8	5.56	2.36
13	11	8	6.20	1.72
14	10	9	6.38	2.06
15	9	10	6.44	2.44
16	9	10	6.44	2.44
17	9	10	6.44	2.44
18	9	10	6.44	2.44
19	9	10	6.44	2.44
20	10	10	6.84	2.04

Profit Table, CSE_p

Quantity

Price		0	1	2	3	4	5	6	7	8	9	10	11	12	13	14	15	16	17	18
1	B	0	1.14	1.80	2.42	3.00	3.54	4.04	4.50	4.92	5.30	5.64	5.94	6.20	6.42	6.60	6.74	6.84	6.90	6.92
	S	0	.90	1.32	1.70	2.04	2.34	2.60	2.82	3.00	3.14	3.24	3.30	3.32	3.30	3.24	3.14	3.00	2.82	2.60
2	B	0	1.10	1.72	2.30	2.84	3.34	3.80	4.22	4.60	4.94	5.24	5.50	5.72	5.90	6.04	6.14	6.20	6.22	6.20
	S	0	.94	1.40	1.82	2.20	2.54	2.84	3.10	3.32	3.50	3.64	3.74	3.80	3.82	3.80	3.74	3.64	3.50	3.32
3	B	0	1.06	1.64	2.18	2.68	3.14	3.56	3.94	4.28	4.58	4.84	5.06	5.24	5.38	5.48	5.54	5.56	5.54	5.48
	S	0	.98	1.48	1.94	2.36	2.74	3.08	3.38	3.64	3.86	4.04	4.18	4.28	4.34	4.36	4.34	4.28	4.18	4.04
4	B	0	1.02	1.56	2.06	2.52	2.94	3.32	3.66	3.96	4.22	4.44	4.62	4.76	4.86	4.92	4.94	4.92	4.86	4.76
	S	0	1.02	1.56	2.06	2.52	2.94	3.32	3.66	3.96	4.22	4.44	4.62	4.76	4.86	4.92	4.94	4.92	4.86	4.76
5	B	0	.98	1.48	1.94	2.36	2.74	3.08	3.38	3.64	3.86	4.04	4.18	4.28	4.34	4.36	4.34	4.28	4.18	4.04
	S	0	1.06	1.64	2.18	2.68	3.14	3.56	3.94	4.28	4.58	4.84	5.06	5.24	5.38	5.48	5.54	5.56	5.54	5.48
6	B	0	.94	1.40	1.82	2.20	2.54	2.84	3.10	3.32	3.50	3.64	3.74	3.80	3.82	3.80	3.74	3.64	3.50	3.32
	S	0	1.10	1.72	2.30	2.84	3.34	3.80	4.22	4.60	4.94	5.24	5.50	5.72	5.90	6.04	6.14	6.20	6.22	6.20
7	B	0	.90	1.32	1.70	2.04	2.34	2.60	2.82	3.00	3.14	3.24	3.30	3.32	3.30	3.24	3.14	3.00	2.82	2.60
	S	0	1.14	1.80	2.42	3.00	3.54	4.04	4.50	4.92	5.30	5.64	5.94	6.20	6.42	6.60	6.74	6.84	6.90	6.92
8	B	0	.86	1.24	1.58	1.88	2.14	2.36	2.54	2.68	2.78	2.84	2.86	2.84	2.78	2.68	2.54	2.36	2.14	1.88
	S	0	1.18	1.88	2.54	3.16	3.74	4.28	4.78	5.24	5.66	6.04	6.38	6.68	6.94	7.16	7.34	7.48	7.58	7.64
9	B	0	.82	1.16	1.46	1.72	1.94	2.12	2.26	2.36	2.42	2.44	2.42	2.36	2.26	2.12	1.94	1.72	1.46	1.16
	S	0	1.12	1.96	2.66	3.32	3.94	4.52	5.06	5.56	6.02	6.44	6.82	7.16	7.46	7.72	7.94	8.12	8.26	8.36
10	B	0	.78	1.08	1.34	1.56	1.74	1.88	1.98	2.04	2.06	2.04	1.98	1.88	1.74	1.56	1.34	1.08	.78	.44
	S	0	1.26	2.04	2.78	3.48	4.14	4.76	5.34	5.88	6.38	6.84	7.26	7.64	7.98	8.28	8.54	8.76	8.94	9.08

Profit Table, CSE_p (Continued)

Quantity

Price		0	1	2	3	4	5	6	7	8	9	10	11	12	13	14	15	16	17	18
11	B	0	.74	1.00	1.22	1.40	1.54	1.64	1.70	1.72	1.70	1.64	1.54	1.40	1.22	1.00	.74	.44	.10	−.28
	S	0	1.30	2.12	2.40	3.64	4.34	5.00	5.62	6.20	6.74	7.24	7.70	8.12	8.50	8.84	9.14	9.40	9.62	9.80
12	B	0	.70	.92	1.10	1.24	1.34	1.40	1.42	1.40	1.34	1.24	1.10	.92	.70	.44	.14	−.20	−.58	−1.00
	S	0	1.34	2.20	3.02	3.80	4.54	5.24	5.90	6.52	7.10	7.64	8.14	8.60	9.02	9.40	9.74	10.04	10.30	10.52
13	B	0	.66	.84	.98	1.08	1.14	1.16	1.14	1.08	.98	.84	.66	.44	.18	−.12	−.46	−.84	−1.26	−1.72
	S	0	1.38	2.28	3.14	3.96	4.74	5.48	6.18	6.84	7.46	8.04	8.58	9.08	9.54	9.96	10.34	10.68	10.98	11.24
14	B	0	.62	.76	.86	.92	.94	.92	.86	.76	.62	.44	.22	−.04	−.34	−.68	−1.06	−1.48	−1.94	−2.44
	S	0	1.42	2.36	3.26	4.12	4.94	5.72	6.46	7.16	7.82	8.44	9.02	9.56	10.06	10.52	10.94	11.32	11.66	11.96
15	B	0	.58	.68	.74	.76	.74	.68	.58	.44	.26	.04	−.22	−.52	−.86	−1.24	−1.66	−2.12	−2.62	−3.16
	S	0	1.46	2.44	3.38	4.28	5.14	5.96	6.74	7.48	8.18	8.84	9.46	10.04	10.58	11.08	11.54	11.96	12.34	12.68
16	B	0	.54	.60	.62	.60	.54	.44	.30	.12	−.10	−.36	−.66	−1.00	−1.38	−1.80	−2.26	−2.76	−3.30	−3.88
	S	0	1.50	2.52	3.50	4.44	5.34	6.20	7.02	7.80	8.54	9.24	9.90	10.52	11.10	11.64	12.14	12.60	13.02	13.40

Key: B = Profit to buyer
     S = Profit to seller

Appendix III

EXPERIMENT 3

BILATERAL MONOPOLY

IRE_p Condition (Incomplete Information, Repeated Bids, Equal-split Payoff on Paretian Optima):

>Instructions for Seller
>Profit Table for Seller
>Instructions for Buyer
>Profit Table for Buyer
>Complete Results for Subjects

Instructions to Seller, IRE_p

The National Science Foundation and the Ford Foundation have provided funds for the conduct of research regarding economic decisions. If you follow instructions carefully and make appropriate decisions, you will earn an appreciable amount of money during the session. *You may keep all the money you earn.* You cannot lose your own money, but poor choices will result in small or no profit to you.

You will be paired, at random, with another person. You will not see this person or speak with him at any time. You will never know the identity of your opponent, nor will he be aware of yours.

You and your anonymous partner will engage in a series of transactions by means of written bids. Imagine that you and he are exchanging some commodity. You have been selected (at random) to act as the *seller* of this commodity; your opponent will act as the buyer. You must deal only with your unknown counterpart and he must deal only with you.

You will be furnished with a table showing the various levels of profit you can attain. Prices are listed on the left-hand side of the table, quantities across the top. The figures in the body of the table represent the profit

222

you will receive, depending on the price and quantity selected. For example, at a price of 10 and a quantity of 2, your profit is 1020, or 10.20 cents. Decimal points have been omitted for simplicity, but may always be considered to be located two places in from the right.

You, as seller, will start the process by quoting a price. You may select any one of the prices on the left-hand side of your table. The price you have selected will be recorded by an experimental assistant on a yellow record sheet provided for that purpose.

The yellow sheet then is taken by the assistant to the buyer. He sees the price that has been established for the first transaction. In the light of this information he selects the quantity to be exchanged, and this choice is recorded on the yellow sheet. He may choose any of the quantities across the top of the table. In other words, you choose the price line, the buyer chooses the quantity column, and the box where these choices intersect indicates the amount of profit you receive for that transaction. You know how much you made from the transaction, but you do not know how much your opponent made. He knows his profit, but not yours.

The process is repeated over and over. You may select the same price each time, and the buyer may select the same quantity each time. You do not have to do so, however. You will be given about one minute for each decision. You will have three practice trials so you may become accustomed to using the profit table.

A white *profit sheet* will be provided so that you can keep a record of the transactions. For each transaction you will record the price and quantity selected and profit you made. At the end we will add up your profit column and give you that amount of money. This will be done in separate counting rooms, so you will not see the person with whom you have been bidding.

Are there any questions?

Profit Table for Seller, IRE_p

Quantity

Price	0	1	2	3	4	5	6	7	8	9	10	11	12	13	14	15	16	17	18
1	0	450	660	850	1020	1170	1300	1410	1500	1570	1620	1650	1660	1650	1620	1570	1500	1410	1300
2	0	470	700	910	1100	1270	1420	1550	1660	1750	1820	1870	1900	1910	1900	1870	1820	1750	1660
3	0	490	740	970	1180	1370	1540	1690	1820	1930	2020	2090	2140	2170	2180	2170	2140	2090	2020
4	0	510	780	1030	1260	1470	1660	1830	1980	2110	2220	2310	2380	2430	2460	2470	2460	2430	2380
5	0	530	820	1090	1340	1570	1780	1970	2140	2290	2420	2530	2620	2690	2740	2770	2780	2770	2740
6	0	550	860	1150	1420	1670	1900	2110	2300	2470	2620	2750	2860	2950	3020	3070	3100	3110	3100
7	0	570	900	1210	1500	1770	2020	2250	2460	2650	2820	2970	3100	3210	3300	3370	3420	3450	3460
8	0	590	940	1270	1580	1870	2140	2390	2620	2830	3020	3190	3340	3470	3580	3670	3740	3790	3820
9	0	610	980	1330	1660	1970	2260	2530	2780	3010	3220	3410	3580	3730	3860	3970	4060	4130	4180
10	0	630	1020	1390	1740	2070	2380	2670	2940	3190	3420	3630	3820	3990	4140	4270	4380	4470	4540
11	0	650	1060	1450	1820	2170	2500	2810	3100	3370	3620	3850	4060	4250	4420	4570	4700	4810	4900
12	0	670	1100	1510	1900	2270	2620	2950	3260	3550	3820	4070	4300	4510	4700	4870	5020	5150	5260
13	0	690	1140	1570	1980	2370	2740	3090	3420	3730	4020	4290	4540	4770	4980	5170	5340	5490	5620
14	0	710	1180	1630	2060	2470	2860	3230	3580	3910	4220	4510	4780	5030	5260	5470	5660	5830	5980
15	0	730	1220	1690	2140	2570	2980	3370	3740	4090	4420	4730	5020	5290	5540	5770	5980	6170	6340
16	0	750	1260	1750	2220	2670	3100	3510	3900	4270	4620	4950	5260	5550	5820	6070	6300	6510	6700

Instructions to Buyer, IRE_p

The National Science Foundation and the Ford Foundation have provided funds for the conduct of research regarding economic decisions. If you follow instructions carefully and make appropriate decisions, you will earn an appreciable amount of money during the session. *You may keep all the money you earn.* You cannot lose your own money, but poor choices will result in small or no profit to you.

You will be paired, at random, with another person. You will not see this person or speak with him at any time. You will never know the identity of your opponent, nor will he be aware of yours.

You and your anonymous partner will engage in a series of transactions by means of written bids. Imagine that you and he are exchanging some commodity. You have been selected (at random) to act as the *buyer* of this commodity; your opponent will act as the seller. You must deal only with your unknown counterpart and he must deal only with you.

You will be furnished with a table showing the various levels of profit you can attain. Prices are listed on the left-hand side of the table, quantities across the top. The figures in the body of the table represent the profit you will receive, depending on the price and quantity selected. For example, at a price of 7 and a quantity of 4, your profit is 1020, or 10.20 cents. Decimal points have been omitted for simplicity but may always be considered to be located two places in from the right.

The seller will start the process by quoting a price. He may select any one of the prices on the left-hand side of his table. The price he has selected will be recorded by an experimental assistant on a yellow record sheet provided for that purpose.

The yellow sheet then is taken by the assistant to you, the buyer. You see the price that has been established for the first transaction. In the light of this information you select the quantity to be exchanged, and this choice is recorded on the yellow sheet. You may choose any one of the quantities across the top of the table. In other words, the seller chooses the price line, you the quantity column, and the box where these choices intersect indicates the amount of profit you receive for that transaction. You know how much you made from the transaction, but you do not know how much your opponent made. He knows his profit, but not yours.

The process is repeated over and over. The seller may select the same price each time, and you may select the same quantity each time. You do not have to do so, however. You will be given about one minute for each decision. You will have three practice trials so you may become accustomed to using the profit table.

A white *profit sheet* will be provided so that you can keep a record of the transactions. For each transaction you will record the price and quantity selected and the profit you made. At the end we will add up your profit column and give you that amount of money. This will be done in separate counting rooms, so you will not see the person with whom you have been bidding.

Are there any questions?

Profit Table for Buyer, IRE_p

Quantity

Price	0	1	2	3	4	5	6	7	8	9	10	11	12	13	14	15	16	17	18
1	0	570	900	1210	1500	1770	2020	2250	2460	2650	2820	2970	3100	3210	3300	3370	3420	3450	3460
2	0	550	860	1150	1420	1670	1900	2110	2300	2470	2620	2750	2860	2950	3020	3070	3100	3110	3100
3	0	530	820	1090	1340	1570	1780	1970	2140	2290	2420	2530	2620	2690	2740	2770	2780	2770	2740
4	0	510	780	1030	1260	1470	1660	1830	1980	2110	2220	2310	2380	2430	2460	2470	2460	2430	2380
5	0	490	740	970	1180	1370	1540	1690	1820	1930	2020	2090	2140	2170	2180	2170	2140	2090	2020
6	0	470	700	910	1100	1270	1420	1550	1660	1750	1820	1870	1900	1910	1900	1870	1820	1750	1660
7	0	450	660	850	1020	1170	1300	1410	1500	1570	1620	1650	1660	1650	1620	1570	1500	1410	1300
8	0	430	620	790	940	1070	1180	1270	1340	1390	1420	1430	1420	1390	1340	1270	1180	1070	940
9	0	410	580	730	860	970	1060	1130	1180	1210	1220	1210	1180	1130	1060	970	860	730	580
10	0	390	540	670	780	870	940	990	1020	1030	1020	990	940	870	780	670	540	390	220
11	0	370	500	610	700	770	820	850	860	850	820	770	700	610	500	370	220	50	−140
12	0	350	460	550	620	670	700	710	700	670	620	550	460	350	220	70	−100	−290	−500
13	0	330	420	490	540	570	580	570	540	490	420	330	220	90	−60	−230	−420	−630	−860
14	0	310	380	430	460	470	460	430	380	310	220	110	−20	−170	−340	−530	−740	−970	−1220
15	0	290	340	370	380	370	340	290	220	130	20	−110	−260	−430	−620	−830	−1060	−1310	−1580
16	0	270	300	310	300	270	220	150	60	−50	−180	−330	−500	−690	−900	−1130	−1380	−1650	−1940

EXPERIMENT 3   Price and Quantity Bids and Total Profits

								Pair Number									
	21		22		23		24		25		26		27		28		29	
PB	P	Q	P	Q	P	Q	P	Q	P	Q	P	Q	P	Q	P	Q	P	Q
A	2	1	2	16	1	18	8	10	4	15	8	11	9	10	5	14	8	11
B	9	17	9	10	16	18	2	4	10	9	6	13	13	6	8	3	1	18
C	16	3	15	4	15	10	14	3	15	4	10	3	8	11	4	6	16	3
T																		
1	10	9	7	11	16	4	10	10	7	12	8	11	10	9	10	9	10	9
2	8	11	8	11	16	3	11	8	9	10	7	12	14	6	7	7	7	10
3	7	12	9	10	16	12	9	12	9	10	9	3	7	9	6	12	9	10
4	9	10	10	10	16	3	10	8	9	3	8	3	11	8	12	1	11	2
5	11	8	9	10	14	5	9	9	16	3	10	1	9	8	11	7	12	0
6	15	4	8	12	13	6	8	11	16	4	13	0	6	9	4	14	9	10
7	9	10	7	13	9	10	7	13	16	10	7	8	12	8	7	10	9	10
8	12	7	8	11	8	10	8	11	16	0	6	6	11	10	3	16	15	0
9	9	10	9	10	9	9	9	13	9	3	5	7	10	8	13	6	9	0
10	8	11	10	9	9	10	11	8	5	15	8	3	12	10	12	6	8	11
11	10	9	11	9	9	10	9	11	7	13	7	3	9	7	9	8	8	5
12	9	10	10	9	9	10	8	12	10	9	5	14	11	9	11	7	6	13
13	6	13	9	11	9	8	10	9	9	11	5	12	12	10	10	10	6	5
14	10	9	8	11	8	11	9	10	9	3	5	8	13	2	8	10	7	4
15	8	11	7	12	9	10	9	13	9	3	8	1	11	2	12	0	5	10
16	9	10	11	9	9	10	9	8	16	0	16	0	6	3	7	10	10	4
17	9	8	10	9	9	10	8	12	3	16	8	11	9	2	9	6	14	0
18	11	8	9	10	9	1	8	8	8	11	7	12	11	2	10	9	5	15
19	8	11	8	12	8	11	10	10	8	11	8	11	7	12	14	5	5	14
20	16	3	11	8	9	10	8	11	8	11	8	11	8	11	6	13	5	14
21	9	10	9	10	9	10	9	10	8	11	8	11	9	10	10	9	5	14
SP	$7.00		$7.43		$6.74		$7.44		$5.73		$4.87		$6.18		$5.99		$4.85	
BP	2.64		2.85		2.18		2.78		2.49		2.81		2.23		2.73		2.94	

Key: PB = Practice bids
  P = Price bid
  Q = Quantity bid
  T = Transactions
  SP = Seller's profit
  BP = Buyer's profit

Appendix IV

EXPERIMENT 4

BILATERAL MONOPOLY

CRE$_b$ Condition (Complete Information, Repeated Bids, Equal-split Payoff at Bowley Point):

    Instructions
    Profit Table
    Complete Results for Subjects

Instructions, CRE$_b$

    The National Science Foundation and the Ford Foundation have provided funds for the conduct of research regarding economic decisions. If you follow instructions carefully and make appropriate decisions, you will earn an appreciable amount of money during the session. *You may keep all the money you earn.* You cannot lose your own money, but poor choices will result in small or no profit to you.

    You will be paired, at random, with another person. You will not see this person or speak with him at any time. You will never know the identity of your opponent, nor will he be aware of yours.

    You and your anonymous partner will engage in a series of transactions by means of written bids. Imagine that you and he are exchanging some commodity. One of you will be selected (at random) to act as the seller of this commodity, the other will act as the buyer. You must deal only with your unknown counterpart and he must deal only with you.

    You will be furnished with a table showing the various levels of profit you can attain. Prices are listed on the left-hand side of the table, quantities across the top. The upper figure in each box of the body of the table represents the profit the *buyer* will receive, depending upon the price and quantity selected. The lower figure in each box represents the profit the *seller* receives for the associated price and quantity choices. For example,

228

at a price of 6 and a quantity of 3, the buyer's profit is 1910 (19.10 cents) and the seller's profit is 150 (1.50 cents). Decimal points have been omitted for simplicity, but may always be considered to be located two places in from the right.

The *seller* will start the process by quoting a price. He may select any one of the prices on the left-hand side of the table. The price he has selected will be recorded by an experimental assistant on a yellow sheet provided for that purpose.

The yellow sheet then is taken by the assistant to the *buyer*. He sees the price that has been established for the first transaction. In the light of this information he selects the quantity to be exchanged, and this choice is recorded on the yellow sheet. He may choose any of the quantities across the top of the table. In other words, the seller chooses the price line, the buyer chooses the quantity column. The box where these choices intersect indicates the amount of profit you receive for that transaction, the upper figure being the buyer's profit, the lower figure being the seller's profit.

The process is repeated over and over. The seller may select the same price each time, and the buyer may select the same quantity each time. They do not have to do so, however. You will be given about one minute for each decision. You will have 3 practice trials so you may become accustomed to using the profit table.

A white *profit sheet* will be provided so that you can keep a record of the transactions. For each transaction you will record the price and quantity selected and the profit you made. At the end we will add up your profit column and give you that amount of money. This will be done in separate counting rooms, so you will not see the person with whom you have been bidding.

Are there any questions?

Profit Table, CRE_b

Quantity

Price		0	1	2	3	4	5	6	7	8	9	10	11	12	13	14	15	16	17	18
1	B	0	1570	1900	2210	2500	2700	3020	3250	3460	3650	3820	3970	4100	4210	4310	4370	4420	4450	4460
	S	0	-550	-340	-150	20	170	300	410	500	570	620	650	660	650	620	570	500	410	300
2	B	0	1550	1860	2150	2420	2670	2900	3110	3300	3470	3620	3750	3860	3950	4020	4070	4100	4110	4100
	S	0	-530	-300	-90	100	270	420	550	660	750	820	870	900	910	900	870	820	750	660
3	B	0	1530	1820	2090	2340	2570	2780	2970	3140	3290	3420	3530	3620	3690	3740	3770	3780	3770	3740
	S	0	-510	-260	-30	180	370	540	690	820	930	1020	1090	1140	1170	1180	1170	1140	1090	1020
4	B	0	1510	1780	2030	2260	2470	2660	2830	2980	3110	3220	3310	3380	3430	3460	3470	3460	3430	3380
	S	0	-490	-220	30	260	470	660	830	980	1110	1220	1310	1380	1430	1460	1470	1460	1430	1380
5	B	0	1490	1740	1970	2180	2370	2540	2690	2820	2930	3020	3090	3140	3170	3180	3170	3140	3090	3020
	S	0	-470	-180	90	340	570	780	970	1140	1290	1420	1530	1620	1690	1740	1770	1780	1770	1740
6	B	0	1470	1700	1910	2100	2270	2420	2550	2660	2750	2820	2870	2900	2910	2900	2870	2820	2750	2660
	S	0	-450	-240	150	420	670	900	1110	1300	1470	1620	1750	1860	1950	2020	2070	2100	2110	2100
7	B	0	1450	1660	1850	2020	2170	2300	2410	2500	2570	2620	2650	2660	2650	2620	2570	2500	2410	2300
	S	0	-420	-100	210	500	770	1020	1250	1460	1650	1820	1970	2100	2210	2300	2370	2420	2450	2460
8	B	0	1430	1620	1790	1940	2070	2180	2270	2340	2390	2420	2430	2420	2390	2340	2270	2180	2070	1940
	S	0	-410	-60	270	580	870	1140	1390	1620	1830	2020	2190	2340	2470	2580	2670	2740	2790	2820
9	B	0	1410	1580	1730	1860	1970	2060	2130	2180	2210	2220	2210	2180	2130	2060	1970	1860	1730	1580
	S	0	-390	-20	330	660	970	1260	1530	1780	2010	2220	2410	2580	2730	2860	2970	3060	3130	3180
10	B	0	1390	1540	1670	1780	1870	1940	1990	2020	2030	2020	1990	1940	1870	1780	1670	1540	1390	1220
	S	0	-370	20	390	740	1070	1380	1670	1940	2190	2420	2630	2820	2990	3140	3270	3380	3470	3540

Profit Table, CRE_b (Continued)

Quantity

Price		0	1	2	3	4	5	6	7	8	9	10	11	12	13	14	15	16	17	18
11	B	0	1370	1500	1610	1700	1770	1820	1850	1860	1850	1820	1770	1700	1610	1500	1370	1220	1050	860
	S	0	-350	60	450	820	1170	1500	1810	2100	2370	2620	2850	3060	3250	3420	3570	3700	3810	3900
12	B	0	1350	1460	1550	1620	1670	1700	1710	1700	1670	1620	1550	1460	1350	1220	1070	900	710	500
	S	0	-330	100	510	900	1270	1620	1950	2260	2550	2820	3070	3300	3510	3700	3870	4020	4150	4260
13	B	0	1330	1420	1490	1540	1570	1580	1570	1540	1490	1420	1330	1220	1090	940	770	580	370	140
	S	0	-310	140	570	980	1370	1740	2090	2420	2730	3020	3290	3540	3770	3980	4170	4340	4490	4620
14	B	0	1310	1380	1430	1460	1470	1460	1430	1380	1310	1220	1110	980	830	660	470	260	30	-220
	S	0	-290	180	630	1060	1470	1860	2230	2580	2910	3220	3510	3780	4030	4260	4470	4660	4830	4980
15	B	0	1290	1340	1370	1380	1370	1340	1290	1220	1130	1020	890	740	570	380	170	-60	-310	-580
	S	0	-270	220	690	1140	1570	1980	2370	2740	3090	3420	3730	4020	4290	4540	4770	4980	5170	5340
16	B	0	1270	1300	1310	1300	1270	1220	1150	1060	950	820	670	500	310	100	-130	-380	-650	-940
	S	0	-250	260	750	1220	1670	2100	2510	2740	3270	3620	3950	4260	4550	4820	5070	5300	5510	5700

Key: B = Profit to buyer
S = Profit to seller

231

EXPERIMENT 4 Price and Quantity Bids and Total Profits

Pair number

	30 P	30 Q	31 P	31 Q	32 P	32 Q	33 P	33 Q	34 P	34 Q	35 P	35 Q	36 P	36 Q	37 P	37 Q	38 P	38 Q	39 P	39 Q
PB																				
A	9	6	5	2	7	12	14	17	14	5	8	11	9	12	9	10	7	16	9	10
B	9	4	1	12	8	11	7	12	10	9	12	14	1	14	11	7	8	12	16	3
C	16	2	16	5	6	13	2	13	12	7	12	7	16	11	7	16	6	15	4	15
T																				
1	10	2	1	12	9	10	11	17	10	9	8	14	9	13	7	16	7	16	10	9
2	6	13	16	4	7	12	13	6	10	6	8	12	16	12	9	10	8	12	11	8
3	7	3	9	8	8	11	8	9	11	7	1	14	16	4	7	16	9	10	9	10
4	6	3	12	8	9	10	14	18	10	2	16	8	9	13	7	16	10	16	6	10
5	9	9	8	13	10	9		1	10	2	3	14	11	4	7	16	7	10	6	13
6	7	12	8	13	9	11	11	1	10	11	13	11	5	16	7	16	9	10	10	9
7	9	9	7	13	8	11	12	4	8	12	8	12	9	17	7	16	8	12	8	11
8	7	11	7	11	9	10	9	10	8	17	8	14	9	6	7	16	6	15	9	10
9	9	2	8	12	9	9	10	9	8	11	8	12	10	3	7	16	7	16	10	9
10	8	8	8	8	10	9	16	14	8	11	8	14	11	2	7	16	8	12	9	10

EXPERIMENT 4 Price and Quantity Bids and Total Profits (Continued)

Pair number

T	30 P	30 Q	31 P	31 Q	32 P	32 Q	33 P	33 Q	34 P	34 Q	35 P	35 Q	36 P	36 Q	37 P	37 Q	38 P	38 Q	39 P	39 Q
11	7	6	10	7	9	10	8	11	8	1	8	12	3	14	7	16	7	16	11	8
12	16	1	8	11	10	9	12	1	8	11	8	14	9	17	7	16	9	10	12	1
13	9	7	7	11	9	10	9	10	8	11	8	13	8	15	7	16	8	12	9	10
14	12	2	9	7	9	10	15	1	8	8	8	12	10	10	7	16	7	16	10	9
15	9	3	16	4	9	10	7	17	8	11	8	13	9	4	7	16	9	10	11	8
16	13	2	8	8	9	10	11	1	8	11	8	12	16	1	7	16	10	10	9	10
17	7	11	3	18	10	9	9	10	8	11	8	13	11	9	7	16	6	15	1	18
18	7	2	14	4	10	8	7	17	8	18	8	12	9	9	7	16	7	16	14	5
19	9	9	7	11	9	9	16	1	8	11	8	13	13	3	7	16	8	12	9	10
20	9	6	9	7	9	10	9	10	8	11	8	12	7	14	7	16	7	16	1	18
21	6	12	9	7	8	12	9	10	9	8	8	13	9	12	7	16	7	16	9	10
SP	$2.56		$3.94		$5.08		$4.71		$4.23		$5.42		$4.32		$5.55		$5.38		$4.02	
BP	4.95		5.33		5.15		4.77		4.95		6.60		4.55		5.72		5.58		5.30	

Key: PB = Practice bids
  P = Price bid
  Q = Quantity bid
  T = Transactions
  SP = Seller's profit
  BP = Buyer's profit

233

Appendix V

EXPERIMENT 5

BILATERAL MONOPOLY

CRE_p Condition (Complete Information, Repeated Bids, Equal-split Payoff on Paretian Optima):

Instructions
Profit Table
Complete Results for Subjects

Instructions, CRE_p

The National Science Foundation and the Ford Foundation have provided funds for the conduct of research regarding economic decisions. If you follow instructions carefully and make appropriate decisions, you will earn an appreciable amount of money during the session. *You may keep all the money you earn.* You cannot lose your own money, but poor choices will result in small or no profit to you.

You will be paired, at random, with another person. You will not see this person or speak with him at any time. You will never know the identity of your opponent, nor will he be aware of yours.

You and your anonymous partner will engage in a series of transactions by means of written bids. Imagine that you and he are exchanging some commodity. One of you will be selected (at random) to act as the seller of this commodity, the other will act as the buyer. You must deal only with your unknown counterpart and he must deal only with you.

You will be furnished with a table showing the various levels of profit you can attain. Prices are listed on the left-hand side of the table, quantities across the top. The upper figure in each box of the body of the table represents the profit the *buyer* will receive, depending upon the price and quantity selected. The lower figure in each box represents the profit the *seller* receives for the associated price and quantity choices. For example, at a

234

price of 6 and a quantity of 3, the buyer's profit is 910 (9.10 cents) and the seller's profit is 1150 (11.50 cents). Decimal points have been omitted for simplicity, but may always be considered to be located two places in from the right.

The *seller* will start the process by quoting a price. He may select any one of the prices on the left-hand side of the table. The price he has selected will be recorded by an experimental assistant on a yellow sheet provided for that purpose.

The yellow sheet then is taken by the assistant to the *buyer*. He sees the price that has been established for the first transaction. In the light of this information he selects the quantity to be exchanged, and this choice is recorded on the yellow sheet. He may choose any of the quantities across the top of the table. In other words, the seller chooses the price line, the buyer chooses the quantity column. The box where these choices intersect indicates the amount of profit you receive for that transaction, the upper figure being the buyer's profit, the lower figure being the seller's profit.

The process is repeated over and over. The seller may select the same price each time, and the buyer may select the same quantity each time. They do not have to do so, however. You will be given about one minute for each decision. You will have 3 practice trials so you may become accustomed to using the profit table.

A white *profit sheet* will be provided so that you can keep a record of the transactions. For each transaction you will record the price and quantity selected and the profit you made. At the end we will add up your profit column and give you that amount of money. This will be done in separate counting rooms, so you will not see the person with whom you have been bidding.

Are there any questions?

Profit Table, CRE_p

Quantity

Price		0	1	2	3	4	5	6	7	8	9	10	11	12	13	14	15	16	17	18
1	B	0	570	900	1210	1500	1770	2020	2250	2460	2650	2820	2970	3100	3210	3300	3370	3420	3450	3460
	S	0	450	660	850	1020	1170	1300	1410	1500	1570	1620	1650	1660	1650	1620	1570	1500	1410	1300
2	B	0	550	860	1150	1420	1670	1900	2110	2300	2470	2620	2750	2860	2950	3020	3070	3100	3110	3100
	S	0	470	700	910	1100	1270	1420	1550	1660	1750	1820	1870	1900	1910	1900	1870	1820	1750	1660
3	B	0	530	820	1090	1340	1570	1780	1970	2140	2290	2420	2530	2620	2690	2740	2770	2780	2770	2740
	S	0	490	740	970	1180	1370	1540	1690	1820	1930	2020	2090	2140	2170	2180	2170	2140	2090	2020
4	B	0	510	780	1030	1260	1470	1660	1830	1980	2110	2220	2310	2380	2430	2460	2470	2460	2430	2380
	S	0	510	780	1030	1260	1470	1660	1830	1980	2110	2220	2310	2380	2430	2460	2470	2460	2430	2380
5	B	0	490	740	970	1180	1370	1540	1690	1820	1930	2020	2090	2140	2170	2180	2170	2140	2090	2020
	S	0	530	820	1090	1340	1570	1780	1970	2140	2290	2420	2530	2620	2690	2740	2770	2780	2770	2740
6	B	0	470	700	910	1100	1270	1420	1550	1660	1750	1820	1870	1900	1910	1900	1870	1820	1750	1660
	S	0	550	860	1150	1420	1670	1900	2110	2300	2470	2620	2750	2860	2950	3020	3070	3100	3110	3100
7	B	0	450	660	850	1020	1170	1300	1410	1500	1570	1620	1650	1660	1650	1620	1570	1500	1410	1300
	S	0	570	900	1210	1500	1770	2020	2250	2460	2650	2820	2970	3100	3210	3300	3370	3420	3450	3460
8	B	0	430	620	790	940	1070	1180	1270	1340	1390	1420	1430	1420	1390	1340	1270	1180	1070	940
	S	0	590	940	1270	1580	1870	2140	2390	2620	2830	3020	3190	3340	3470	3580	3670	3740	3790	3820
9	B	0	410	580	730	860	970	1060	1130	1180	1210	1220	1210	1180	1130	1060	970	860	730	580
	S	0	610	980	1330	1660	1970	2260	2530	2780	3010	3220	3410	3580	3730	3860	3970	4060	4130	4180
10	B	0	390	540	670	780	870	940	990	1020	1030	1020	990	940	870	780	670	540	390	220
	S	0	630	1020	1390	1740	2070	2380	2670	2940	3190	3420	3630	3820	3990	4140	4270	4380	4470	4540

Profit Table, CRE_p (Continued)

Quantity

Price		0	1	2	3	4	5	6	7	8	9	10	11	12	13	14	15	16	17	18
11	B	0	370	500	610	700	770	820	850	860	850	820	770	700	610	500	370	220	50	−140
	S	0	650	1060	1450	1820	2170	2500	2810	3100	3370	3620	3850	4060	4250	4420	4570	4700	4810	4900
12	B	0	350	460	550	620	670	700	710	700	670	620	550	460	350	220	70	−100	−290	−500
	S	0	670	1100	1510	1900	2270	2620	2950	3260	3550	3820	4070	4300	4510	4700	4870	5020	5150	5260
13	B	0	330	420	490	540	570	580	570	540	490	420	330	220	90	−60	−230	−420	−630	−860
	S	0	690	1140	1570	1980	2370	2740	3090	3420	3730	4020	4290	4540	4770	4980	5170	5340	5490	5620
14	B	0	310	380	430	460	470	460	430	380	310	220	110	−20	−170	−340	−530	−740	−970	−1220
	S	0	710	1180	1630	2060	2470	2860	3230	3580	3910	4220	4510	4780	5030	5260	5470	5660	5830	5980
15	B	0	290	340	370	380	370	340	290	220	130	20	−110	−260	−430	−620	−830	−1060	−1310	−1580
	S	0	730	1220	1690	2140	2570	2980	3370	3740	4090	4420	4730	5020	5290	5540	5770	5980	6170	6340
16	B	0	270	300	310	300	270	220	150	60	−50	−180	−330	−500	−690	−900	−1130	−1380	−1650	−1940
	S	0	750	1260	1750	2220	2670	3100	3510	3900	4270	4620	4950	5260	5550	5820	6070	6300	6510	6700

Key: B = Profit to buyer
    S = Profit to seller

237

EXPERIMENT 5   Price and Quantity Bids and Total Profits

Pair number

	40 P	40 Q	41 P	41 Q	42 P	42 Q	43 P	43 Q	44 P	44 Q	45 P	45 Q	46 P	46 Q	47 P	47 Q	48 P	48 Q	49 P	49 Q	50 P	50 Q	51 P	51 Q
PB																								
A	9	10	3	16	2	18	4	15	9	1	12	0	14	3	4	15	11	8	5	14	10	1	4	18
B	10	9	2	17	4	18	4	15	6	13	6	0	15	1	13	6	4	15	4	15	8	5	9	10
C	8	11	5	14	12	7	4	15	5	14	3	17	16	0	15	0	15	0	9	10	4	15	4	18
T																								
1	9	10	9	10	6	14	4	15	15	1	4	15	6	15	4	15	9	1	9	10	12	3	9	10
2	9	10	9	1	11	8	4	15	7	10	3	14	8	8	4	15	4	15	9	10	11	3	11	8
3	9	10	9	10	7	11	4	15	13	1	5	0	7	10	4	15	6	7	9	10	10	4	9	10
4	9	10	9	10	10	9	4	15	6	12	5	0	5	9	4	15	4	15	9	10	8	5	9	10
5	9	10	9	10	8	9	4	15	1	15	5	0	7	7	4	15	5	9	9	1	6	7	9	10
6	9	10	9	10	9	7	4	15	2	12	4	15	8	5	4	15	4	15	16	1	4	15	9	10
7	9	10	9	0	8	8	4	15	6	10	4	15	6	7	4	15	4	15	5	14	4	15	9	6
8	9	10	8	11	10	6	4	15	7	8	5	0	5	8	4	15	4	15	4	15	4	15	10	0
9	10	9	8	0	6	12	4	15	8	5	5	0	7	1	4	15	4	15	4	1	4	0	1	18
10	11	1	7	12	7	11	4	15	10	1	4	1	8	0	4	15	4	15	16	1	16	0	1	18

238

EXPERIMENT 5 Price and Quantity Bids and Total Profits (Continued)

Pair number

T	40		41		42		43		44		45		46		47		48		49		50		51	
	P	Q	P	Q	P	Q	P	Q	P	Q	P	Q	P	Q	P	Q	P	Q	P	Q	P	Q	P	Q
11	10	9	9	0	11	5	4	15	16	1	4	15	6	6	4	15	4	15	16	0	4	9	9	10
12	10	7	9	10	9	7	4	15	6	12	4	1	5	7	4	15	4	15	3	9	4	8	1	18
13	8	11	7	12	8	9	4	15	6	10	4	15	6	1	4	15	4	15	4	9	6	5	9	14
14	9	10	1	18	7	11	4	15	6	9	5	0	5	1	4	15	4	15	4	6	5	5	1	18
15	9	10	9	10	10	5	4	15	14	1	5	0	6	0	4	15	4	15	7	1	4	9	9	14
16	9	10	9	10	8	6	4	15	7	9	5	0	4	15	4	15	4	15	4	15	4	9	1	18
17	9	10	7	12	9	6	4	15	7	8	5	0	5	0	4	15	4	15	3	16	4	9	9	14
18	9	10	1	18	5	14	4	15	5	14	5	0	4	15	4	15	4	15	4	15	4	9	1	18
19	9	10	9	10	11	4	4	15	5	14	5	0	5	0	4	15	4	15	4	15	4	8	9	14
20	9	10	9	10	6	12	6	13	5	14	4	15	4	15	4	15	4	15	4	15	4	15	1	18
21	9	10	9	10	6	13	4	15	5	14	4	15	5	0	4	15	4	15	4	15	4	9	4	15
SP	$7.09		$5.76		$6.14		$5.73		$4.91		$2.54		$3.21		$5.68		$5.44		$4.64		$4.26		$5.66	
BP	2.68		2.96		3.40		5.63		3.74		2.60		2.45		5.68		5.33		3.76		3.79		4.51	

Key: PB = Practice bids
 P = Price bid
 Q = Quantity bid
 T = Transactions
 SP = Seller's profit
 BP = Buyer's profit

239

Appendix VI

Instructions

Funds have been provided for the conduct of research regarding economic decisions. If you follow instructions carefully and make appropriate decisions, you will earn an appreciable amount of money during the session. *You may keep all the money you earn.* You cannot lose your own money, but poor choices will result in small or no profit to you.

You will be paired, at random, with another person. You will not see this person or speak with him at any time. You will never know the identity of your opponent, nor will he be aware of yours.

You and your anonymous partner will engage in a series of transactions by means of written bids. Imagine that you and he are exchanging some commodity. One of you will be selected (at random) to act as the seller of this commodity, the other will act as the buyer. You must deal only with your unknown counterpart and he must deal only with you.

You will be furnished with a table showing the various levels of profit you and the other person can attain on each transaction. Prices are listed on the left-hand side of the table, quantities across the top. The upper figure in each box of the body of the table represents the profit the *buyer* will receive, depending upon the price and quantity selected. The lower figure

240

in each box represents the profit the *seller* receives for the associated price and quantity choices.   For example, at a price of 6 and a quantity of 3, the buyer's profit is 0.46 (46 cents) and the seller's profit is 0.58 (58 cents).

The *seller* will start the process by quoting a price.   He may select any one of the prices on the left-hand side of the table.   The price he has selected will be recorded on a yellow sheet provided for that purpose.

The yellow sheet then is taken to the *buyer*.   He sees the price that has been established for the first transaction.   In the light of this information he selects the quantity to be exchanged, and this choice is recorded on the yellow sheet.   He may choose any of the quantities across the top of the table.   In other words, the seller chooses the price line, the buyer chooses the quantity column.   The box where these choices intersect indicates the amount of profit you receive for that transaction, the upper figure being the buyer's profit, the lower figure being the seller's profit.

The process is repeated over and over.   The seller may select the same price each time, and the buyer may select the same quantity each time.   They do not have to do so, however.   You will be given about one minute for each decision.   You will have 3 practice trials so that you may become accustomed to using the profit table.

A white *profit sheet* will be provided so that you can keep a record of the transactions.   For each transaction you will record the price and quantity selected and the profit you made.   At the end we will add up your profit column and give you that amount of money.   This will be done in separate rooms, so you will not see the person with whom you have been bidding.

Are there any questions?

Profit Table

Quantity

Price		0	1	2	3	4	5	6	7	8	9	10	11	12	13	14	15	16	17	18
1	B	0.00	0.28	0.45	0.60	0.75	0.88	1.01	1.12	1.23	1.32	1.41	1.48	1.55	1.60	1.65	1.68	1.71	1.72	1.73
	S	0.00	0.22	0.33	0.42	0.51	0.58	0.65	0.70	0.75	0.78	0.81	0.82	0.83	0.82	0.81	0.78	0.75	0.70	0.65
2	B	0.00	0.28	0.43	0.58	0.71	0.84	0.95	1.06	1.15	1.24	1.31	1.38	1.43	1.48	1.51	1.54	1.55	1.56	1.55
	S	0.00	0.24	0.35	0.46	0.55	0.64	0.71	0.78	0.83	0.88	0.91	0.94	0.95	0.96	0.95	0.94	0.91	0.88	0.83
3	B	0.00	0.26	0.41	0.54	0.67	0.78	0.89	0.98	1.07	1.14	1.21	1.26	1.31	1.34	1.37	1.38	1.39	1.38	1.37
	S	0.00	0.24	0.37	0.48	0.59	0.68	0.77	0.84	0.91	0.96	1.01	1.04	1.07	1.08	1.09	1.08	1.07	1.04	1.01
4	B	0.00	0.26	0.39	0.52	0.63	0.74	0.83	0.92	0.99	1.06	1.11	1.16	1.19	1.22	1.23	1.24	1.23	1.22	1.19
	S	0.00	0.26	0.39	0.52	0.63	0.74	0.83	0.92	0.99	1.06	1.11	1.16	1.19	1.22	1.23	1.24	1.23	1.22	1.19
5	B	0.00	0.24	0.37	0.48	0.59	0.68	0.77	0.84	0.91	0.96	1.01	1.04	1.07	1.08	1.09	1.08	1.07	1.04	1.01
	S	0.00	0.26	0.41	0.54	0.67	0.78	0.89	0.98	1.07	1.14	1.21	1.26	1.31	1.34	1.37	1.38	1.39	1.38	1.37
6	B	0.00	0.24	0.35	0.46	0.55	0.64	0.71	0.78	0.83	0.88	0.91	0.94	0.95	0.96	0.95	0.94	0.91	0.88	0.83
	S	0.00	0.28	0.43	0.58	0.71	0.84	0.95	1.06	1.15	1.24	1.31	1.38	1.43	1.48	1.51	1.54	1.55	1.56	1.55
7	B	0.00	0.22	0.33	0.42	0.51	0.58	0.65	0.70	0.75	0.78	0.81	0.82	0.83	0.82	0.81	0.78	0.75	0.70	0.65
	S	0.00	0.28	0.45	0.60	0.75	0.88	1.01	1.12	1.23	1.32	1.41	1.48	1.55	1.60	1.65	1.68	1.71	1.72	1.73
8	B	0.00	0.22	0.31	0.40	0.47	0.54	0.59	0.64	0.67	0.70	0.71	0.72	0.71	0.70	0.67	0.64	0.59	0.54	0.47
	S	0.00	0.28	0.47	0.64	0.79	0.94	1.07	1.20	1.31	1.42	1.51	1.60	1.67	1.74	1.79	1.84	1.87	1.90	1.91
9	B	0.00	0.20	0.29	0.36	0.43	0.48	0.53	0.56	0.59	0.60	0.61	0.60	0.59	0.56	0.53	0.48	0.43	0.36	0.29
	S	0.00	0.30	0.49	0.66	0.83	0.98	1.13	1.26	1.39	1.50	1.61	1.70	1.79	1.86	1.93	1.98	2.03	2.06	2.09
10	B	0.00	0.20	0.27	0.34	0.39	0.44	0.47	0.50	0.51	0.52	0.51	0.50	0.47	0.44	0.39	0.34	0.27	0.20	0.11
	S	0.00	0.32	0.51	0.70	0.87	1.04	1.19	1.34	1.47	1.60	1.71	1.82	1.91	2.00	2.07	2.14	2.19	2.24	2.27

Profit Table (Continued)

Quantity

Price		0	1	2	3	4	5	6	7	8	9	10	11	12	13	14	15	16	17	18
11	B	0.00	0.18	0.25	0.30	0.35	0.38	0.41	0.42	0.43	0.42	0.41	0.38	0.35	0.30	0.25	0.18	0.11	0.02	−0.07
	S	0.00	0.32	0.53	0.72	0.91	1.08	1.25	1.40	1.55	1.68	1.81	1.92	2.03	2.12	2.21	2.28	2.35	2.40	2.45
12	B	0.00	0.18	0.23	0.28	0.31	0.34	0.35	0.36	0.35	0.34	0.31	0.28	0.23	0.18	0.11	0.04	−0.05	−0.14	−0.25
	S	0.00	0.34	0.55	0.76	0.95	1.14	1.31	1.48	1.63	1.78	1.91	2.04	2.15	2.26	2.35	2.44	2.51	2.58	2.63
13	B	0.00	0.16	0.21	0.24	0.27	0.28	0.29	0.28	0.27	0.24	0.21	0.16	0.11	0.04	−0.03	−0.12	−0.21	−0.32	−0.43
	S	0.00	0.34	0.57	0.78	0.99	1.18	1.37	1.54	1.71	1.86	2.01	2.14	2.27	2.38	2.49	2.58	2.67	2.74	2.81
14	B	0.00	0.16	0.19	0.22	0.23	0.24	0.23	0.22	0.19	0.16	0.11	0.06	−0.01	−0.08	−0.17	−0.26	−0.37	−0.48	−0.61
	S	0.00	0.36	0.59	0.82	1.03	1.24	1.43	1.62	1.79	1.96	2.11	2.26	2.39	2.52	2.63	2.74	2.83	2.92	2.99
15	B	0.00	0.14	0.17	0.18	0.19	0.18	0.17	0.14	0.11	0.06	0.01	−0.06	−0.13	−0.22	−0.31	−0.42	−0.53	−0.66	−0.79
	S	0.00	0.36	0.61	0.84	1.07	1.28	1.49	1.68	1.87	2.04	2.21	2.36	2.51	2.64	2.77	2.88	2.99	3.08	3.17
16	B	0.00	0.14	0.15	0.16	0.15	0.14	0.11	0.08	0.03	−0.02	−0.09	−0.16	−0.25	−0.34	−0.45	−0.56	−0.69	−0.82	−0.97
	S	0.00	0.38	0.63	0.88	1.11	1.34	1.55	1.76	1.95	2.14	2.31	2.48	2.63	2.78	2.91	3.04	3.15	3.26	3.35

Key: B = Profit to buyer
S = Profit to seller

Instructions and Profit Table for Incomplete Information (Buyer), Replication of Experiment 3

Instructions to Buyer

Funds have been provided for the conduct of research regarding economic decisions. If you follow instructions carefully and make appropriate decisions, you will earn an appreciable amount of money during the session. *You may keep all the money you earn.* You cannot lose your own money, but poor choices will result in small or no profit to you.

You will be paired, at random, with another person. You will not see this person or speak with him at any time. You will never know the identity of your opponent, nor will he be aware of yours.

You and your anonymous partner will engage in a series of transactions by means of written bids. Imagine that you and he are exchanging some commodity. You have been selected (at random) to act as the *buyer* of this commodity; your opponent will act as the seller. You must deal only with your unknown counterpart and he must deal only with you.

You will be furnished with a table showing the various levels of profit you can attain. Prices are listed on the left-hand side of the table, quantities across the top. The figures in the body of the table represent the profit you will receive, depending on the price and quantity selected. For example, at a price of 7 and a quantity of 4, your profit is 0.51 or 51 cents.

The seller will start the process by quoting a price. He may select any one of the prices on the left-hand side of his table. The price he has selected will be recorded on a yellow record sheet provided for that purpose.

The yellow sheet then is taken to you, the buyer. You see the price that has been established for the first transaction. In the light of this information you select the quantity to be exchanged, and this choice is recorded on the yellow sheet. You may choose any one of the quantities across the top of the table. In other words, the seller chooses the price line, you the quantity column, and the box where these choices intersect indicates the amount of profit you receive for that transaction. You know how much you made from the transaction, but you do not know how much the seller made. He knows his profit, but not yours.

The process is repeated over and over. The seller may select the same price each time, and you may select the same quantity each time. You do not have to do so, however. You will be given several minutes for each decision. You will have three practice trials so you may become accustomed to using the profit table.

A white *profit sheet* will be provided so that you can keep a record of the transactions. For each transaction you will record the price and quantity selected and the profit you made. At the end we will add up your profit column and give you that amount of money. This will be done in separate rooms, so you will not see the person with whom you have been bidding.

Are there any questions?

244

Profit Table for Buyer

Quantity

Price	0	1	2	3	4	5	6	7	8	9	10	11	12	13	14	15	16	17	18
1	0.00	0.28	0.45	0.60	0.75	0.88	1.01	1.12	1.23	1.32	1.41	1.48	1.55	1.60	1.65	1.68	1.71	1.72	1.73
2	0.00	0.28	0.43	0.58	0.71	0.84	0.95	1.06	1.15	1.24	1.31	1.38	1.43	1.48	1.51	1.54	1.55	1.56	1.55
3	0.00	0.26	0.41	0.54	0.67	0.78	0.89	0.98	1.07	1.14	1.21	1.26	1.31	1.34	1.37	1.38	1.39	1.38	1.37
4	0.00	0.26	0.39	0.52	0.63	0.74	0.83	0.92	0.99	1.06	1.11	1.16	1.19	1.22	1.23	1.24	1.23	1.22	1.19
5	0.00	0.24	0.37	0.48	0.59	0.68	0.77	0.84	0.91	0.96	1.01	1.04	1.07	1.08	1.09	1.08	1.07	1.04	1.01
6	0.00	0.24	0.35	0.46	0.55	0.64	0.71	0.78	0.83	0.88	0.91	0.94	0.95	0.96	0.95	0.94	0.91	0.88	0.83
7	0.00	0.22	0.33	0.42	0.51	0.58	0.65	0.70	0.75	0.78	0.81	0.82	0.83	0.82	0.81	0.78	0.75	0.70	0.65
8	0.00	0.22	0.31	0.40	0.47	0.54	0.59	0.64	0.67	0.70	0.71	0.72	0.71	0.70	0.67	0.64	0.59	0.54	0.47
9	0.00	0.20	0.29	0.36	0.43	0.48	0.53	0.56	0.59	0.60	0.61	0.60	0.59	0.56	0.53	0.48	0.43	0.36	0.29
10	0.00	0.20	0.27	0.34	0.39	0.44	0.47	0.50	0.51	0.52	0.51	0.50	0.47	0.44	0.39	0.34	0.27	0.20	0.11
11	0.00	0.18	0.25	0.30	0.35	0.38	0.41	0.42	0.43	0.42	0.41	0.38	0.35	0.30	0.25	0.18	0.11	0.02	−0.07
12	0.00	0.18	0.23	0.28	0.31	0.34	0.35	0.36	0.35	0.34	0.31	0.28	0.23	0.18	0.11	0.04	−0.05	−0.14	−0.25
13	0.00	0.16	0.21	0.24	0.27	0.28	0.29	0.28	0.27	0.24	0.21	0.16	0.11	0.04	−0.03	−0.12	−0.21	−0.32	−0.43
14	0.00	0.16	0.19	0.22	0.23	0.24	0.23	0.22	0.19	0.16	0.11	0.06	−0.01	−0.08	−0.17	−0.26	−0.37	−0.48	−0.61
15	0.00	0.14	0.17	0.18	0.19	0.18	0.17	0.14	0.11	0.06	0.01	−0.06	−0.13	−0.22	−0.31	−0.42	−0.53	−0.66	−0.79
16	0.00	0.14	0.15	0.16	0.15	0.14	0.11	0.08	0.03	−0.02	−0.09	−0.16	−0.25	−0.34	−0.45	−0.56	−0.69	−0.82	−0.97

245

Instructions and Profit Table for Incomplete Information (Seller), Replication of Experiment 3

Instructions to Seller

Funds have been provided for the conduct of research regarding economic decisions. If you follow instructions carefully and make appropriate decisions, you will earn an appreciable amount of money during the session. *You may keep all the money you earn.* You cannot lose your own money, but poor choices will result in small or no profit to you.

You will be paired, at random, with another person. You will not see this person or speak with him at any time. You will never know the identity of your opponent, nor will he be aware of yours.

You and your anonymous partner will engage in a series of transactions by means of written bids. Imagine that you and he are exchanging some commodity. You have been selected (at random) to act as the *seller* of this commodity; your opponent will act as the buyer. You must deal only with your unknown counterpart and he must deal only with you.

You will be furnished with a table showing the various levels of profit you can attain. Prices are listed on the left-hand side of the table, quantities across the top. The figures in the body of the table represent the profit you will receive, depending on the price and quantity selected. For example, at a price of 10 and a quantity of 2, your profit is 0.51 or 51 cents.

You, as seller, will start the process by quoting a price. You may select any one of the prices on the left-hand side of your table. The price you have selected will be recorded on a yellow record sheet provided for that purpose.

The yellow sheet then is taken to the buyer. He sees the price that has been established for the first transaction. In the light of this information he selects the quantity to be exchanged, and this choice is recorded on the yellow sheet. He may choose any of the quantities across the top of the table. In other words, you choose the price line, the buyer chooses the quantity column, and the box where these choices intersect indicates the amount of profit you receive for that transaction. You know how much you made from the transaction, but you do not know how much the buyer made. He knows his profit, but not yours.

The process is repeated over and over. You may select the same price each time, and the buyer may select the same quantity each time. You do not have to do so, however. You will be given several minutes for each decision. You will have three practice trials so you may become accustomed to using the profit table.

A white *profit sheet* will be provided so that you can keep a record of the transactions. For each transaction you will record the price and quantity selected and the profit you made. At the end we will add up your profit column and give you that amount of money. This will be done in separate rooms, so you will not see the person with whom you have been bidding.

Are there any questions?

Profit Table for Seller

Price	Quantity																		
	0	1	2	3	4	5	6	7	8	9	10	11	12	13	14	15	16	17	18
1	0.00	0.22	0.33	0.42	0.51	0.58	0.65	0.70	0.75	0.78	0.81	0.82	0.83	0.82	0.81	0.78	0.75	0.70	0.65
2	0.00	0.24	0.35	0.46	0.55	0.64	0.71	0.78	0.83	0.88	0.91	0.94	0.95	0.96	0.95	0.94	0.91	0.88	0.83
3	0.00	0.24	0.37	0.48	0.59	0.68	0.77	0.84	0.91	0.96	1.01	1.04	1.07	1.08	1.09	1.08	1.07	1.04	1.01
4	0.00	0.26	0.39	0.52	0.63	0.74	0.83	0.92	0.99	1.06	1.11	1.16	1.19	1.22	1.23	1.24	1.23	1.22	1.19
5	0.00	0.26	0.41	0.54	0.67	0.78	0.89	0.98	1.07	1.14	1.21	1.26	1.31	1.34	1.37	1.38	1.39	1.38	1.37
6	0.00	0.28	0.43	0.58	0.71	0.84	0.95	1.06	1.15	1.24	1.31	1.38	1.43	1.48	1.51	1.54	1.55	1.56	1.55
7	0.00	0.28	0.45	0.60	0.75	0.88	1.01	1.12	1.23	1.32	1.41	1.48	1.55	1.60	1.65	1.68	1.71	1.72	1.73
8	0.00	0.30	0.47	0.64	0.79	0.94	1.07	1.20	1.31	1.42	1.51	1.60	1.67	1.74	1.79	1.84	1.87	1.90	1.91
9	0.00	0.30	0.49	0.66	0.83	0.98	1.13	1.26	1.39	1.50	1.61	1.70	1.79	1.86	1.93	1.98	2.03	2.06	2.09
10	0.00	0.32	0.51	0.70	0.87	1.04	1.19	1.34	1.47	1.60	1.71	1.82	1.91	2.00	2.07	2.14	2.19	2.24	2.27
11	0.00	0.32	0.53	0.72	0.91	1.08	1.25	1.40	1.55	1.68	1.81	1.92	2.03	2.12	2.21	2.28	2.35	2.40	2.45
12	0.00	0.34	0.55	0.76	0.95	1.14	1.31	1.48	1.63	1.78	1.91	2.04	2.15	2.26	2.35	2.44	2.51	2.58	2.63
13	0.00	0.34	0.57	0.78	0.99	1.18	1.37	1.54	1.71	1.86	2.01	2.14	2.27	2.38	2.49	2.58	2.67	2.74	2.81
14	0.00	0.36	0.59	0.82	1.03	1.24	1.43	1.62	1.79	1.96	2.11	2.26	2.39	2.52	2.63	2.74	2.83	2.92	2.99
15	0.00	0.36	0.61	0.84	1.07	1.28	1.49	1.68	1.87	2.04	2.21	2.36	2.51	2.64	2.77	2.88	2.99	3.08	3.17
16	0.00	0.38	0.63	0.88	1.11	1.34	1.55	1.76	1.95	2.14	2.31	2.48	2.63	2.78	2.91	3.04	3.15	3.26	3.35

247

248   Appendix VI

EXPERIMENT 6   Replication of Experiment 5 (Complete Information): Price and Quantity Bids and Total Profits

Pair Number

PB	1 P	1 Q	2 P	2 Q	3 P	3 Q	4 P	4 Q	5 P	5 Q	6 P	6 Q	7 P	7 Q	8 P	8 Q
A	4	15	12	2	8	7	8	11	4	15	1	18	16	3	4	14
B	4	15	11	2	10	5	7	12	1	18	5	14	13	6	7	12
C	1	18	16	2	13	3	9	10	11	0	4	15	15	4	10	12

T																
1	12	1	9	2	4	15	6	13	1	18	4	15	16	0	10	16
2	1	18	8	1	5	10	7	12	10	9	3	16	10	0	11	6
3	12	7	6	3	3	16	5	14	1	18	7	14	4	15	9	12
4	1	18	5	7	8	1	4	15	10	9	4	15	4	0	8	9
5	12	8	5	6	4	15	5	14	1	18	1	16	1	18	9	9
6	7	1	4	15	4	15	9	10	8	11	4	15	5	0	12	7
7	4	15	5	1	4	15	8	1	2	17	4	15	3	16	13	1
8	4	15	4	14	6	6	4	15	8	11	4	15	4	15	11	9
9	4	15	4	14	4	15	4	15	2	17	4	15	4	15	10	11
10	4	15	4	15	4	15	9	1	9	10	4	15	4	15	10	9
11	4	15	4	15	4	15	4	15	9	10	7	12	10	0	9	10
SP	\$11.21		\$ 9.68		\$12.21		\$12.94		\$12.01		\$13.70		\$ 7.10		\$16.68	
BP	10.77		9.00		12.01		9.96		13.33		13.42		8.08		5.14	

Key: PB = Practice bids
    P = Price bid
    Q = Quantity bid
    T = Transactions
    SP = Seller's profit
    BP = Buyer's profit

EXPERIMENT 6   Replication of Experiment 3 (Incomplete Information): Price and Quantity Bids and Total Profits

Pair Number

	9		10		11		12		13		14		15		16	
PB	*P*	*Q*	*P*	*Q*	*P*	*Q*	*P*	*Q*	*P*	*Q*	*P*	*Q*	*P*	*Q*	*P*	*Q*
A	10	9	9	10	8	11	5	14	10	9	12	7	15	8	7	6
B	3	16	16	3	6	13	5	14	11	8	5	14	9	3	12	10
C	16	3	3	16	10	9	6	14	8	11	15	4	2	3	3	3
T																
1	11	8	10	9	8	11	8	11	14	5	7	12	16	8	8	11
2	8	11	9	10	7	12	9	9	10	5	9	10	14	10	12	5
3	13	6	9	10	12	7	6	13	10	9	9	8	12	8	16	1
4	14	5	8	11	9	10	12	7	9	4	8	11	13	6	4	15
5	9	5	9	10	11	8	16	3	9	10	10	12	15	4	8	8
6	9	10	9	10	16	3	8	11	9	4	10	5	6	16	10	7
7	10	5	9	10	11	8	7	12	10	10	11	4	16	3	9	7
8	8	11	9	10	10	9	8	11	10	9	8	6	6	13	10	7
9	9	10	9	10	12	7	11	9	10	3	13	2	8	11	8	5
10	9	10	9	10	9	10	11	7	9	10	9	7	14	5	13	6
11	9	10	9	10	10	9	8	11	9	10	9	10	10	9	9	10
SP	$15.82		$17.69		$16.51		$16.37		$14.38		$14.52		$16.48		$13.63	
BP	5.76		6.73		5.55		6.63		5.26		5.98		4.48		6.11	

Key: *PB* = Practice bids
  P = Price bid
  Q = Quantity bid
  T = Transactions
  SP = Seller's profit
  BP = Buyer's profit

Appendix VII

Profit Sheet

Number_____   Name_____

Cubicle_____   Date_____   Phone_____

Transaction	My quantity bid	Seller B's quantity bid	My profit or loss
Practice A			
trials B			
C			

Table of Profit to Seller A

Quantity produced

	8	9	10	11	12	13	14	15	16	17	18	19
8	1400	1500	1650	1800	1900	2000	2100	2200	2300	2350	2400	2500
9	1350	1500	1600	1750	1850	1950	2050	2150	2220	2300	2350	2400
10	1300	1450	1600	1700	1800	1900	2000	2100	2150	2250	2300	2350
11	1300	1400	1550	1650	1750	1850	1950	2000	2100	2150	2200	2250
12	1250	1400	1500	1600	1700	1800	1900	1950	2000	2100	2150	2200
13	1200	1350	1450	1550	1650	1750	1850	1900	1950	2000	2050	2100
14	1200	1300	1400	1500	1600	1700	1750	1850	1900	1950	2000	2050
15	1150	1250	1400	1450	1550	1650	1700	1800	1850	1900	1900	1950
16	1150	1250	1350	1450	1500	1600	1650	1700	1750	1800	1850	1900
17	1100	1200	1300	1400	1450	1550	1600	1650	1700	1750	1800	1800
18	1050	1150	1250	1350	1400	1500	1550	1600	1650	1700	1700	1700
19	1050	1150	1200	1300	1350	1450	1500	1550	1600	1600	1650	1650
20	1000	1100	1200	1250	1300	1400	1450	1500	1500	1550	1550	1550
21	950	1050	1150	1200	1250	1350	1400	1400	1450	1450	1500	1500
22	950	1000	1100	1150	1200	1300	1300	1350	1400	1400	1400	1400
23	900	1000	1050	1100	1200	1200	1250	1300	1300	1350	1350	1350
24	850	950	1000	1100	1150	1150	1200	1250	1250	1250	1250	1250
25	850	900	1000	1050	1100	1100	1150	1200	1200	1200	1200	1200
26	800	900	950	1000	1050	1050	1100	1100	1150	1150	1150	1100
27	800	850	900	950	1000	1000	1050	1050	1050	1050	1050	1050
28	750	800	850	900	950	950	1000	1000	1050	1000	1000	950
29	700	750	800	850	900	900	950	1000	950	950	900	900
30	700	750	800	800	850	850	850	900	850	850	850	800
31	650	700	750	750	800	800	800	850	800	800	750	750
32	600	650	700	700	750	750	750	750	750	700	700	650
33	600	600	650	700	700	700	700	700	700	650	600	600
34	550	600	600	650	650	650	650	650	600	600	550	500
35	500	550	600	600	600	600	600	600	550	500	500	450
36	500	500	550	550	550	550	550	500	500	450	400	350

Quantity produced by seller A's competition

by seller A

20	21	22	23	24	25	26	27	28	29	30	31	32
2550	2600	2600	2650	2650	2700	2700	2700	2650	2650	2600	2600	2550
2450	2500	2550	2550	2550	2600	2600	2550	2550	2550	2500	2450	2400
2400	2400	2450	2450	2450	2500	2450	2450	2450	2400	2400	2350	2300
2300	2350	2350	2350	2400	2400	2350	2350	2350	2300	2250	2200	2150
2200	2250	2250	2300	2300	2300	2250	2250	2200	2200	2150	2100	2000
2150	2150	2200	2200	2200	2200	2150	2150	2100	2050	2000	1950	1900
2050	2100	2100	2100	2100	2100	2050	2050	2000	1950	1900	1850	1750
2000	2000	2000	2000	2000	2000	1950	1900	1900	1850	1800	1700	1650
1900	1900	1900	1900	1900	1900	1850	1800	1750	1700	1650	1600	1500
1800	1800	1800	1800	1800	1800	1750	1700	1650	1600	1550	1450	1400
1750	1750	1750	1700	1700	1700	1650	1600	1550	1500	1400	1350	1250
1700	1650	1650	1650	1600	1600	1550	1500	1450	1350	1300	1200	1150
1600	1550	1550	1550	1500	1500	1450	1400	1300	1250	1200	1100	1000
1550	1500	1450	1450	1400	1400	1350	1250	1200	1150	1050	950	850
1400	1400	1400	1350	1300	1300	1200	1150	1100	1000	950	850	750
1350	1300	1300	1250	1200	1200	1100	1050	1000	900	800	700	600
1250	1250	1200	1150	1150	1100	1000	950	850	800	700	600	500
1200	1150	1100	1100	1050	1000	900	850	750	650	600	450	350
1100	1050	1050	1000	950	900	800	750	650	550	450	350	250
1000	1000	950	900	850	800	700	600	550	450	350	250	100
950	900	850	800	750	700	600	500	400	300	200	100	000
850	800	750	700	650	600	500	400	300	200	100	000	−100
800	750	700	600	550	500	400	300	200	100	000	−100	−250
700	650	600	550	450	400	300	200	100	000	−100	−250	−350
600	550	500	450	350	300	200	100	000	−100	−200	−350	−500
550	500	400	350	250	200	100	000	−100	−200	−350	−450	−600
450	400	350	250	200	100	000	−100	−200	−300	−450	−600	−750
400	300	250	150	50	000	−100	−200	−300	−450	−600	−700	−850
300	250	150	50	00	−100	−200	−300	−400	−550	−700	−850	−1000

Table of Profit to Seller A (Continued)

Quantity produced

		8	9	10	11	12	13	14	15	16	17	18	19
	37	450	500	500	500	500	500	500	450	400	400	350	300
	38	400	450	450	450	450	450	400	400	350	300	250	200
	39	400	400	400	400	400	400	350	350	300	250	200	150
	40	350	350	400	350	350	350	300	300	250	200	100	50
	41	350	350	350	350	300	300	250	200	150	100	50	00
	42	300	300	300	300	250	250	200	150	100	50	00	−50
	43	250	250	250	250	200	200	150	100	50	00	−50	−150
Quantity produced by seller A's competition	44	250	250	200	200	150	150	100	50	00	−50	−100	−200
	45	200	200	200	150	100	100	50	00	−50	−100	−200	−300
	46	150	150	150	100	50	50	00	−50	−100	−200	−250	−350
	47	150	100	100	50	00	00	−50	−100	−150	−250	−350	−450
	48	100	100	50	00	00	00	−100	−150	−250	−300	−400	−500
	49	50	50	00	00	000	−50	−150	−200	−300	−400	−500	−600
	50	50	00	00	00	−50	−100	−200	−300	−350	−450	−550	−650
	51	00	00	00	−50	−100	−150	−250	−350	−400	−500	−600	−750
	52	00	00	−50	−100	−150	−200	−300	−400	−500	−600	−700	−800
	53	0	−50	−100	−150	−200	−250	−350	−450	−550	−650	−750	−900
	54	−50	−100	−150	−200	−250	−300	−400	−500	−600	−700	−850	−950
	55	−50	−100	−200	−250	−300	−350	−500	−600	−700	−800	−900	−1050
	56	−100	−150	−200	−300	−350	−400	−550	−650	−750	−850	−1000	−1100
	57	−150	−200	−250	−350	−400	−450	−600	−700	−800	−950	−1050	−1200
	58	−150	−250	−300	−350	−450	−500	−650	−750	−850	−1000	−1150	−1250
	59	−200	−250	−350	−400	−500	−550	−700	−850	−950	−1050	−1200	−1350
	60	−250	−300	−400	−450	−550	−600	−750	−900	−1050	−1150	−1250	−1400
	61	−250	−350	−400	−500	−600	−650	−800	−1000	−1050	−1200	−1350	−1500
	62	−300	−350	−450	−550	−650	−700	−850	−1000	−1150	−1250	−1400	−1550
	63	−350	−400	−500	−600	−700	−750	−950	−1050	−1200	−1350	−1500	−1650
	64	−350	−450	−550	−650	−750	−800	−1000	−1100	−1250	−1400	−1550	−1700

by seller A

20	21	22	23	24	25	26	27	28	29	30	31	32
200	150	50	00	−50	−200	−300	−400	−550	−650	−800	−950	−1150
150	50	00	−50	−200	−300	−400	−500	−650	−800	−950	−1100	−1250
50	00	−50	−150	−250	−400	−500	−600	−750	−900	−1050	−1200	−1400
00	−50	−150	−250	−350	−500	−600	−750	−850	−1000	−1200	−1350	−1500
−50	−150	−250	−350	−450	−600	−700	−850	−1000	−1150	−1300	−1450	−1650
−150	−250	−350	−450	−550	−700	−800	−950	−1100	−1250	−1400	−1600	−1750
−200	−300	−400	−550	−650	−800	−900	−1050	−1200	−1350	−1550	−1700	−1900
−300	−400	−500	−600	−750	−900	−1000	−1150	−1300	−1500	−1650	−1850	−2000
−400	−500	−600	−700	−850	−1000	−1100	−1250	−1450	−1600	−1800	−1950	−2150
−450	−550	−700	−800	−950	−1100	−1200	−1400	−1550	−1700	−1900	−2100	−2300
−550	−650	−750	−900	−1050	−1200	−1350	−1500	−1650	−1850	−2000	−2200	−2400
−600	−750	−850	−1000	−1150	−1300	−1450	−1600	−1750	−1950	−2150	−2350	−2550
−700	−800	−950	−1100	−1200	−1400	−1550	−1700	−1900	−2050	−2250	−2450	−2650
−800	−900	−1050	−1150	−1300	−1500	−1650	−1800	−2000	−2200	−2400	−2600	−2800
−850	−1000	−1100	−1250	−1400	−1600	−1750	−1900	−2100	−2300	−2500	−2700	−2900
−950	−1050	−1200	−1350	−1500	−1700	−1850	−2050	−2200	−2400	−2600	−2850	−3050
−1000	−1150	−1300	−1450	−1600	−1800	−1950	−2150	−2350	−2550	−2750	−2950	−3150
−1100	−1250	−1400	−1550	−1700	−1900	−2050	−2250	−2450	−2650	−2850	−3100	−3300
−1200	−1300	−1450	−1650	−1800	−2000	−2150	−2350	−2550	−2750	−3000	−3200	−3450
−1250	−1400	−1550	−1700	−1900	−2100	−2250	−2450	−2650	−2900	−3100	−3350	−3550
−1350	−1500	−1650	−1800	−2000	−2200	−2350	−2550	−2800	−3000	−3200	−3450	−3700
−1400	−1550	−1750	−1900	−2100	−2300	−2450	−2700	−2900	−3100	−3350	−3600	−3800
−1550	−1650	−1800	−2000	−2200	−2400	−2600	−2800	−3000	−3250	−3450	−3700	−3950
−1650	−1750	−1900	−2100	−2300	−2500	−2700	−2900	−3100	−3350	−3600	−3850	−4050
−1700	−1800	−2000	−2200	−2400	−2600	−2800	−3000	−3250	−3450	−3700	−3950	−4200
−1750	−1900	−2100	−2300	−2450	−2700	−2900	−3100	−3350	−3600	−3800	−4100	−4300
−1800	−2000	−2200	−2350	−2550	−2800	−3000	−3200	−3450	−3700	−3950	−4200	−4450
−1900	−2100	−2250	−2450	−2650	−2900	−3100	−3350	−3550	−3800	−4050	−4350	−4600

EXPERIMENT 7 Quantity Bids and Total Profits

	Group number																																
	1		**2**		**3**		**4**		**5**		**6**		**7**		**8**		**9**		**10**		**11**		**12**		**13**		**14**		**15**		**16**	
PB	Qa	Qb	Qa	Qb	Qa	Qb	Qa	Qb	Qa	Qb	Qa	Qb	Qa	Qb	Qa	Qb	Qa	Qb	Qa	Qb	Qa	Qb	Qa	Qb	Qa	Qb	Qa	Qb	Qa	Qb	Qa	Qb
A	15	20	17	19	25	27	21	21	15	18	20	25	20	10	17	8	8	8	20	21	22	10	8	30	20	20	25	8	15	21	14	20
B	8	30	17	29	15	28	28	16	17	21	16	20	20	15	13	32	32	10	23	19	28	10	16	20	24	32	25	8	15	21	18	17
C	25	10	17	9	32	20	25	25	22	20	28	15	20	20	26	9	9	9	18	22	14	10	8	21	16	8	25	8	15	21	30	24
T																																
1	18	15	17	19	32	19	20	20	25	20	32	20	20	20	20	16	15	8	20	21	23	15	22	24	16	18	25	20	20	21	16	21
2	19	20	17	19	20	16	10	24	25	20	20	15	20	20	24	18	20	9	22	21	27	25	25	18	20	20	25	15	20	20	17	21
3	24	17	17	19	21	22	21	28	19	20	21	20	22	20	19	30	14	10	25	19	18	18	16	30	21	16	28	16	20	23	18	22
4	20	10	17	19	25	20	16	16	19	20	20	18	20	14	8	20	17	11	26	19	21	20	23	27	21	22	26	15	20	23	19	20
5	17	22	20	19	20	19	17	24	20	20	20	20	21	20	26	25	25	12	22	15	20	17	15	8	16	16	27	15	19	12	21	19
6	26	22	20	8	30	20	19	26	20	20	20	20	21	20	20	20	21	13	25	21	23	15	32	29	25	19	27	14	21	25	23	24
7	22	13	20	20	20	20	26	20	20	20	20	25	25	20	22	20	21	14	24	20	25	25	23	27	18	18	28	14	19	25	23	23
8	15	20	20	20	20	20	27	25	20	20	20	25	25	20	20	20	20	15	25	19	23	27	18	14	24	20	28	16	32	25	22	22
9	21	20	20	20	22	20	18	16	17	17	16	25	25	20	30	16	20	16	25	18	19	20	15	20	18	25	19	16	32	20	20	21
10	11	19	19	20	20	20	15	18	23	16	16	26	25	20	8	16	18	17	25	22	20	19	15	20	21	27	25	15	20	20	20	20
11	25	25	15	20	21	20	15	22	17	18	18	26	22	19	11	25	21	18	16	22	23	23	20	20	16	20	15	15	20	20	20	20
12	22	22	20	32	22	22	20	20	18	18	18	23	20	20	9	25	20	19	22	22	23	27	17	17	21	30	24	15	20	20	20	20
13	18	22	25	32	20	20	16	23	25	19	20	22	21	20	26	25	20	20	26	21	17	20	16	21	21	30	25	16	20	20	23	23
14	27	19	25	20	19	20	23	18	18	20	21	21	21	20	18	25	20	21	27	22	20	20	21	21	15	20	25	16	30	20	23	20
15	19	12	25	19	21	20	23	27	22	21	23	20	20	20	20	25	16	22	25	18	27	19	19	23	20	24	25	15	20	20	25	20
16	23	18	25	19	20	20	23	25	20	20	25	20	20	20	10	23	17	23	22	18	20	25	25	11	20	20	25	16	21	19	18	18
17	20	20	20	20	20	20	23	20	20	20	20	16	20	20	20	24	20	24	22	20	20	25	25	22	20	23	26	16	22	20	20	20
18	24	25	20	20	32	20	23	22	17	20	25	20	20	20	20	25	20	25	25	19	24	24	25	21	20	23	19	16	22	20	20	23
19	25	17	20	20	8	17	23	24	17	20	16	16	20	20	20	25	18	24	25	18	25	25	14	20	18	23	19	16	20	20	15	20
20	21	14	18	20	32	20	18	18	20	20	25	25	20	20	24	32	18	23	27	19	10	21	20	23	18	25	25	18	20	20	25	20
21	16	20	18	20	19	19	20	20	20	20	20	20	20	20	15	25	18	22	22	19	19	22	23	20	18	25	25	20	31	15	27	20
22	25	25	18	20	19	20	20	20	24	20	20	20	20	20	18	25	18	22	22	19	19	20	22	22	15	25	25	20	20	20	20	20
πa	$3.68		$3.37		$3.27		$2.92		$3.52		$3.26		$3.46		$2.68		$3.81		$3.39		$3.15		$3.09		$3.07		$4.10		$3.14		$3.22	
πb	$3.14		$3.43		$3.13		$3.49		$3.39		$3.27		$3.27		$3.45		$3.30		$2.89		$3.12		$3.07		$3.45		$2.60		$2.82		$3.32	

Key: PB = Practice bids
 Qa = Quantity choice by player a
 T = Transactions
 πa = Profit to player a

256

Appendix VIII

EXPERIMENT 8

OLIGOPOLY

Triopoly, Incomplete Information, Quantity Variation

Instructions
Profit Table Same as in Appendix VII
Complete Results for Subjects

Instructions to Seller A

The National Science Foundation, the Ford Foundation, and the Office of Naval Research have provided funds for the conduct of research regarding economic decisions. If you follow instructions carefully and make appropriate decisions, you may earn an appreciable amount of money. *You may keep all the money that you earn.* You cannot lose your own money, but poor choices will result in small or no profit to you.

You will be paired at random with two other persons. You will not see these persons or speak with them at any time. You will never know the identity of your competition, called seller *B* and seller *C*, nor will they be aware of yours.

Imagine that you, seller *B*, and seller *C* are the sole producers of some standardized commodity. You and they will engage in a series of transactions by means of written bids, the bids on each transaction representing the quantity of the commodity produced for that transaction. You must bid on each transaction.

You will be furnished with a table which shows the various levels of profit or loss you can attain. The quantities you may produce are listed across the top of the table, while the sum of the quantities produced by seller *B* and seller *C* are listed down the left-hand margin. Your profits are represented within the body of the table by the intersection of the quantity produced by you and the sum of the quantities produced by seller *B* and seller *C*. For example, on a given transaction you might select a quantity of 24; you would receive one of the profits in the 24th column. If seller *B* together with seller *C* had selected a total quantity of 28, then your profit would be at the intersection of column 24 (your bid) and row 28 (their total bid). The profit shown at this point is 750, or 7.50 cents. Decimal points have been omitted for simplicity, but may always be considered to be located two places in from the right.

The process is started by each player selecting and recording a quantity on the white sheet provided for that purpose. You may select any quantity across the top of the table, and then record it. An experimental assistant will then inform you of the total quantity chosen by seller *B* and seller *C* and the amount of profit or loss you made on that transaction. After each transaction your white sheet should show your quantity bid, the sum of seller *B*'s and seller *C*'s quantity bids, and your profit or loss from that transaction.

The process is repeated over and over. You may select the same quantity each time; you do not have to do so, however. Decisions will ordinarily be made every few minutes, but extra time will be granted when necessary.

In order for you to become accustomed to using the profit table, the first 3 bids will be for practice, and will involve no profit or loss. At the end of the session we will add up your profit and loss column and give you the resulting amount of money. This will be done in separate counting rooms, so you will not see the person with whom you have been bidding.

Are there any questions?

EXPERIMENT 8 Quantity Bids and Total Profits

Group number

	17			18			19			20			21			22			23			24			25			26			27		
PB	Qa	Qb	Qc	Qa	Qb	Qc	Qa	Qb	Qc	Qa	Qb	Qc	Qa	Qb	Qc	Qa	Qb	Qc	Qa	Qb	Qc	Qa	Qb	Qc	Qa	Qb	Qc	Qa	Qb	Qc	Qa	Qb	Qc
A	29	25	10	25	25	8	13	25	15	20	10	13	30	18	14	20	14	25	18	17	25	24	30	30	20	15	16	15	16	14	8	15	21
B	30	23	8	25	15	8	10	8	10	19	30	15	19	9	8	17	12	18	14	14	17	14	30	30	26	15	12	14	21	18	8	11	10
C	25	30	32	20	12	8	17	27	20	8	20	8	9	12	15	18	18	13	15	15	9	8	14	21	28	13	14	18	27	14	32	26	30
T																																	
1	12	16	20	20	12	25	14	11	15	14	23	14	19	12	19	15	18	18	16	13	18	8	14	20	18	10	12	15	15	8	23	15	18
2	14	14	20	14	8	25	12	8	17	17	32	12	14	15	15	14	14	17	13	11	21	9	17	20	17	15	16	15	20	15	23	11	23
3	14	18	16	16	13	25	13	14	15	11	17	16	16	16	20	15	8	18	15	15	20	10	16	18	20	15	14	14	18	8	23	15	13
4	15	20	16	16	12	25	13	15	15	15	17	12	11	14	13	13	9	19	11	16	18	11	16	16	18	25	13	17	21	24	23	20	20
5	10	21	15	8	10	25	15	8	20	16	9	8	19	15	17	14	22	22	23	15	12	12	17	15	18	30	19	13	13	24	23	22	20
6	16	16	17	16	21	25	11	16	15	18	20	10	15	11	15	14	22	21	15	15	18	13	17	15	12	23	18	14	15	21	20	23	20
7	16	15	18	8	18	25	14	13	15	15	16	15	18	15	16	13	15	19	20	14	17	15	17	15	8	21	18	14	15	28	20	25	8
8	15	22	32	16	18	25	16	12	20	18	18	15	17	13	13	15	15	18	24	18	26	16	18	15	9	23	22	13	20	28	20	15	10
9	10	15	15	17	11	25	16	15	17	14	18	15	11	11	15	16	13	18	12	14	15	15	18	9	15	19	20	12	21	15	20	20	12
10	15	15	15	18	16	25	14	15	15	15	12	15	16	17	15	16	17	12	15	15	15	16	18	15	8	25	20	16	22	15	20	25	11
11	15	15	15	16	26	25	15	15	20	17	12	11	18	16	17	15	15	13	13	15	14	17	16	15	10	20	20	16	19	21	20	14	15
12	13	15	20	16	16	25	15	15	15	16	15	15	19	19	11	16	16	14	14	16	18	17	14	15	11	15	20	15	20	15	20	28	16
13	14	13	8	19	26	25	15	8	20	16	15	15	25	20	13	17	18	15	16	15	15	17	14	15	14	15	22	15	18	10	20	25	20
14	16	18	30	8	14	25	15	13	14	15	15	13	25	20	17	14	16	15	15	15	20	18	14	15	12	15	22	20	21	10	20	15	11
15	14	15	15	8	18	25	15	14	15	15	17	16	15	15	20	20	20	15	25	15	15	19	14	15	14	16	20	20	18	10	20	26	10
16	15	23	10	8	10	25	15	15	20	15	17	13	17	16	14	16	20	20	15	12	16	15	20	15	14	15	16	20	21	10	20	15	10
17	11	16	10	8	15	25	15	10	13	15	18	14	16	14	16	17	15	20	16	12	19	14	18	13	15	15	24	20	21	10	20	20	10
18	13	20	10	8	15	25	15	22	14	15	14	16	17	15	15	17	16	20	25	15	20	15	20	15	15	18	21	20	14	15	20	20	10
19	14	16	15	8	12	25	15	13	19	15	14	15	17	18	16	14	10	20	15	14	17	15	20	14	15	21	15	19	19	15	20	23	19
20	13	10	15	14	15	25	15	16	15	15	15	15	16	15	17	14	15	19	23	14	12	15	20	14	15	16	15	20	13	11	20	23	19
21	15	10	15	8	10	25	14	15	17	15	16	15	15	15	16	12	15	20	16	16	16	15	21	14	16	15	20				20	20	19
22	15	15	17	8	12	25	15	15	18	15	16	15	16	15	15	17	20	20	17	13	19	15	11	13	14	14	18				20	15	20
πa	$1.51			$ .61			$1.86			$1.80			$1.69			$1.38			$1.40			$1.67			$1.21			$1.12			$ .91		
πb	$1.80			$ .75			$1.70			$1.79			$1.59			$1.40			$1.33			$1.95			$1.40			$1.11			$ .77		
πc	$1.59			$1.83			$2.16			$1.58			$1.64			$1.63			$1.55			$1.80			$1.62			$ .87			$ .47		

Key: PB = Practice bids
Qa = Quantity choice by player a
T = Transactions
πa = Profit to player a

259

Appendix IX

EXPERIMENT 9

OLIGOPOLY

Triopoly, Complete Information, Quantity Variation

Instructions
Profit Sheet
Profit Table
Complete Results for Subjects

Instructions

The National Science Foundation, the Ford Foundation, and the Office of Naval Research have provided funds for the conduct of research regarding economic decisions. If you follow instructions carefully and make appropriate decisions, you may earn an appreciable amount of money. *You may keep all the money that you earn.* You cannot lose your own money, but poor choices will result in small or no profit to you.

You will be grouped at random with two other persons. You will not see these persons or speak with them at any time. You will never know the identity of your competition, nor will they be aware of yours.

Imagine that you and your competition are the sole producers of some standardized commodity. You and they will engage in a series of transactions by means of written bids, the bids on each transaction representing the quantity of the commodity produced for that transaction. You must bid on each transaction.

You will be furnished with a table showing the various levels of profit or loss you and your competition can attain. The quantities you may produce are listed across the top of the table, while the sum of quantities produced by your competition is listed down the left-hand margin. Both your profits and their profits are represented within the body of the table by the intersection of the quantities produced. The left figure at each intersection is your

261

profit for that transaction, while the right figure is the sum of the profits earned by your competition. For example, on a given transaction you might select a quantity of 24; you would receive one of the profits in the 24th column. If your competition had selected a total quantity of 28, then both profits would be at the intersection of column 24 (your bid) and row 28 (their bid). The profit for you at this point is 750 (7.50 cents) and the total profit for your competition is 850 (8.50 cents). Decimal points have been omitted for simplicity, but may always be considered to be located two places in from the right.

The process is started by each player selecting and recording a quantity on the profit sheet provided for that purpose. You may select any quantity across the top of the table, and then record it. An experimental assistant will then inform you of the quantity chosen by each of your competitors, and the amount of profit or loss you made on that transaction. After each transaction your profit sheet should show your quantity bid, each of your competition's quantity bids, and your profit or loss from that transaction.

The process is repeated over and over. You may select the same quantity each time; you do not have to do so, however. Decisions will ordinarily be made every few minutes, but extra time will be granted when necessary.

In order for you to become accustomed to using the profit table, the first 3 bids will be for practice, and will involve no profit or loss. At the end of the session we will add up your profit and loss column and give you the resulting amount of money. This will be done in separate counting rooms, so you will not see the persons with whom you have been bidding.

Are there any questions?

Profit Sheet

Number_____   Name_____

Cubicle_____   Date_____   Phone_____

Transaction		My quantity bid	Seller B's bid–profit	Seller C's bid–profit	My profit or loss
Practice trials	_A_				
	_B_				
	_C_				

Profit Table

Quantity produced

	8 M	8 C	9 M	9 C	10 M	10 C	11 M	11 C	12 M	12 C	13 M	13 C
8	1400	1400	1500	1350	1650	1300	1800	1300	1900	1250	2000	1200
9	1350	1500	1500	1500	1600	1450	1750	1400	1850	1400	1950	1350
10	1300	1650	1450	1600	1600	1600	1700	1550	1800	1500	1900	1450
11	1300	1800	1400	1750	1550	1700	1650	1650	1750	1600	1850	1550
12	1250	1900	1400	1850	1500	1800	1600	1750	1700	1700	1800	1650
13	1200	2000	1350	1950	1450	1900	1550	1850	1650	1800	1750	1750
14	1200	2100	1300	2050	1400	2000	1500	1950	1600	1900	1700	1850
15	1150	2200	1250	2150	1400	2100	1450	2000	1550	1950	1650	1900
16	1150	2300	1250	2200	1350	2150	1450	2100	1500	2000	1600	1950
17	1100	2350	1200	2300	1300	2250	1400	2150	1450	2100	1550	2000
18	1050	2400	1150	2350	1250	2300	1350	2200	1400	2150	1500	2050
19	1050	2500	1150	2400	1200	2350	1300	2250	1350	2200	1450	2100
20	1000	2550	1100	2450	1200	2400	1250	2300	1300	2200	1400	2150
21	950	2600	1050	2500	1150	2400	1200	2350	1250	2250	1350	2150
22	950	2600	1000	2500	1100	2450	1150	2350	1200	2250	1300	2200
23	900	2650	1000	2550	1050	2450	1100	2350	1200	2300	1200	2200
24	850	2650	950	2550	1000	2450	1100	2400	1150	2300	1150	2200
25	850	2700	900	2600	1000	2500	1050	2400	1100	2300	1100	2200
26	800	2700	900	2600	950	2450	1000	2350	1050	2250	1050	2150
27	800	2700	850	2550	900	2450	950	2350	1000	2250	1000	2150
28	750	2650	800	2550	850	2450	900	2350	950	2200	950	2100
29	700	2650	750	2550	800	2400	850	2300	900	2200	900	2050
30	700	2600	750	2500	800	2400	800	2250	850	2150	850	2000
31	650	2600	700	2450	750	2350	750	2200	800	2100	800	1950
32	600	2550	650	2400	700	2300	700	2150	750	2000	750	1900
33	600	2500	600	2350	650	2250	700	2100	700	1950	700	1850
34	550	2400	600	2300	600	2150	650	2000	650	1900	650	1750
35	500	2350	550	2200	600	2100	600	1950	600	1800	600	1650
36	500	2300	500	2150	550	2000	550	1850	550	1700	550	1550
37	450	2200	500	2050	500	1900	500	1750	500	1600	500	1450
38	400	2100	450	1950	450	1800	450	1650	450	1500	450	1350
39	400	2000	400	1850	400	1700	400	1550	400	1400	400	1200
40	350	1900	350	1750	400	1600	350	1400	350	1250	350	1100
41	350	1800	350	1600	350	1450	350	1300	300	1100	300	950
42	300	1650	300	1500	300	1300	300	1150	250	1000	250	800
43	250	1500	250	1350	250	1200	250	1000	200	850	200	650
44	250	1400	250	1200	200	1050	200	850	150	700	150	500
45	200	1250	200	1050	200	900	150	700	100	500	100	350
46	150	1100	150	900	150	700	100	550	50	350	50	150
47	150	900	100	750	100	550	50	350	00	150	00	00
48	100	750	100	550	50	350	00	150	00	00	00	−150
49	50	550	50	350	00	150	00	00	000	−150	−50	−350
50	50	400	00	200	00	00	00	−200	−50	−400	−100	−600
51	00	200	00	00	00	−200	−50	−400	−100	−600	−150	−800
52	00	00	00	−200	−50	−400	−100	−600	−150	−800	−200	−1000.
53	00	−200	−50	−400	−100	−600	−150	−800	−200	−1050	−250	−1250
54	−50	−400	−100	−600	−150	−850	−200	−1050	−250	−1250	−300	−1500
55	−50	−650	−100	−850	−200	−1100	−250	−1300	−300	−1500	−350	−1750
56	−100	−850	−150	−1100	−200	−1300	−300	−1550	−350	−1750	−400	−2000
57	−150	−1100	−200	−1350	−250	−1550	−350	−1800	−400	−2050	−450	−2250
58	−150	−1350	−250	−1600	−300	−1850	−350	−2050	−450	−2300	−500	−2550
59	−200	−1650	−300	−1850	−350	−2100	−400	−2350	−500	−2550	−550	−2800
60	−250	−1900	−300	−2150	−400	−2400	−450	−2600	−550	−2850	−600	−3100
61	−250	−2150	−350	−2400	−400	−2650	−500	−2900	−600	−3150	−650	−3400
62	−300	−2450	−350	−2700	−450	−2950	−550	−3200	−650	−3450	−700	−3700
63	−350	−2750	−400	−3000	−500	−3250	−600	−3500	−700	−3750	−750	−4000
64	−350	−3050	−450	−3300	−550	−3550	−650	−3800	−750	−4050	−800	−4350

Quantity produced by my competition

M = Profit by me C = Profit by my competition

by me

14		15		16		17		18		19	
M	C	M	C	M	C	M	C	M	C	M	C
2100	1200	2200	1150	2300	1150	2350	1100	2400	1050	2500	1050
2050	1300	2150	1250	2200	1250	2300	1200	2350	1150	2400	1150
2000	1400	2100	1400	2150	1350	2250	1300	2300	1250	2350	1200
1950	1500	2000	1450	2100	1450	2150	1400	2200	1350	2250	1300
1900	1600	1950	1550	2000	1500	2100	1450	2150	1400	2200	1350
1850	1770	1900	1650	1950	1600	2000	1550	2050	1500	2100	1450
1750	1750	1850	1700	1900	1650	1950	1660	2000	1550	2050	1500
1700	1850	1800	1800	1850	1770	1900	1650	1900	1600	1950	1550
1650	1900	1700	1850	1750	1750	1800	1700	1850	1650	1900	1600
1600	1950	1650	1900	1700	1800	1750	1750	1880	1700	1800	1600
1550	2000	1600	1900	1650	1850	1700	1800	1700	1700	1700	1650
1500	2050	1550	1950	1600	1900	1600	1800	1650	1700	1650	1650
1450	2050	1550	2000	1500	1900	1550	1800	1550	1750	1550	1700
1400	2100	1400	2000	1450	1900	1450	1800	1500	1750	1500	1650
1300	2100	1350	2000	1400	1900	1400	1800	1400	1750	1400	1650
1250	2100	1300	2000	1300	1900	1350	1800	1350	1700	1350	1650
1200	2100	1250	2000	1250	1900	1250	1800	1250	1700	1250	1600
1150	2100	1200	2000	1200	1900	1200	1800	1200	1700	1200	1600
1100	2050	1100	1950	1150	1850	1150	1750	1150	1650	1100	1550
1050	2050	1050	1900	1050	1800	1050	1700	1050	1600	1050	1500
1000	2000	1000	1900	1050	1750	1000	1650	1000	1550	950	1450
950	1950	1000	1850	950	1700	950	1600	900	1500	900	1350
850	1900	900	1800	850	1650	850	1550	850	1400	800	1300
800	1850	850	1700	800	1600	800	1450	750	1350	750	1200
750	1750	750	1650	750	1550	700	1400	700	1250	650	1150
700	1700	700	1550	700	1450	650	1300	600	1150	600	1050
650	1600	650	1450	600	1350	600	1200	550	1050	500	950
600	1500	600	1400	550	1250	500	1100	500	950	450	800
550	1400	500	1250	500	1150	450	1000	400	850	350	700
500	1300	450	1150	400	1000	400	850	350	700	300	550
400	1200	400	1050	350	900	300	750	250	600	200	450
350	1050	350	900	300	750	250	600	200	450	150	300
300	950	300	800	250	600	200	450	100	300	50	150
250	800	200	650	150	450	100	300	50	150	00	00
200	650	150	500	100	300	50	150	00	00	−50	−150
150	500	100	300	50	150	00	00	−50	−150	−150	−300
100	350	50	150	00	00	−50	−150	−100	−350	−200	−500
50	150	00	00	−50	−150	−100	−350	−200	−500	−300	−700
00	00	−50	−150	−100	−350	−200	−550	−250	−700	−350	−900
−50	−150	−100	−350	−150	−550	−250	−750	−350	−900	−450	−1100
−100	−350	−150	−550	−250	−750	−300	−950	−400	−1150	−500	−1300
−150	−550	−200	−750	−300	−950	−400	−1150	−500	−1350	−600	−1550
−200	−800	−300	−1000	−350	−1200	−450	−1400	−550	−1600	−650	−1800
−250	−1000	−350	−1200	−400	−1400	−500	−1600	−600	−1800	−750	−2000
−300	−1200	−400	−1450	−500	−1650	−600	−1850	−700	−2050	−800	−2250
−350	−1450	−450	−1650	−550	−1900	−650	−2100	−750	−2300	−900	−2500
−400	−1700	−500	−1900	−600	−2150	−700	−2350	−850	−2550	−950	−2800
−500	−1950	−600	−2200	−700	−2400	−800	−2600	−900	−2850	−1050	−3050
−550	−2200	−650	−2450	−750	−2650	−850	−2900	−1000	−3100	−1100	−3350
−600	−2500	−700	−2700	−800	−2950	−950	−3150	−1050	−3400	−1200	−3600
−650	−2750	−750	−3000	−850	−3200	−1000	−3450	−1150	−3700	−1250	−3900
−700	−3050	−850	−3300	−950	−3500	−1050	−3750	−1200	−4000	−1350	−4200
−750	−3350	−900	−3600	−1050	−3800	−1150	−4050	−1250	−4300	−1400	−4550
−800	−3650	−1000	−3900	−1050	−4100	−1200	−4350	−1350	−4600	−1500	−4850
−850	−3950	−1000	−4200	−1150	−4450	−1250	−4700	−1400	−4950	−1150	−5200
−950	−4250	−1050	−4500	−1200	−4750	−1350	−5000	−1500	−5250	−1650	−5500
−1000	−4600	−1100	−4850	−1250	−5100	−1400	−5350	−1550	−5600	−1700	−5850

Profit Table (Continued)

Quantity produced

	20		21		22		23		24		25	
	M	C	M	C	M	C	M	C	M	C	M	C
8	2550	1000	2600	950	2600	950	2650	900	2650	850	2700	850
9	2450	1100	2500	1050	2550	1000	2500	1000	2500	950	2600	900
10	2400	1200	2400	1150	2450	1100	2450	1050	2450	1000	2500	1000
11	2300	1250	2350	1200	2350	1150	2350	1100	2400	1100	2400	1050
12	2200	1300	2250	1250	2250	1200	2300	1200	2300	1150	2300	1100
13	2150	1400	2150	1350	2200	1300	2200	1200	2200	1150	2200	1100
14	2050	1450	2100	1400	2100	1300	2100	1250	2100	1200	2100	1150
15	2000	1500	2000	1400	2000	1350	2000	1300	2000	1250	2000	1200
16	1900	1500	1900	1450	1900	1400	1900	1300	1900	1250	1900	1200
17	1800	1550	1800	1450	1800	1400	1800	1350	1800	1250	1800	1200
18	1750	1550	1750	1550	1750	1400	1700	1350	1700	1250	1700	1200
19	1700	1550	1650	1500	1650	1400	1650	1350	1600	1250	1600	1200
20	1600	1600	1550	1550	1550	1400	1550	1350	1500	1250	1500	1200
21	1550	1550	1500	1500	1450	1400	1450	1300	1400	1250	1400	1150
22	1400	1550	1400	1450	1400	1400	1350	1300	1300	1200	1300	1100
23	1350	1550	1300	1450	1300	1350	1250	1250	1200	1150	1200	1100
24	1250	1500	1250	1400	1200	1300	1150	1200	1150	1150	1100	1050
25	1200	1500	1150	1400	1100	1300	1100	1100	1050	1100	1000	1000
26	1100	1450	1050	1350	1050	1200	1000	1100	950	1000	900	900
27	1000	1400	1000	1250	950	1150	900	1050	850	950	800	850
28	950	1300	900	1200	850	1100	800	1000	750	850	700	750
29	850	1250	800	1150	750	1000	700	900	650	800	600	650
30	800	1200	750	1050	700	950	600	800	550	700	550	600
31	700	1100	650	950	600	850	550	700	450	600	400	450
32	600	1000	550	850	500	750	450	600	350	500	300	350
33	550	900	500	750	400	650	350	500	250	350	200	250
34	450	800	400	650	350	500	250	400	200	250	100	100
35	400	700	300	550	250	400	150	250	50	100	000	000
36	300	550	250	400	150	250	50	100	00	00	−100	−100
37	200	400	150	250	50	100	00	00	−50	−100	−200	−250
38	150	300	50	150	00	00	−50	−150	−200	−300	−300	−450
39	50	150	00	00	−50	−150	−150	−300	−250	−450	−400	−600
40	00	00	−50	−150	−150	−300	−250	−450	−350	−600	−500	−800
41	−50	−150	−150	−300	−250	−450	−350	−650	−450	−800	−600	−950
42	−150	−300	−250	−500	−350	−650	−450	−800	−550	−1000	−700	−1150
43	−200	−500	−300	−650	−400	−850	−550	−1000	−650	−1200	−800	−1350
44	−300	−700	−400	−850	−500	−1050	−600	−1200	−750	−1400	−900	−1550
45	−400	−900	−500	−1050	−600	−1250	−700	−1400	−850	−1600	−1000	−1800
46	−450	−1100	−550	−1250	−700	−1450	−800	−1650	−950	−1800	−1100	−2000
47	−550	−1300	−650	−1500	−750	−1650	−900	−1850	−1050	−2050	−1200	−2250
48	−600	−1500	−750	−1750	−850	−1900	−1000	−2100	−1150	−2300	−1300	−2450
49	−700	−1750	−800	−1950	−950	−2150	−1100	−2350	−1200	−2500	−1400	−2700
50	−800	−2000	−900	−2200	−1050	−2400	−1150	−2600	−1300	−2800	−1500	−3000
51	−850	−2200	−1000	−2400	−1100	−2650	−1250	−2850	−1400	−3050	−1600	−3250
52	−950	−2450	−1050	−2700	−1200	−2900	−1350	−3100	−1500	−3300	−1700	−3500
53	−1000	−2750	−1150	−2950	−1300	−3150	−1450	−3350	−1600	−3600	−1800	−3800
54	−1100	−3000	−1250	−3200	−1400	−3450	−1550	−3650	−1700	−3850	−1900	−4100
55	−1200	−3300	−1300	−3500	−1450	−3700	−1650	−3950	−1800	−4150	−2000	−4400
56	−1250	−3550	−1400	−3800	−1550	−4000	−1700	−4250	−1900	−4450	−2100	−4700
57	−1350	−3850	−1500	−4100	−1650	−4300	−1800	−4550	−2000	−4750	−2200	−5000
58	−1400	−4150	−1550	−4400	−1750	−4600	−1900	−4850	−2100	−5100	−2300	−5300
59	−1550	−4450	−1650	−4700	−1800	−4950	−2000	−5150	−2200	−5400	−2400	−5650
60	−1650	−4800	−1750	−5000	−1900	−5250	−2100	−5500	−2300	−5750	−2500	−6000
61	−1700	−5100	−1800	−5350	−2000	−5600	−2200	−5850	−2400	−6100	−2600	−6300
62	−1750	−5450	−1900	−5700	−2100	−5950	−2300	−6200	−2450	−6400	−2700	−6650
63	−1800	−5750	−2000	−6000	−2200	−6300	−2350	−6550	−2550	−6800	−2800	−7050
64	−1900	−6100	−2100	−6400	−2050	−6650	−2450	−6900	−2650	−7150	−2900	−7400

Quantity produced by my competition

M = Profit by me C = Profit by my competition

by me

26		27		28		29		30		31		32	
M	C	M	C	M	C	M	C	M	C	M	C	M	C
2700	800	2700	800	2650	750	2650	700	2600	700	2600	650	2550	600
2600	900	2550	850	2550	800	2550	750	2500	750	2450	700	2400	650
2450	950	2450	900	2450	850	2400	800	2400	800	2350	750	2300	700
2350	1000	2350	950	2350	900	2300	850	2250	800	2200	750	2150	700
2250	1050	2250	1000	2200	950	2200	900	2150	800	2100	800	2000	750
2150	1050	2150	1000	2000	950	2050	900	2000	850	2000	850	1900	750
2050	1100	2050	1050	1900	1000	1950	950	1900	850	1950	800	1750	750
1950	1100	1900	1050	1750	1050	1850	1000	1800	900	1850	800	1650	750
1850	1150	1800	1050	1650	1000	1700	950	1650	850	1700	850	1500	750
1750	1150	1700	1050	1550	1000	1600	950	1550	850	1600	800	1400	700
1650	1150	1600	1050	1450	950	1500	900	1400	850	1450	800	1250	700
1550	1100	1500	1050	1300	950	1350	900	1300	800	1350	750	1150	650
1450	1100	1400	1000	1200	900	1250	850	1200	800	1200	750	1000	600
1350	1050	1250	1000	1100	850	1150	800	1050	750	1100	700	850	550
1200	1050	1150	950	1000	800	1000	750	950	700	950	650	750	500
1100	1000	1050	900	850	750	900	700	800	600	850	600	600	450
1000	950	950	850	750	700	800	650	700	550	700	550	500	350
900	900	850	800	650	600	650	600	600	500	600	450	350	300
800	800	750	700	550	500	550	500	450	400	450	400	250	200
700	750	600	600	400	400	450	400	350	300	350	300	100	100
600	650	500	550	300	300	300	300	200	200	250	200	000	000
500	550	400	450	200	200	200	200	100	100	100	100	-100	-100
400	450	300	350	100	100	100	100	000	000	000	000	-250	-200
300	350	200	250	000	000	000	000	-100	-100	-100	-100	-350	-350
200	250	100	100	-100	-100	-100	-100	-200	-250	-250	-250	-500	-500
100	100	000	000	-200	-250	-200	-250	-350	-350	-350	-350	-600	-650
000	000	-100	-100	-300	-400	-300	-400	-450	-500	-450	-500	-750	-800
-100	-100	-200	-250	-400	-550	-450	-550	-600	-650	-600	-650	-850	-950
-200	-250	-300	-400	-550	-700	-550	-700	-700	-850	-700	-800	-1000	-1150
-300	-400	-400	-550	-650	-900	-650	-850	-800	-1000	-850	-1000	-1150	-1300
-400	-600	-500	-750	-750	-1050	-800	-1050	-950	-1200	-950	-1150	-1250	-1500
-500	-750	-600	-900	-850	-1250	-900	-1200	-1050	-1400	-1100	-1350	-1400	-1700
-600	-950	-750	-1100	-1000	-1450	-1000	-1400	-1200	-1600	-1200	-1550	-1500	-1900
-700	-1100	-850	-1300	-1100	-1650	-1150	-1600	-1300	-1800	-1350	-1750	-1650	-2100
-800	-1300	-950	-1500	-1200	-1850	-1250	-1800	-1400	-2000	-1450	-1950	-1750	-2350
-900	-1500	-1050	-1700	-1300	-2100	-1350	-2050	-1550	-2200	-1600	-2150	-1900	-2550
-1000	-1750	-1150	-1900	-1450	-2300	-1500	-2250	-1650	-2450	-1700	-2400	-2000	-2800
-1100	-1950	-1250	-2150	-1550	-2550	-1600	-2500	-1800	-2700	-1850	-2600	-2150	-3050
-1200	-2200	-1400	-2350	-1650	-2800	-1700	-2750	-1900	-2900	-1950	-2850	-2300	-3300
-1350	-2400	-1500	-2600	-1750	-3050	-1850	-3000	-2000	-3150	-2100	-3100	-2400	-3550
-1450	-2750	-1600	-2850	-1900	-3300	-1950	-3250	-2150	-3450	-2200	-3350	-2550	-3800
-1550	-2900	-1700	-3100	-2000	-3600	-2050	-3500	-2250	-3700	-2350	-3600	-2650	-4100
-1650	-3200	-1800	-3400	-2100	-3850	-2200	-3800	-2400	-4000	-2450	-3900	-2800	-4400
-1750	-3450	-1900	-3650	-2200	-4150	-2300	-4050	-2500	-4250	-2600	-4200	-2900	-4650
-1850	-3700	-2050	-3950	-2350	-4450	-2400	-4350	-2600	-4550	-2700	-4450	-3050	-4950
-1950	-4000	-2150	-4200	-2450	-4750	-2550	-4650	-2750	-4850	-2850	-4750	-3150	-5300
-2050	-4300	-2250	-4500	-2550	-5050	-2650	-4950	-2850	-5150	-2950	-5050	-3300	-5600
-2150	-4600	-2350	-4800	-2650	-5350	-2750	-5250	-3000	-5500	-3100	-5400	-3450	-5900
-2250	-4900	-2450	-5150	-2800	-5700	-2900	-5600	-3100	-5800	-3200	-5700	-3550	-6250
-2350	-5200	-2550	-5450	-2900	-6000	-3000	-5900	-3200	-6150	-3350	-6050	-3700	-6600
-2450	-5550	-2700	-5800	-3000	-6350	-3100	-6250	-3350	-6450	-3450	-6350	-3800	-6950
-2600	-5900	-2800	-6100	-3100	-6700	-3250	-6600	-3450	-6800	-3600	-6700	-3950	-7300
-2700	-6200	-2900	-6450	-3250	-7050	-3350	-6950	-3600	-7200	-3700	-7050	-4050	-7650
-2800	-6550	-3000	-6800	-3350	-7400	-3450	-7300	-3700	-7550	-3850	-7400	-4200	-8050
-2900	-6900	-3100	-7150	-3450	-7800	-3600	-7650	-3800	-7900	-3950	-7800	-4300	-8400
-3000	-7300	-3200	-7550	-3550	-8150	-3700	-8050	-3950	-8300	-4100	-8150	-4450	-8800
-3100	-7650	-3350	-7900			-3800	-8400	-4050	-8700	-4200	-8550	-4600	-9200
										-4350	-8950		

EXPERIMENT 9 Quantity Bids and Total Profits

Group number

PB	28 Qa	28 Qb	28 Qc	29 Qa	29 Qb	29 Qc	30 Qa	30 Qb	30 Qc	31 Qa	31 Qb	31 Qc	32 Qa	32 Qb	32 Qc	33 Qa	33 Qb	33 Qc	34 Qa	34 Qb	34 Qc	35 Qa	35 Qb	35 Qc	36 Qa	36 Qb	36 Qc	37 Qa	37 Qb	37 Qc	38 Qa	38 Qb	38 Qc
A	8	20	17	13	12	19	16	15	16	15	15	11	24	10	30	32	16	11	25	20	17	17	25	19	12	23	30	8	21	25	11	16	15
B	14	18	25	18	11	22	14	20	9	17	16	14	18	10	32	32	22	25	30	12	20	24	17	10	20	26	17	14	26	10	14	20	15
C	28	12	13	15	10	16	15	22	24	20	20	21	10	8	15	32	10	28	17	15	28	26	9	30	10	19	10	8	16	12	17	13	11
T																																	
1	18	8	22	17	10	15	18	20	11	19	16	20	10	10	21	11	12	12	8	10	26	26	15	10	18	20	8	8	15	9	8	15	15
2	26	14	10	17	15	17	13	17	12	16	15	18	11	15	19	11	9	12	18	15	16	23	12	22	15	15	15	25	16	14	12	22	15
3	26	16	14	14	14	15	18	15	18	16	16	16	15	15	18	12	12	14	18	23	11	16	15	17	20	14	12	14	14	20	20	18	20
4	20	15	19	13	12	13	14	14	20	18	14	14	15	12	16	9	10	12	13	17	13	16	18	21	20	21	18	13	20	14	9	23	20
5	27	21	17	15	10	24	18	18	18	18	13	13	15	15	15	13	13	15	26	17	15	24	12	15	20	19	8	25	15	18	25	20	20
6	15	25	22	18	10	24	15	20	25	10	12	14	15	16	30	13	10	17	23	11	17	24	10	18	16	17	15	12	16	11	8	19	12
7	20	14	10	17	30	15	16	13	15	15	11	10	15	8	30	14	10	12	24	15	20	20	20	22	15	21	20	14	16	15	15	10	12
8	25	16	10	15	10	9	17	15	16	15	10	15	20	12	15	14	10	12	23	9	18	16	8	15	11	14	15	13	19	22	17	10	10
9	20	20	10	16	10	15	14	19	18	14	9	15	15	13	19	15	10	17	20	21	16	16	10	16	17	21	18	8	19	23	11	12	10
10	22	23	11	16	30	15	16	17	17	15	8	12	15	13	15	17	30	16	19	18	10	20	15	18	18	20	16	25	15	18	15	24	10
11	15	21	17	16	10	15	15	12	16	15	22	20	17	16	16	19	10	15	25	15	21	23	20	20	12	17	20	25	15	20	13	18	20
12	23	18	12	16	15	15	15	15	20	13	22	20	15	16	14	15	30	15	23	9	22	16	10	17	15	23	15	20	16	20	19	16	16
13	15	15	16	15	14	15	17	13	20	18	22	15	16	16	16	19	10	14	14	12	23	13	20	16	13	14	21	18	10	20	14	22	10
14	10	15	12	15	18	15	16	16	15	16	16	16	14	16	29	19	10	12	20	20	20	20	11	20	17	20	15	18	16	17	17	16	25
15	25	8	15	16	16	15	15	20	16	15	18	16	14	11	20	17	30	12	22	13	21	17	15	15	19	16	18	17	16	14	20	19	10
16	20	15	17	15	15	15	14	16	16	13	17	20	14	14	20	15	10	15	16	25	22	16	15	14	10	15	20	15	18	14	16	16	25
17	15	15	16	16	14	17	15	17	21	15	16	15	20	13	16	16	30	15	21	18	18	16	14	20	18	22	17	20	18	8	21	20	25
18	15	15	18	15	16	8	18	15	18	16	18	15	12	14	17	14	30	8	8	21	23	16	10	15	15	17	18	17	18	13	17	11	10
19	26	10	26	15	15	15	15	15	15	16	15	8	15	16	18	14	10	16	23	20	23	16	20	20	18	14	13	19	16	22	17	15	10
20	10	10	20	14	14	15	15	16	15	17	14	20	15	14	20				22	17	23	16	20	18	19	16	18	20	20	25	17	28	25
21	10	10	20	14	14	15	15	16	16	12	12	20	15	16	20	17	30	15	20	15	23	19	20	20	17	20	22	8	15	28	17	14	10
22	20	15	15	15	15	15	15	16	15	16	23	20	15	15	23	19	10	12	10	14	22	20	20	26	16	20	18	8	8	24	17	17	10
πa	$1.39			$1.85			$1.48			$1.71			$1.39			$1.98			$.71			$1.22			$1.30			$1.13			$1.15		
πb	$1.05			$1.55			$1.53			$1.56			$1.37			$1.43			$.68			$.87			$1.40			$1.32			$1.32		
πc	$1.32			$1.78			$1.56			$1.69			$1.69			$1.90			$.88			$1.14			$1.35			$1.28			$.93		

Key: PB = Practice bids
Qa = Quantity choice by player a
T = Transactions
πa = Profit to player a

Appendix X

EXPERIMENT 10

OLIGOPOLY

Duopoly, Complete Information, Quantity Variation

Instructions
Profit Table Same as in Appendix IX
Complete Results for Subjects

Instructions

The National Science Foundation, the Ford Foundation, and the Offic
of Naval Research have provided funds for the conduct of research regarding
economic decisions. If you follow instructions carefully and make appropriate decisions, you may earn an appreciable amount of money. *You may
keep all the money that you earn.* You cannot lose your own money, but
poor choices will result in small or no profit to you.

You will be paired at random with one other person. You will not see
this person or speak with him at any time. You will never know the identity
of your competition, nor will he be aware of yours.

Imagine that you and your competition are the sole producers of some
standardized commodity. You and he will engage in a series of transactions
by means of written bids, the bids on each transaction representing the quantity of the commodity produced for that transaction. You must bid on
each transaction.

You will be furnished with a table showing the various levels of profit or
loss you and your competition can attain. The quantities you may produce
are listed across the top of the table, while the quantities produced by your
competition are listed down the left-hand margin. Both your profits and
his profits are represented within the body of the table by the intersection
of the quantities produced. The left figure at each intersection is your
profit for that transaction, while the right figure is the profit earned by your

269

competition. For example, on a given transaction you might select a quantity of 24; you would receive one of the profits in the 24th column. If your competition had selected a quantity of 28, then both profits would be at the intersection of column 24 (your bid) and row 28 (his bid). The profit for you at this point is 750 (7.50 cents) and the profit for your competition is 850 (8.50 cents). Decimal points have been omitted for simplicity but may always be considered to be located two places in from the right.

The process is started by each player selecting and recording a quantity on the profit sheet provided for that purpose. You may select any quantity across the top of the table, and then record it. An experimental assistant will then inform you of the quantity chosen by your competition, and the amount of profit or loss you made on that transaction. After each transaction your profit sheet should show your quantity bid, your competition's quantity bid, and your profit or loss from that transaction.

The process is repeated over and over. You may select the same quantity each time; you do not have to do so, however. Decisions will ordinarily be made every few minutes, but extra time will be granted when necessary.

In order for you to become accustomed to using the profit table, the first 3 bids will be for practice, and will involve no profit or loss. At the end of the session we will add up your profit and loss column and give you the resulting amount of money. This will be done in separate counting rooms, so you will not see the person with whom you have been bidding.

Are there any questions?

EXPERIMENT 10 Quantity Bids and Total Profits

Group number

PB	39		40		41		42		43		44		45		46		47		48		49		50		51		52		53		54	
	Qa	Qb	Qa	Qb	Qa	Qb	Qa	Qb	Qa	Qb	Qa	Qb	Qa	Qb	Qa	Qb	Qa	Qb	Qa	Qb	Qa	Qb	Qa	Qb	Qa	Qb	Qa	Qb	Qa	Qb	Qa	Qb
A	20	30	15	15	19	14	32	20	26	26	21	15	12	18	19	13	8	23	25	18	13	8	10	26	19	15	28	15	12	13	12	25
B	17	25	18	15	17	25	23	8	26	18	26	15	24	10	16	30	23	17	18	15	28	21	25	18	17	28	21	22	24	16	15	30
C	26	32	15	15	20	26	15	23	8	18	27	15	20	17	21	27	17	23	28	20	32	20	23	30	20	21	16	30	32	25	15	15
T																																
1	26	23	15	15	21	21	29	27	18	25	25	15	24	22	19	17	18	18	30	28	13	32	18	18	19	22	24	29	28	17	15	24
2	28	27	15	15	21	18	32	24	22	8	28	24	20	19	21	32	18	18	25	27	31	29	21	18	22	19	22	25	17	21	15	29
3	24	24	15	15	20	20	25	17	8	27	28	15	20	16	8	25	22	15	11	25	32	29	23	29	27	27	28	27	29	14	15	27
4	22	28	15	15	20	19	19	23	27	8	25	15	19	20	21	20	18	15	26	25	24	27	18	30	27	20	13	28	30	28	32	23
5	29	29	15	15	18	18	27	16	8	25	28	22	23	20	23	20	15	15	18	23	27	27	20	26	27	18	25	24	31	21	30	21
6	20	26	15	15	17	17	28	20	25	8	28	15	20	18	26	25	15	15	22	24	19	27	24	25	26	18	26	30	30	27	31	15
7	20	18	15	15	16	16	25	23	8	25	28	15	20	17	23	25	15	15	25	20	25	27	29	18	32	30	27	27	13	25	15	29
8	20	15	15	15	15	15	25	27	25	8	26	30	18	20	19	26	20	20	27	25	28	27	19	27	27	16	28	28	30	23	31	22
9	15	15	15	15	15	15	21	26	8	25	28	30	17	18	27	25	15	15	23	23	28	28	19	22	27	29	23	26	23	19	31	17
10	15	20	15	15	15	15	30	19	25	8	27	30	20	18	26	25	15	15	21	23	25	28	20	22	30	29	24	32	12	21	30	30
11	17	16	15	15	15	15	20	13	25	8	32	32	18	18	25	20	15	15	20	26	18	28	18	22	30	28	8	31	28	22	31	28
12	17	14	15	15	15	15	20	13	8	25	28	32	19	17	21	20	15	15	20	25	22	20	23	25	28	16	14	28	32	18	30	15
13	16	21	15	15	15	15	20	13	25	8	24	32	19	20	21	20	15	15	32	23	20	20	19	22	27	28	25	23	29	27	32	15
14	22	20	15	15	15	15	18	13	8	25	25	32	20	20	26	20	15	15	32	25	20	20	22	16	25	28	25	23	30	21	15	30
15	23	23	15	15	15	15	15	13	25	8	22	32	20	20	25	30	15	25	32	27	17	20	22	22	25	28	16	27	32	26	15	21
16	19	22	15	15	15	15	13	13	8	25	22	22	20	19	22	20	8	15	21	23	17	20	18	22	28	28	27	31	27	24	24	21
17	18	20	15	15	15	15	16	13	25	8	14	24	20	20	20	20	15	15	23	21	26	20	16	25	27	27	31	28	25	32	32	23
18	18	17	15	15	15	15	25	16	8	25	30	21	20	20	20	20	15	15	21	25	20	20	17	22	25	18	30	30	31	15	31	23
19	17	8	15	15	15	15	29	15	25	8	25	15	20	18	21	20	15	15	20	26	20	20	26	17	25	19	27	27	32	20	32	23
20	15	25	15	15	15	15	23	23	8	25	24	22	20	20	20	20	15	15	20	23	20	20	22	22	25	19	27	32	30	16	27	18
21	17	8	15	15	19	13	19	23	25	8	15	23	19	20	20	20	15	25	20	20	25	25	26	23	30	20	28	28	30	25	30	30
22	23	25	20	15	20	20	13	23	8	25	15	15	19	20	20	20	25	25	20	21	25	25	15	22	23	18	27	15	29	28	32	23
πa	$3.37		$3.98		$3.84		$3.32		$3.81		$1.85		$3.63		$2.93		$3.46		$2.34		$2.31		$2.76		$2.46		$1.61		$2.07		$2.14	
πb	$3.19		$3.93		$3.87		$2.61		$3.93		$1.72		$3.51		$3.12		$4.01		$2.70		$2.57		$3.16		$1.83		$2.50		$1.81		$2.09	

Key: PB = Practice bids
Qa = Quantity choice by player a
T = Transactions
πa = Profit to player a

271

Appendix XI

EXPERIMENT 11

OLIGOPOLY

Duopoly, Complete Information, Quantity Variation
Experiment Designed to Induce Cooperative Behavior

> Instructions
> Profit Sheet
> Profit Table
> Complete Results for Subjects

Instructions

The National Science Foundation, the Ford Foundation, and the Office of Naval Research have provided funds for the conduct of research regarding economic decisions. If you follow instructions carefully and make appropriate decisions, you may earn an appreciable amount of money. You cannot lose your own money, but a poor choice will result in small or no profit to you. *You may keep all the money that you earn.*

You will be paired at random with one other person. You will not see this person or speak with him at any time. You will never know the identity of your competition, nor will he be aware of yours.

Imagine that you and your competition are the sole producers of some standardized commodity. You and he will engage in a *single* transaction by means of a written bid, the bid representing the quantity of the commodity each of you will produce for the transaction.

You will be furnished with a table showing the various levels of profit or loss you and your competition can attain. You may produce any quantity listed across the top of the table, while the quantity produced by your competition is listed down the left-hand margin. Both your profits and his profits are represented within the body of the table by the intersection of the quantities produced. The left figure at each intersection is your profit for the transaction, while the right figure is the profit earned by your competition. For example, you might select a quantity of 24; you would receive one of the profits in the 24th column. If your competition had selected a quantity of 28, then both profits would be at the intersection of column 24 (your bid) and row 28 (his bid). The profit for you at this point is 750 (75.0 cents) and the profit for your competition is 850 (85.0 cents). Decimal points have been omitted for simplicity, but may always be considered to be located one place in from the right.

In addition to the profits in the table, it is possible for both you and your competitor to earn an additional $4.00 apiece. You will each receive this extra $4.00 if your profit *plus* your opponent's profit exceeds $3.55. Thus, in the example above, where you produced 24 and your competitor 28, the sum of your profits was only $1.60 (75 + 85), and you could *not* have received the additional $4.00. If, however, you had produced a quantity of 10 and he had produced 20, then you would have made $1.20 and he would have made $2.40. The sum of these profits ($1.20 + $2.40 = $3.60) *does* exceed $3.55, so you would each get the additional $4.00. Your total for the session would be $5.20 ($4.00 + $1.20) and your competitor's total would be $6.40 ($4.00 + $2.40).

Only one bid will determine the amount of profit you can earn. Preceding this one transaction, however, you will be given 10 practice trials so you may become accustomed to using the profit table. These bids will involve no profit or loss to you, and will not count toward determining whether or not you receive the additional $4.00.

For each practice trial and the final transaction you will select and record a quantity on the profit sheet provided for that purpose. You may select any quantity across the top of the table, and then record it. An experimental assistant will then inform you of the quantity chosen by your competition and, for each practice trial, will indicate the amount of money you would have made. At the end of 10 practice trials we will announce that the next trial will be the final transaction, and the money you earn from that decision will be the amount you take home.

You will be paid in separate counting rooms, so you will not see the person with whom you have been bidding.

Are there any questions?

Profit Sheet

Number_____   Name_____

Cubicle_____   Date_____   Phone_____

Transaction, practice trials	My quantity bid	Competition's quantity bid	My profit or loss	His profit or loss
1				
2				
3				
4				
5				
6				
7				
8				
9				
10				
Final payoff transaction				

Profit Table

	Quantity produced											
	8		**9**		**10**		**11**		**12**		**13**	
	M	*C*	*M*	*C*	*M*	*C*	*M*	*C*	*M*	*C*	*M*	*C*
8	1400	1400	1500	1350	1650	1300	1800	1300	1900	1250	2000	1200
9	1350	1500	1500	1500	1600	1450	1750	1400	1850	1400	1950	1350
10	1300	1650	1450	1600	1600	1600	1700	1550	1800	1500	1900	1450
11	1300	1800	1400	1750	1550	1700	1650	1650	1750	1600	1850	1550
12	1250	1900	1400	1850	1500	1800	1600	1750	1700	1700	1800	1650
13	1200	2000	1350	1950	1450	1900	1550	1850	1650	1800	1750	1750
14	1200	2100	1300	2050	1400	2000	1500	1950	1600	1900	1700	1850
15	1150	2200	1250	2150	1400	2100	1450	2000	1550	1950	1650	1900
16	1150	2300	1250	2200	1350	2150	1450	2100	1500	2000	1600	1950
17	1100	2350	1200	2300	1300	2250	1400	2150	1450	2100	1550	2050
18	1050	2400	1150	2350	1250	2300	1350	2200	1400	2200	1500	2050
19	1050	2500	1150	2400	1200	2350	1300	2300	1350	2200	1450	2100
20	1000	2550	1100	2450	1200	2400	1250	2300	1300	2200	1400	2150
21	950	2600	1050	2550	1150	2400	1200	2350	1250	2250	1350	2150
22	950	2650	1000	2550	1100	2450	1150	2350	1200	2250	1300	2200
23	900	2650	1000	2550	1050	2450	1100	2350	1200	2300	1200	2200
24	850	2650	950	2550	1000	2450	1100	2400	1150	2300	1150	2200
25	850	2700	900	2600	1000	2500	1050	2400	1100	2300	1100	2200
26	800	2700	900	2600	950	2450	1000	2350	1050	2250	1050	2150
27	800	2700	850	2550	900	2450	950	2350	1000	2250	1000	2150
28	750	2650	800	2550	850	2450	900	2350	950	2200	950	2100
29	700	2650	750	2550	800	2400	850	2300	900	2200	900	2050
30	700	2600	750	2500	800	2400	800	2250	850	2150	850	2000
31	650	2600	700	2450	750	2350	750	2200	800	2100	800	1950
32	600	2550	650	2400	700	2300	700	2150	750	2000	750	1900
33	600	2500	600	2350	650	2250	700	2100	700	1950	700	1850
34	550	2400	600	2300	600	2150	650	2000	650	1900	650	1750
35	500	2350	550	2200	600	2100	600	1950	600	1800	600	1650
36	500	2300	500	2150	550	2000	550	1850	550	1700	550	1550
37	450	2200	500	2050	500	1900	500	1750	500	1600	500	1450
38	400	2100	450	1950	450	1800	450	1650	450	1500	450	1350
39	400	2000	400	1850	400	1700	400	1550	400	1400	400	1200
40	350	1900	350	1750	400	1600	350	1400	350	1250	350	1100
41	350	1800	350	1600	350	1450	350	1300	300	1100	300	950
42	300	1650	300	1500	300	1300	300	1150	250	1000	250	800
43	250	1500	250	1350	250	1200	250	1000	200	850	200	650
44	250	1400	250	1200	200	1050	200	850	150	700	150	500
45	200	1250	200	1050	200	900	150	700	100	500	100	350
46	150	1100	150	900	150	700	100	550	50	350	50	150
47	150	900	100	750	100	550	50	350	00	150	00	00
48	100	750	100	550	50	350	00	150	00	00	00	−150
49	50	550	50	350	00	150	00	00	000	−150	−50	−350
50	50	400	00	200	00	00	00	−200	−50	−400	−100	−600
51	00	200	00	00	00	−200	−50	−400	−100	−600	−150	−800
52	00	00	00	−200	−50	−400	−100	−600	−150	−800	−200	−1000
53	00	−200	−50	−400	−100	−600	−150	−800	−200	−1050	−250	−1250
54	−50	−400	−100	−600	−150	−850	−200	−1050	−250	−1250	−300	−1500
55	−50	−650	−100	−850	−200	−1100	−250	−1300	−300	−1501	−350	−1750
56	−100	−850	−150	−1100	−200	−1300	−300	−1550	−350	−1750	−400	−2000
57	−150	−1100	−200	−1350	−250	−1550	−350	−1800	−400	−2050	−450	−2250
58	−150	−1350	−250	−1600	−300	−1850	−350	−2050	−450	−2300	−500	−2550
59	−200	−1650	−250	−1850	−350	−2100	−400	−2350	−500	−2550	−550	−2800
60	−250	−1900	−300	−2150	−400	−2400	−450	−2600	−550	−2850	−600	−3100
61	−250	−2150	−350	−2400	−400	−2650	−500	−2900	−600	−3150	−650	−3400
62	−300	−2450	−350	−2700	−450	−2950	−550	−3200	−650	−3450	−700	−3700
63	−350	−2750	−400	−3000	−500	−3250	−600	−3500	−700	−3750	−750	−4000
64	−350	−3050	−450	−3300	−550	−3550	−650	−3800	−750	−4050	−800	−4350

(Left axis label: Quantity produced by my competition)

M = Profit to me   *C* = Profit to my competition

by me

14		15		16		17		18		19	
M	C	M	C	M	C	M	C	M	C	M	C
2100	1200	2200	1150	2300	1150	2350	1100	2400	1050	2500	1050
2050	1300	2150	1250	2200	1250	2300	1200	2350	1150	2400	1150
2000	1400	2100	1400	2150	1350	2250	1300	2300	1250	2350	1200
1950	1500	2000	1450	2100	1450	2150	1400	2200	1350	2300	1300
1900	1600	1950	1550	2000	1500	2100	1450	2200	1400	2200	1350
1850	1700	1900	1650	1950	1600	2050	1550	2050	1500	2100	1450
1750	1750	1850	1700	1950	1650	1950	1660	2000	1550	2050	1500
1700	1850	1800	1800	1850	1770	1900	1650	1900	1600	1950	1550
1650	1950	1700	1850	1750	1750	1800	1700	1850	1650	1900	1600
1600	1950	1650	1900	1700	1800	1750	1750	1800	1700	1800	1600
1550	2000	1600	1900	1650	1850	1700	1800	1700	1700	1700	1650
1500	2050	1550	1950	1600	1900	1600	1800	1650	1700	1650	1650
1450	2050	1500	2000	1500	1900	1550	1800	1550	1750	1550	1700
1400	2100	1400	2000	1450	1900	1450	1800	1500	1750	1500	1650
1300	2100	1350	2000	1400	1900	1400	1800	1400	1750	1400	1650
1250	2100	1300	2000	1300	1900	1350	1800	1350	1700	1350	1650
1200	2100	1250	2000	1250	1900	1250	1800	1250	1700	1250	1600
1150	2100	1200	2000	1200	1900	1200	1800	1200	1700	1200	1600
1100	2050	1100	1950	1150	1850	1150	1750	1150	1650	1100	1550
1050	2050	1050	1900	1050	1800	1050	1700	1050	1600	1050	1500
1000	2000	1000	1850	1050	1750	1000	1650	1000	1550	950	1450
950	1950	900	1800	950	1700	950	1600	900	1500	900	1350
850	1900	850	1700	850	1650	850	1550	850	1400	800	1300
800	1850	750	1650	800	1600	800	1450	750	1350	750	1200
750	1750	700	1550	750	1500	700	1400	700	1250	650	1150
700	1700	650	1450	700	1450	650	1300	600	1150	600	1050
650	1600	600	1400	600	1350	600	1200	550	1050	500	950
600	1500	500	1250	550	1250	500	1100	500	950	450	800
550	1400	450	1150	500	1150	450	1000	400	850	350	700
500	1300			400	1000	400	850	350	700	300	550
400	1200	400	1050	350	900	300	750	250	600	200	450
350	1050	350	900	300	750	250	600	200	450	150	300
300	950	300	800	250	600	200	450	100	300	50	150
250	800	200	650	150	450	100	300	50	150	00	00
200	650	150	500	100	300	50	150	00	00	−50	−150
150	500	100	300	50	150	00	00	−50	−150	−150	−300
100	350	50	150	00	00	−50	−150	−100	−350	−200	−500
50	150	00	00	−50	−150	−100	−350	−200	−500	−300	−700
00	00	−50	−150	−100	−350	−200	−550	−250	−700	−350	−900
−50	−150	−100	−350	−150	−550	−250	−750	−350	−900	−450	−1100
−100	−350	−150	−550	−250	−750	−300	−950	−400	−1150	−500	−1300
−150	−550	−200	−750	−300	−950	−400	−1150	−500	−1350	−600	−1550
−200	−800	−300	−1000	−350	−1200	−450	−1400	−550	−1600	−650	−1800
−250	−1000	−350	−1200	−400	−1400	−500	−1600	−600	−1800	−750	−2000
−300	−1200	−400	−1450	−500	−1650	−600	−1850	−700	−2050	−800	−2250
−350	−1450	−450	−1650	−550	−1900	−650	−2100	−750	−2300	−900	−2500
−400	−1700	−500	−1900	−600	−2150	−700	−2350	−850	−2550	−950	−2800
−500	−1850	−600	−2200	−700	−2400	−800	−2600	−900	−2850	−1050	−3050
−550	−2200	−650	−2450	−750	−2650	−850	−2900	−1000	−3100	−1100	−3350
−600	−2500	−700	−2700	−800	−2950	−950	−3150	−1050	−3400	−1200	−3600
−650	−2750	−750	−3000	−850	−3200	−1000	−3450	−1150	−3700	−1250	−3900
−700	−3050	−850	−3300	−950	−3500	−1050	−3750	−1200	−4000	−1350	−4200
−750	−3350	−900	−3600	−1050	−3800	−1150	−4050	−1250	−4300	−1400	−4550
−800	−3650	−1000	−3900	−1050	−4100	−1200	−4350	−1350	−4600	−1500	−4850
−850	−3950	−1000	−4200	−1150	−4450	−1250	−4700	−1400	−4950	−1550	−5200
−950	−4250	−1050	−4500	−1200	−4750	−1350	−5000	−1500	−5250	−1650	−5500
−1000	−4600	−1100	−4850	−1250	−5100	−1400	−5350	−1550	−5600	−1700	−5850

Profit Table (Continued)

Quantity produced

Quantity produced by my competition	20 M	20 C	21 M	21 C	22 M	22 C	23 M	23 C	24 M	24 C	25 M	25 C
8	2550	1000	2600	950	2650	950	2650	900	2650	850	2700	850
9	2450	1100	2550	1050	2550	1000	2550	1000	2550	950	2600	900
10	2400	1200	2400	1150	2450	1100	2450	1050	2450	1000	2500	1000
11	2300	1250	2350	1200	2350	1150	2350	1100	2400	1100	2400	1050
12	2200	1300	2250	1250	2250	1200	2300	1200	2300	1150	2300	1100
13	2150	1400	2150	1350	2200	1300	2200	1200	2200	1150	2200	1100
14	2050	1450	2100	1400	2100	1300	2100	1250	2100	1200	2100	1150
15	2000	1500	2000	1400	2000	1350	2000	1300	2000	1250	2000	1200
16	1900	1500	1900	1450	1900	1400	1900	1300	1900	1250	1900	1200
17	1800	1550	1800	1450	1800	1400	1800	1350	1800	1250	1800	1200
18	1750	1550	1750	1500	1750	1400	1700	1350	1700	1250	1700	1200
19	1700	1550	1650	1500	1650	1400	1650	1350	1600	1250	1600	1200
20	1600	1600	1550	1550	1550	1400	1550	1350	1500	1250	1500	1200
21	1550	1550	1500	1500	1450	1400	1450	1300	1400	1250	1400	1150
22	1400	1550	1400	1450	1400	1400	1350	1300	1300	1200	1300	1100
23	1350	1550	1300	1450	1300	1350	1250	1250	1200	1150	1200	1100
24	1250	1500	1250	1400	1200	1300	1150	1200	1150	1150	1100	1050
25	1200	1500	1150	1400	1100	1300	1100	1200	1050	1100	1000	1000
26	1100	1450	1050	1350	1050	1200	1000	1100	950	1000	900	900
27	1000	1400	1000	1250	950	1150	900	1050	850	950	800	850
28	950	1300	900	1200	850	1100	800	1000	750	850	700	750
29	850	1250	800	1150	750	1000	700	900	650	800	600	650
30	800	1200	750	1050	700	950	600	800	550	700	500	600
31	700	1100	650	950	600	850	550	700	450	600	400	450
32	600	1000	550	850	500	750	450	600	350	500	300	350
33	550	900	500	750	400	650	350	500	250	350	200	250
34	450	800	400	650	350	500	250	400	200	250	100	150
35	400	700	300	550	250	400	150	250	50	100	000	000
36	300	550	250	400	150	250	50	100	00	00	-100	-150
37	200	400	150	250	50	100	00	00	-50	-100	-200	-250
38	150	300	50	150	00	00	-50	-150	-200	-300	-300	-450
39	50	150	00	00	-50	-150	-150	-300	-250	-450	-400	-600
40	00	00	-50	-150	-150	-300	-250	-450	-350	-600	-500	-800
41	-50	-150	-150	-300	-250	-450	-350	-650	-450	-800	-600	-950
42	-150	-300	-250	-500	-350	-650	-450	-800	-550	-1000	-700	-1150
43	-200	-500	-300	-650	-400	-850	-550	-1000	-650	-1200	-800	-1350
44	-300	-700	-400	-850	-500	-1050	-600	-1200	-750	-1400	-900	-1550
45	-400	-900	-500	-1050	-600	-1250	-700	-1400	-850	-1600	-1000	-1800
46	-450	-1100	-550	-1250	-700	-1450	-800	-1650	-950	-1800	-1100	-2000
47	-550	-1300	-650	-1500	-750	-1650	-900	-1850	-1050	-2050	-1200	-2250
48	-600	-1500	-750	-1750	-850	-1900	-1000	-2100	-1150	-2300	-1300	-2450
49	-700	-1750	-800	-1950	-950	-2150	-1100	-2350	-1200	-2500	-1400	-2700
50	-800	-2000	-900	-2200	-1050	-2400	-1150	-2600	-1300	-2800	-1500	-3000
51	-850	-2200	-1000	-2400	-1100	-2650	-1250	-2850	-1400	-3050	-1600	-3250
52	-950	-2450	-1050	-2700	-1200	-2900	-1350	-3100	-1500	-3300	-1700	-3500
53	-1000	-2750	-1150	-2950	-1300	-3150	-1450	-3350	-1600	-3600	-1800	-3800
54	-1100	-3000	-1250	-3200	-1400	-3450	-1550	-3650	-1700	-3850	-1900	-4100
55	-1200	-3300	-1300	-3500	-1450	-3700	-1650	-3950	-1800	-4150	-2000	-4400
56	-1250	-3550	-1400	-3800	-1550	-4000	-1700	-4250	-1900	-4450	-2100	-4700
57	-1350	-3850	-1500	-4100	-1650	-4300	-1800	-4550	-2000	-4750	-2200	-5000
58	-1400	-4150	-1550	-4400	-1750	-4600	-1900	-4850	-2100	-5100	-2300	-5300
59	-1550	-4450	-1650	-4700	-1800	-4950	-2000	-5150	-2200	-5400	-2400	-5650
60	-1650	-4800	-1750	-5000	-1900	-5250	-2100	-5500	-2300	-5750	-2500	-6000
61	-1700	-5100	-1800	-5350	-2000	-5600	-2200	-5850	-2400	-6100	-2600	-6300
62	-1750	-5450	-1900	-5700	-2100	-5950	-2300	-6200	-2450	-6400	-2700	-6650
63	-1800	-5750	-2000	-6000	-2200	-6300	-2350	-6550	-2550	-6800	-2800	-7050
64	-1900	-6100	-2100	-6400	-2250	-6650	-2450	-6900	-2650	-7150	-2900	-7400

M = Profit to me C = Profit to my competition

by me

26		27		28		29		30		31		32	
M	C	M	C	M	C	M	C	M	C	M	C	M	C
2700	800	2700	800	2650	750	2650	700	2600	700	2600	650	2550	600
2600	900	2550	850	2550	800	2550	750	2500	750	2450	700	2400	650
2450	950	2450	900	2450	850	2400	800	2400	800	2350	750	2300	700
2350	1000	2350	950	2350	900	2300	850	2250	800	2200	750	2150	700
2250	1050	2250	1000	2200	950	2200	900	2150	800	2100	800	2000	750
2150	1050	2150	1000	2100	950	2050	900	2000	850	1950	800	1900	750
2050	1100	2050	1050	2000	1000	1950	950	1900	850	1850	800	1750	750
1950	1100	1900	1050	1900	1000	1850	1000	1800	900	1700	850	1650	750
1850	1150	1800	1050	1750	1050	1700	950	1650	850	1600	800	1500	750
1750	1150	1700	1050	1650	1000	1600	950	1550	850	1450	800	1400	700
1650	1150	1600	1050	1550	1000	1500	900	1400	850	1350	750	1250	700
1550	1100	1500	1050	1450	950	1350	900	1300	800	1200	750	1150	650
1450	1100	1400	1000	1300	950	1250	850	1200	800	1100	700	1000	600
1350	1050	1250	1000	1200	900	1150	800	1050	750	950	650	850	550
1200	1050	1150	950	1100	850	1000	750	950	700	850	600	750	500
1100	1000	1050	900	1000	800	900	700	800	600	700	550	600	450
1000	950	950	850	850	750	800	650	700	550	600	450	500	350
900	900	850	800	750	700	650	600	600	500	450	400	350	300
800	800	750	700	650	600	550	500	450	400	350	300	250	200
700	750	600	600	550	500	450	400	350	300	250	200	150	100
600	650	500	550	400	400	350	300	250	200	150	100	000	000
500	550	400	450	300	350	200	200	150	100	000	000	-150	-100
400	450	300	350	200	250	100	150	000	000	-150	-100	-250	-200
300	350	200	250	100	150	000	000	-100	-150	-250	-250	-350	-300
200	250	100	150	000	000	-100	-150	-200	-250	-300	-350	-500	-500
100	150	000	000	-100	-150	-200	-250	-350	-400	-450	-500	-600	-650
000	000	-100	-150	-200	-250	-300	-400	-450	-500	-600	-650	-750	-800
-100	-150	-200	-250	-300	-400	-450	-550	-600	-700	-700	-800	-850	-950
-200	-250	-300	-400	-400	-550	-550	-700	-700	-850	-850	-1000	-1000	-1150
-300	-400	-400	-550	-550	-700	-650	-850	-800	-1000	-950	-1150	-1150	-1300
-400	-600	-500	-750	-650	-900	-800	-1050	-950	-1200	-1100	-1350	-1250	-1500
-500	-750	-600	-900	-750	-1050	-900	-1200	-1050	-1400	-1200	-1550	-1400	-1700
-600	-950	-750	-1100	-850	-1250	-1000	-1400	-1200	-1600	-1350	-1750	-1500	-1900
-700	-1100	-850	-1300	-1000	-1450	-1150	-1600	-1300	-1800	-1450	-1950	-1650	-2100
-800	-1300	-950	-1500	-1100	-1650	-1250	-1800	-1400	-2000	-1600	-2150	-1750	-2350
-900	-1500	-1050	-1700	-1200	-1850	-1350	-2050	-1550	-2200	-1700	-2400	-1900	-2550
-1000	-1750	-1150	-1900	-1300	-2100	-1500	-2250	-1650	-2450	-1850	-2600	-2000	-2800
-1100	-1950	-1250	-2150	-1450	-2300	-1600	-2500	-1800	-2700	-1950	-2850	-2150	-3050
-1200	-2200	-1400	-2350	-1550	-2500	-1700	-2750	-1900	-2900	-2100	-3100	-2300	-3300
-1350	-2400	-1500	-2600	-1650	-2800	-1850	-3000	-2000	-3150	-2200	-3350	-2400	-3550
-1450	-2750	-1600	-2850	-1750	-3050	-1950	-3250	-2150	-3450	-2350	-3600	-2550	-3800
-1550	-2900	-1700	-3100	-1900	-3300	-2050	-3500	-2250	-3700	-2450	-3900	-2650	-4100
-1650	-3200	-1800	-3400	-2000	-3600	-2200	-3800	-2400	-4000	-2600	-4200	-2900	-4400
-1750	-3450	-1900	-3650	-2100	-3850	-2300	-4050	-2500	-4250	-2700	-4450	-2900	-4650
-1850	-3700	-2050	-3950	-2200	-4150	-2400	-4350	-2600	-4550	-2850	-4750	-3050	-4950
-1950	-4000	-2150	-4200	-2350	-4450	-2550	-4650	-2750	-4850	-2950	-5050	-3150	-5300
-2050	-4300	-2250	-4500	-2450	-4750	-2650	-4950	-2850	-5150	-3100	-5400	-3300	-5600
-2150	-4600	-2350	-4800	-2550	-5050	-2750	-5250	-3000	-5500	-3200	-5700	-3450	-5900
-2250	-4900	-2450	-5150	-2650	-5350	-2900	-5600	-3100	-5800	-3350	-6050	-3550	-6250
-2350	-5200	-2550	-5450	-2800	-5700	-3000	-5900	-3250	-6150	-3450	-6350	-3700	-6600
-2450	-5550	-2700	-5800	-2900	-6000	-3100	-6250	-3350	-6450	-3600	-6700	-3800	-6950
-2600	-5900	-2800	-6100	-3000	-6350	-3250	-6600	-3450	-6800	-3700	-7050	-3950	-7300
-2700	-6200	-2900	-6450	-3100	-6700	-3350	-6950	-3600	-7200	-3850	-7400	-4050	-7650
-2800	-6550	-3000	-6800	-3250	-7050	-3450	-7300	-3700	-7550	-3950	-7800	-4200	-8050
-2900	-6900	-3100	-7150	-3350	-7400	-3600	-7650	-3800	-7900	-4100	-8150	-4300	-8400
-3000	-7300	-3200	-7550	-3450	-7800	-3700	-8050	-3950	-8300	-4200	-8550	-4450	-8800
-3100	-7650	-3350	-7900	-3550	-8150	-3800	-8400	-4050	-8700	-4350	-8950	-4600	-9200

EXPERIMENT 11   Quantity Bids and Total Profits

Group number

PB	55		56		57		58		59		60	
	Qa	Qb	Qa	Qb	Qa	Qb	Qa	Qb	Qa	Qb	Qa	Qb
1	15	12	15	15	15	16	14	15	15	15	8	21
2	15	13	15	22	15	19	15	15	15	15	9	22
3	15	14	15	22	16	20	15	15	25	15	10	22
4	15	15	15	22	15	12	15	15	25	15	11	22
5	15	16	22	22	15	14	15	15	28	25	8	18
6	15	17	15	21	15	29	15	15	15	16	12	22
7	15	18	21	21	15	22	15	15	15	15	8	22
8	15	19	15	20	15	10	15	15	28	15	8	22
9	15	15	15	20	15	24	15	15	15	15	8	22
10	15	15	15	15	15	13	15	15	15	15	8	22
Qi	15	15	15	15	15	15	15	15	15	15	8	22
πa	\$5.80		\$5.80		\$5.80		\$5.80		\$5.80		\$4.95	
πb	\$5.80		\$5.80		\$5.80		\$5.80		\$5.80		\$6.65	

Key: PB = Practice bids
Qa = Quantity choice by player a
Qi = Quantity choice which determines profits
πa = Profit to player a

Appendix XII

EXPERIMENT 12

OLIGOPOLY

Duopoly, Complete Information, Quantity Variation
Experiment Designed to Induce Rivalistic Behavior

Instructions
Profit Sheet Same as in Experiment 11
Profit Table Same as in Appendix XI
Complete Results for Subjects

Instructions

The National Science Foundation, the Ford Foundation, and the Office of Naval Research have provided funds for the conduct of research regarding economic decisions. If you follow instructions carefully and make appropriate decisions, you may earn an appreciable amount of money. You cannot lose your own money, but a poor choice will result in small or no profit to you. *You may keep all the money that you earn.*

You will be paired at random with one other person. You will not see this person or speak with him at any time. You will never know the identity of your competition, nor will he be aware of yours.

Imagine that you and your competition are the sole producers of some standardized commodity. You and he will engage in a *single* transaction by means of a written bid, the bid representing the quantity of the commodity each of you will produce for the transaction.

You will be furnished with a table showing the various levels of profit or loss you and your competition can attain. You may produce any quantity listed across the top of the table, while the quantity produced by your competition is listed down the left-hand margin. Both your profits and his profits are represented within the body of the table by the intersection of

the quantities produced.   The left figure at each intersection is your profit
for the transaction, while the right figure is the profit earned by your competition.   For example, you might select a quantity of 24; you would receive
one of the profits in the 24th column.   If your competition had selected a
quantity of 28, then both profits would be at the intersection of column 24
(your bid) and row 28 (his bid).   The profit for you at this point is 750
(75.0 cents) and the profit for your competition is 850 (85.0 cents).   Decimal
points have been omitted for simplicity, but may always be considered to
be located one place in from the right.

In addition to the profits represented in the body of the table, the person
who *makes the larger amount of money, or who loses the least,* will receive an
additional profit of $8.00.   Thus, in the example you produced a quantity
of 24 and your competition a quantity of 28; you would have received a
total profit of 75.0 cents, and he would have received 85.0 cents.   Since he
made $.10 more he would receive an extra $8.00, or a total of $8.85.   Should
both your bids have been for the same quantity, say 24, then you would
share the $8.00 equally and each of you would make an additional 1150
($1.15), for a total of $5.15.

Preceding the one transaction on which you can earn money, you will be
given ten practice trials so you may become accustomed to using the profit
table.   These bids will involve no profit or loss to you, and will not count
toward determining who will receive the additional $8.00.

For each practice trial and the final transaction you will select and record
a quantity on the profit sheet provided for that purpose.   You may select
any quantity across the top of the table, and then record it.   An experimental assistant will then inform you of the quantity chosen by your competition, and, for each practice trial, will indicate the amount of money you
would have made.   At the end of the ten practice trials we will announce
that the next trial will be the final transaction, and the money you earn from
that decision will be the amount you take home.

You will be paid in separate counting rooms, so you will not see the person
with whom you have been bidding.

Are there any questions?

EXPERIMENT 12   Quantity Bids and Total Profits

Group number

PB	61 Qa	61 Qb	62 Qa	62 Qb	63 Qa	63 Qb	64 Qa	64 Qb	65 Qa	65 Qb	66 Qa	66 Qb	67 Qa	67 Qb
1	8	20	28	17	27	23	19	20	17	24	18	24	18	22
2	11	21	22	11	11	25	9	18	20	18	12	19	28	20
3	13	19	18	26	9	27	26	28	19	19	15	13	15	25
4	15	22	23	31	11	25	16	25	12	20	13	32	14	10
5	19	8	32	28	10	20	24	29	14	20	17	11	14	13
6	20	11	26	21	8	21	32	15	16	32	14	15	16	17
7	21	13	24	24	20	13	13	16	27	30	19	10	16	9
8	22	15	31	32	22	12	21	14	25	30	20	25	16	12
9	22	13	29	27	23	8	20	19	17	30	11	17	25	24
10	22	15	25	21	20	11	10	17	19	30	16	21	16	19
Qi	30	30	30	30	30	30	30	30	30	30	30	30	28	30
πa	$4.00		$4.00		$4.00		$4.00		$4.00		$4.00		$0.20	
πb	$4.00		$4.00		$4.00		$4.00		$4.00		$4.00		$8.25	

Key: PB = Practice bids
Qa = Quantity choice by player a
Qi = Quantity choice which determines profits
πa = Profit to player a

Appendix XIII

OLIGOPOLY

Duopoly, Incomplete Information, Price Variation

Profit Table
Complete Results for Subjects
(Instructions Reproduced in Chapter 10)

Table of Profit to Seller A

My price	Profit when I have the lower price	Profit when I am tied for low price	Loss when I have the higher price
0.5	.13	.00	
1.0	.35	.11	−.25
1.5	.53	.20	−.25
2.0	.67	.27	−.25
2.5	.77	.32	−.25
3.0	.83	.35	−.25
3.5	.85	.36	−.25
4.0	.83	.35	−.25
4.5	.77	.32	−.25
5.0		.27	−.25

EXPERIMENT 13 Price Bids and Total Profits

Group number

PB	1 Pa	1 Pb	2 Pa	2 Pb	3 Pa	3 Pb	4 Pa	4 Pb	5 Pa	5 Pb	6 Pa	6 Pb	7 Pa	7 Pb	8 Pa	8 Pb	9 Pa	9 Pb	10 Pa	10 Pb	11 Pa	11 Pb	12 Pa	12 Pb	13 Pa	13 Pb	14 Pa	14 Pb	15 Pa	15 Pb	16 Pa	16 Pb	17 Pa	17 Pb
A	1.5	3.5	1.0	3.0	1.0	3.5	3.0	1.5	2.5	3.5	1.0	0.5	2.0	3.5	2.5	3.5	3.0	0.5	2.5	2.0	3.5	3.5	1.0	1.5	3.5	2.5	1.5	4.0	2.0	2.0	3.0	3.5	4.0	0.5
B	1.5	2.5	3.0	1.0	2.0	3.5	1.5	1.5	3.0	3.0	2.5	0.5	1.0	4.0	3.0	1.5	5.0	3.0	5.0	5.0	3.5	3.5	1.5	0.5	1.0	0.5	3.0	3.5	2.5	0.5	4.0	2.0	2.5	1.0
C	1.0	1.5	3.5	1.0	2.5	4.5	2.0	1.0	2.5	3.0	0.5	2.0	3.5	0.5	3.0	1.5	2.0	1.5	5.0	3.5	2.0	3.5	0.5	1.0	1.0	0.5	4.0	2.5	2.5	1.5	3.5	3.0	1.5	1.5

T	1 Pa	1 Pb	2 Pa	2 Pb	3 Pa	3 Pb	4 Pa	4 Pb	5 Pa	5 Pb	6 Pa	6 Pb	7 Pa	7 Pb	8 Pa	8 Pb	9 Pa	9 Pb	10 Pa	10 Pb	11 Pa	11 Pb	12 Pa	12 Pb	13 Pa	13 Pb	14 Pa	14 Pb	15 Pa	15 Pb	16 Pa	16 Pb	17 Pa	17 Pb
1	2.0	1.0	0.5	3.0	1.5	3.5	0.5	2.0	2.0	0.5	0.5	0.5	1.5	1.5	2.5	1.5	0.5	0.5	1.5	1.0	2.0	3.5	0.5	0.5	2.0	2.5	1.5	1.5	2.0	1.5	2.5	4.0	1.5	2.0
2	1.0	1.0	0.5	1.5	1.0	1.0	0.5	1.0	1.5	1.0	1.0	0.5	1.0	1.0	1.0	1.5	1.0	1.0	1.0	0.5	2.5	2.5	2.0	2.0	5.0	1.5	3.0	1.5	1.5	1.5	2.0	3.0	1.0	1.5
3	0.5	1.0	0.5	0.5	0.5	0.5	0.5	0.5	1.0	0.5	0.5	1.0	5.0	1.0	1.5	1.0	0.5	0.5	0.5	1.0	2.5	2.0	1.5	0.5	1.5	1.5	1.5	2.5	1.5	1.5	2.0	2.0	1.0	1.0
4	1.0	1.0	0.5	0.5	1.5	3.5	0.5	1.0	0.5	1.0	0.5	0.5	3.0	1.0	1.0	1.5	0.5	0.5	1.5	0.5	1.5	1.0	1.5	1.5	2.0	1.5	1.0	1.5	2.5	1.5	2.0	2.0	1.0	1.5
5	0.5	0.5	0.5	0.5	1.0	1.0	0.5	0.5	1.0	0.5	0.5	0.5	0.5	0.5	1.0	1.5	1.0	1.0	1.5	0.5	1.5	1.0	1.5	2.5	1.5	2.0	1.5	1.5	1.5	1.5	1.5	1.5	1.5	2.0
6	1.5	1.0	0.5	1.0	0.5	0.5	1.0	0.5	0.5	0.5	0.5	0.5	0.5	1.5	1.0	1.5	0.5	0.5	2.0	3.0	1.0	1.5	1.0	1.0	1.5	1.5	1.5	1.5	2.0	2.0	2.5	1.5	1.0	1.5
7	1.0	1.0	0.5	1.0	1.0	0.5	0.5	0.5	0.5	1.0	0.5	0.5	1.5	0.5	1.0	1.0	0.5	0.5	0.5	1.5	1.0	1.5	1.0	1.0	1.0	1.5	1.5	1.5	2.0	2.5	2.0	2.0	2.5	1.0
8	0.5	1.0	0.5	0.5	1.0	0.5	0.5	0.5	0.5	1.0	0.5	0.5	1.5	0.5	1.0	1.0	0.5	1.0	1.5	1.0	1.0	1.5	1.0	1.0	1.0	1.5	1.5	1.0	2.0	1.5	2.0	1.5	2.0	1.5
9	0.5	0.5	0.5	0.5	0.5	1.0	0.5	0.5	3.0	0.5	0.5	0.5	3.5	1.0	1.0	0.5	2.0	0.5	1.0	2.0	1.0	1.5	1.0	1.0	1.0	1.5	1.0	1.5	2.5	1.5	2.0	1.5	2.0	2.0
10	0.5	0.5	0.5	0.5	0.5	0.5	0.5	1.0	0.5	1.5	0.5	1.0	0.5	1.0	0.5	0.5	0.5	0.5	1.5	1.5	1.0	1.5	1.0	1.0	1.0	1.5	1.5	2.0	2.0	2.0	2.0	2.0	2.5	2.5
11	0.5	0.5	0.5	0.5	0.5	0.5	0.5	0.5	0.5	0.5	0.5	0.5	1.0	1.0	1.0	1.0	0.5	0.5	0.5	0.5	1.0	0.5	1.0	1.0	1.0	1.5	2.0	1.5	2.0	1.5	1.5	1.5	3.0	3.0
12	1.0	0.5	0.5	0.5	0.5	1.0	0.5	0.5	0.5	0.5	0.5	0.5	1.0	0.5	0.5	0.5	2.5	0.5	1.5	1.0	1.0	1.0	1.0	1.0	1.0	1.0	2.0	1.0	1.5	2.5	1.5	2.0	3.5	3.5
13	1.0	0.5	0.5	0.5	0.5	0.5	0.5	0.5	2.5	0.5	0.5	0.5	0.5	4.5	1.0	0.5	0.5	1.0	1.5	1.0	1.0	1.5	1.0	1.0	1.0	1.0	1.0	1.0	1.5	1.5	1.0	1.0	3.0	3.5
14	0.5	0.5	0.5	0.5	0.5	0.5	0.5	0.5	0.5	0.5	0.5	0.5	1.0	0.5	0.5	1.0	0.5	0.5	1.5	1.0	1.0	0.5	1.0	1.0	1.5	1.0	1.0	1.0	1.5	1.5	1.0	2.0	1.5	3.0
15	0.5	1.0	0.5	0.5	1.5	0.5	0.5	1.0	1.0		0.5	0.5	2.0	2.0	0.5	0.5	2.0	1.0	2.0	1.5	2.5	2.0	0.5	1.0	1.0	1.5	1.0	1.0	1.5	1.5	1.0	3.0	3.0	2.0

	1 Pa	1 Pb	2 Pa	2 Pb	3 Pa	3 Pb	4 Pa	4 Pb	5 Pa	5 Pb	6 Pa	6 Pb	7 Pa	7 Pb	8 Pa	8 Pb	9 Pa	9 Pb	10 Pa	10 Pb	11 Pa	11 Pb	12 Pa	12 Pb	13 Pa	13 Pb	14 Pa	14 Pb	15 Pa	15 Pb	16 Pa	16 Pb	17 Pa	17 Pb
πa	$2.60		$2.76		$2.53		$2.89		$0.52		$2.13		$3.66		$2.85		$2.01		$0.57		$3.45		$3.40		$3.96		$3.19		$2.94		$5.77		$6.93	
πb	$2.44		$2.00		$2.27		$1.37		$3.24		$2.51		$2.20		$3.41		$2.01		$5.29		$4.75		$3.60		$4.78		$5.35		$5.88		$4.01		$3.83	

Key: PB = Practice bids
Pa = Price choice by player a
T = Transactions
πa = Profit to player a

285

Appendix XIV

Instructions to Seller A

The National Science Foundation, the Ford Foundation, and the Office of Naval Research have provided funds for the conduct of research regarding economic decisions. If you follow instructions carefully and make appropriate decisions, you may earn an appreciable amount of money.

We will give you $2.50 of capital to start with. *You may keep this money plus all that you earn during the session.* It is possible to end the session with considerably more than $2.50. However, you can lose part or all of the $2.50 you are given if your decisions are not made carefully, but you cannot lose more than that amount. The session will be stopped if, at any time, you should happen to lose all of your earnings as well as the $2.50 of capital.

You will be grouped at random with two other players. *You will not see these persons or speak with them at any time.* You will never know the identities of your counterparts, called sellers *B* and *C*, nor will they be aware of yours.

You and your anonymous counterparts will engage in a series of transactions by means of written bids. Imagine that you and they are engaged in selling some standardized commodity. *You must bid on each transaction.* The bids are in terms of the price you will charge for the commodity for that transaction. If your price bid for a given transaction is lower than both seller *B*'s and seller *C*'s bids, you will earn some amount of money. If

286

either one or both of your counterparts has a price bid lower than yours, you will lose money on that transaction. If your price bid is tied for low price with either one or both of your counterparts, you will not lose money, but you may not gain any either.

You will be furnished with a table showing the various levels of profit or loss you can attain. The figures within the table are the profits that you will receive depending on the prices set by you, seller *B*, and seller *C*. For example, on a given transaction you might select a price of 2.0; you would receive one of the profits in the fourth row, depending upon the prices selected by your counterparts for that transaction. If they both bid prices higher than 2.0, then you would receive 67¢. However, if on the same transaction one of them also had bid a price of 2.0, and the other some higher price, then you would receive a profit of 27¢. Similarly, if both of your counterparts had bid prices of 2.0, you would have received a profit of 14¢ on the transaction. However, if either one or both of your counterparts had bid a price lower than your price bid of 2.0, you would have lost 25¢ on the transaction.

The process is started by each player selecting and recording a price on the yellow sheet provided for that purpose. You may select any price on the left-hand side of the table, and then record it. An experimental assistant will then inform you of the amount of profit or loss you made on that transaction. After each transaction your yellow sheet should show both your price bid and your profit from that transaction.

The process is repeated over and over. You may select the same price each time; you do not have to do so, however. You will be given a few minutes for each decision. You will have three practice trials so that you may become accustomed to using the profit table.

For each transaction you will record the price selected as well as the profit or loss resulting from your decision. At the end of the session we will add up your profit column and give you that amount of money, or take back any losses you incurred, up to the $2.50 you receive initially. This will be done in separate counting rooms, so you will not see the persons with whom you have been bidding.

Are there any questions?

Table of Profit to Seller A

My price	Profit when I have the lowest price	Profit when I am tied for low price with one other person	Profit when I am tied for low price with two other persons	Loss when any other price is lower than mine
0.5	.13	.00	.00	
1.0	.35	.11	.03	−.25
1.5	.53	.20	.09	−.25
2.0	.67	.27	.14	−.25
2.5	.77	.32	.17	−.25
3.0	.83	.35	.19	−.25
3.5	.85	.36	.20	−.25
4.0	.83	.35	.19	−.25
4.5	.77	.32	.17	−.25
5.0		.27	.14	−.25

EXPERIMENT 14 Price Bids and Total Profits

Group number

	18			19			20			21			22			23			24			25			26			27			28			
PB	Pa	Pb	Pc	Pa	Pb	Pc	Pa	Pb	Pc	Pa	Pb	Pc	Pa	Pb	Pc	Pa	Pb	Pc	Pa	Pb	Pc	Pa	Pb	Pc	Pa	Pb	Pc	Pa	Pb	Pc	Pa	Pb	Pc	Pc
A	0.5	1.0	2.0	1.5	3.5	1.5	1.0	1.0	3.0	1.5	3.0	1.0	2.5	1.5	1.0	1.0	2.5	2.5	1.5	1.5	2.0	1.5	2.5	5.0	1.5	1.5	2.0	3.5	1.5	1.5	4.5	3.5	3.0	1.0
B	0.5	0.5	2.0	1.0	1.5	1.0	1.0	1.0	3.5	1.0	2.0	0.5	3.0	3.0	0.5	2.0	1.0	2.0	1.5	1.5	3.0	2.0	2.0	0.5	3.0	5.0	3.0	2.0	3.0	1.5	4.0	3.5	3.5	4.0
C	0.5	0.5	1.5	3.5	0.5	2.5	1.5	1.5	0.5	1.0	1.0	1.0	2.0	2.5	1.0	1.5	1.5	0.5	2.0	2.0	1.5	2.0	1.5	2.5	2.0	3.5	3.2	1.0	2.5	1.5	1.5	3.5	3.5	2.5
T																																		
1	0.5	1.0	0.5	1.0	0.5	1.0	1.0	1.0	3.5	1.0	1.0	1.0	2.0	1.0	1.0	1.0	0.5	1.0	1.5	1.0	1.5	2.0	1.5	1.0	1.5	1.5	1.0	1.0	1.5	1.0	2.0	3.0	1.0	1.5
2	0.5	0.5	0.5	0.5	1.0	0.5	0.5	0.5	2.0	0.5	0.5	0.5	1.5	1.5	0.5	2.0	1.0	0.5	1.5	0.5	1.0	1.0	1.0	0.5	0.5	1.0	1.0	1.0	1.0	1.0	2.5	1.5	1.5	1.5
3	0.5	0.5	0.5	1.0	0.5	0.5	2.0	0.5	0.5	1.0	0.5	1.5	1.0	0.5	0.5	1.0	0.5	0.5	1.5	0.5	0.5	1.0	0.5	0.5	1.0	1.0	0.5	0.5	1.0	0.5	2.0	2.0	1.5	1.5
4	0.5	0.5	0.5	0.5	0.5	0.5	0.5	1.0	3.5	1.0	1.0	0.5	0.5	0.5	0.5	0.5	0.5	0.5	0.5	0.5	1.5	0.5	0.5	0.5	1.0	1.0	0.5	0.5	0.5	0.5	2.0	2.0	1.5	1.5
5	0.5	1.0	1.0	2.0	0.5	0.5	1.0	0.5	1.5	1.0	1.0	0.5	0.5	1.0	0.5	0.5	0.5	0.5	0.5	1.5	0.5	0.5	1.0	1.0	1.0	1.0	0.5	1.0	1.0	0.5	3.5	3.5	1.5	1.5
6	0.5	1.0	0.5	0.5	0.5	0.5	1.0	1.0	1.5	0.5	0.5	0.5	1.0	1.0	0.5	0.5	0.5	1.0	0.5	1.0	1.0	0.5	0.5	1.0	0.5	0.5	1.5	0.5	0.5	0.5	0.5	1.0	1.0	1.0
7	0.5	0.5	0.5	0.5	0.5	0.5	1.0	1.0	0.5	0.5	1.0	0.5	0.5	0.5	0.5	0.5	0.5	0.5	0.5	0.5	1.0	0.5	0.5	0.5	0.5	0.5	1.0	0.5	0.5	1.0	0.5	1.0	1.0	1.0
8	0.5	0.5	0.5	0.5	0.5	0.5	1.0	1.0	0.5	0.5	0.5	0.5	0.5	0.5	0.5	1.0	0.5	0.5	1.0	0.5	1.0	0.5	0.5	0.5	0.5	0.5	0.5	1.0	0.5	0.5	1.5	1.0	1.5	0.5
9	0.5	0.5	2.0	2.0	0.5	0.5	1.0	1.0	0.5	0.5	0.5	0.5	0.5	0.5	0.5	0.5	0.5	0.5	0.5	1.0	0.5	1.0	0.5	1.0	0.5	0.5	0.5	0.5	0.5	0.5	1.5	1.0	1.0	0.5
10	0.5	3.5	1.0	1.0	0.5	0.5	1.0	1.0	1.0	0.5	1.0	0.5	0.5	0.5	0.5	0.5	0.5	0.5	0.5	0.5	1.0	0.5	1.0	0.5	0.5	0.5	0.5	0.5	4.0	0.5	1.5	0.5	0.5	0.5
11	0.5	0.5	0.5	0.5	0.5	0.5	0.5	0.5	1.0	0.5	0.5	0.5	0.5	1.0	0.5	0.5	0.5	0.5	0.5	0.5	0.5	0.5	0.5	1.0	0.5	0.5	0.5	0.5	0.5	0.5	0.5	1.5	1.0	1.0
12	0.5	0.5	0.5	0.5	0.5	0.5	1.5	0.5	0.5	0.5	0.5	0.5	0.5	0.5	0.5	0.5	1.0	0.5	0.5	0.5	0.5	0.5	0.5	0.5	0.5	0.5	0.5	0.5	1.0	1.0	1.0	1.0	0.5	0.5
13	0.5	0.5	0.5	0.5	0.5	0.5	0.5	0.5	0.5	1.0	0.5	0.5	0.5	0.5	0.5	1.0	0.5	0.5	0.5	0.5	0.5	0.5	0.5	0.5	0.5	0.5	1.0	0.5	0.5	0.5	1.0	1.0	0.5	0.5
14	0.5	0.5	0.5	0.5	0.5	0.5	0.5	0.5	0.5	0.5	0.5	2.0	0.5	0.5	0.5	0.5	0.5	0.5	0.5	0.5	0.5	0.5	0.5	0.5	0.5	0.5	1.0	1.0	0.5	1.0	1.0	1.0	0.5	0.5
15	0.5	0.5	0.5	3.5	0.5	0.5	0.5	0.5	1.0	0.5	0.5	0.5	0.5	0.5	0.5	0.5	0.5	0.5	0.5	0.5	1.0	0.5	0.5	0.5	0.5	0.5	1.0	0.5	1.0	0.5	3.0	5.0	2.0	
πa	$2.63			$1.13			$0.74			$2.03			$1.75			$1.75			$1.63			$1.00			$1.75			$3.10			$0.36			
πb	$2.00			$2.38			$1.60			$2.03			$1.61			$2.13			$1.74			$2.15			$2.22			$1.11			$0.12			
πc	$1.00			$2.00			$2.09			$1.91			$2.74			$2.00			$1.74			$1.73			$1.85			$0.50			$3.43			

Key: PB = Practice bids
Pa = Price choice by player a
T = Transactions
πa = Profit to player a

289

Appendix XV

EXPERIMENT 15

OLIGOPOLY

Triopoly, Complete Information, Price Variation

Instructions
Profit Table
Complete Results for Subjects

Instructions

The National Science Foundation, the Ford Foundation, and the Office of Naval Research have provided funds for the conduct of research regarding economic decisions. If you follow instructions carefully and make appropriate decisions, you may earn an appreciable amount of money.

We will give you $2.50 of capital to start with. *You may keep this money plus all that you earn during the session.* It is possible to end the session with considerably more than $2.50. However, you can lose part or all of the $2.50 you are given if your decisions are not made carefully; but you cannot lose more than that amount. The session will be stopped, if, at any time, you should happen to lose all of your earnings as well as the $2.50 of capital.

You will be grouped at random with two other persons. *You will not see these persons or speak with them at any time.* You will never know the identities of your counterparts, nor will they be aware of yours.

You and your anonymous counterparts will engage in a series of transactions by means of written bids. Imagine that you and the others are engaged in selling some standardized commodity. *You must bid on each transaction.* The bids are in terms of the price you will charge for the commodity for that transaction.

You will be furnished with a table showing various levels of profit or loss you can attain. Down the left-hand side of the table are listed the various

290

prices that you may set for the commodity for a given transaction. Each of your counterparts has a table identical to the one which you have. The figures within the body of the table represent the profits that you can make depending on the prices bid by you and your counterparts. For example, on a given transaction you might select a price of 2.0; you would receive one of the profits in the fourth row. Since you are bidding with two other players, their price decisions affect your profits. If you name a price of 2.0 for the given transaction and both of your counterparts select higher prices than yours, then you would receive a profit of 67¢ and they would each incur a loss of 25¢ for that transaction If one of them also bids 2.0 for the transaction and the other bids higher than 2.0, then both you and your counterpart who bid 2.0 would receive 27¢ profit, while the person who bid higher would lose 25¢.   If all three of you were to select a price of 2.0, then each of you would receive a profit of 14¢ on that transaction.   Had either one or both of the other players bid a price which was lower than your price of 2.0, then you would have lost 25¢.

The process is started by each player selecting and recording a price in the space provided for that purpose on the yellow sheet you received. You may select any price on the left-hand side of the table; then record your selection. An experimental assistant will then inform you of the price choices made by the other persons, as well as your profit or loss for that transaction. You should record both your counterparts' price bids and your profit or loss from the transaction on your yellow sheet.

The process is repeated over and over. The players may select the same price each time; they do not have to do so, however. You will be given a few minutes for each decision. You will have three practice trials so that you may become accustomed to using the profit tables.

For each transaction you will record the price you selected, the prices your counterparts' selected, and your profit or loss from that transaction. At the end of the session we will add up your profit column and give you that amount of money, or take back any losses you incurred, up to the $2.50 you received initially. This will be done in separate counting rooms, so you will not see the persons with whom you have been bidding.

Are there any questions?

Table of Profit to Seller A

My price	Profit when I have the lowest price	Profit when I am tied for low price with one other person	Profit when I am tied for low price with two other persons	Loss when any other price is lower than mine
0.5	.13	.00	.00	
1.0	.35	.11	.03	−.25
1.5	.53	.20	.09	−.25
2.0	.67	.27	.14	−.25
2.5	.77	.32	.17	−.25
3.0	.83	.35	.19	−.25
3.5	.85	.36	.20	−.25
4.0	.83	.35	.19	−.25
4.5	.77	.32	.17	−.25
5.0		.27	.14	−.25

EXPERIMENT 15 Price Bids and Total Profits

PB	Group 29 Pa	Pb	Pc	Group 30 Pa	Pb	Pc	Group 31 Pa	Pb	Pc	Group 32 Pa	Pb	Pc	Group 33 Pa	Pb	Pc	Group 34 Pa	Pb	Pc	Group 35 Pa	Pb	Pc	Group 36 Pa	Pb	Pc	Group 37 Pa	Pb	Pc	Group 38 Pa	Pb	Pc
A	3.5	3.0	1.5	3.0	1.0	2.5	3.5	3.5	3.5	4.0	4.5	1.5	2.5	1.5	3.5	1.5	2.0	1.5	1.5	1.0	2.0	2.5	3.0	3.0	3.5	3.5	4.5	2.5	1.5	3.5
B	3.5	3.5	2.5	3.0	0.5	3.0	4.0	4.0	3.5	4.5	4.0	2.0	3.0	1.5	3.5	1.0	2.5	2.0	2.5	0.5	1.0	2.5	2.5	3.0	3.5	3.0	2.5	2.0	2.5	2.5
C	3.5	3.5	3.5	3.0	2.0	2.0	4.5	3.5	3.5	4.0	4.0	2.0	3.0	2.5	3.5	3.5	2.5	1.5	3.5	1.5	1.0	2.5	2.5	3.5	3.5	1.5	3.5	1.0	3.5	2.5
T																														
1	1.0	1.0	3.0	1.0	1.5	0.5	1.5	3.0	2.5	2.0	0.5	1.5	3.0	2.0	1.5	1.5	1.0	2.0	0.5	0.5	1.0	2.5	1.0	3.5	2.0	2.0	2.0	0.5	1.5	2.0
2	0.5	1.0	1.0	0.5	1.0	1.5	1.5	1.5	1.0	2.0	0.5	1.5	2.0	1.0	1.5	1.5	2.0	1.5	0.5	1.5	1.0	2.5	1.5	2.0	1.5	3.5	2.0	1.0	2.5	0.5
3	0.5	0.5	1.0	0.5	0.5	1.5	0.5	1.5	1.0	1.0	3.5	0.5	2.0	2.5	1.0	1.0	1.5	1.5	0.5	0.5	1.0	1.0	1.5	1.0	1.5	0.5	3.5	1.0	1.5	1.0
4	0.5	1.0	0.5	1.0	0.5	0.5	1.0	0.5	0.5	0.5	1.0	0.5	2.0	1.5	3.0	1.0	1.0	1.0	0.5	1.0	1.0	1.0	1.5	0.5	1.5	0.5	1.0	1.0	1.5	0.5
5	1.0	1.0	0.5	0.5	0.5	0.5	0.5	0.5	0.5	3.5	1.0	1.0	1.0	1.0	1.5	0.5	0.5	1.0	0.5	1.0	0.5	0.5	1.0	0.5	1.5	0.5	0.5	0.5	1.0	0.5
6	0.5	0.5	0.5	0.5	0.5	0.5	0.5	0.5	0.5	1.5	1.5	1.0	1.5	1.0	0.5	2.0	2.0	0.5	0.5	0.5	0.5	0.5	0.5	0.5	1.0	2.5	3.5	1.0	0.5	1.0
7	0.5	0.5	0.5	0.5	0.5	0.5	0.5	0.5	0.5	0.5	1.5	1.0	1.0	2.0	1.0	1.0	1.0	1.0	0.5	3.5	0.5	0.5	0.5	1.0	0.5	1.5	0.5	1.5	0.5	1.0
8	0.5	0.5	0.5	3.5	0.5	3.5	0.5	0.5	0.5	1.0	0.5	0.5	1.5	1.0	1.5	0.5	2.0	0.5	0.5	1.0	3.5	0.5	3.0	1.5	0.5	0.5	0.5	0.5	0.5	0.5
9	1.0	0.5	0.5	3.5	0.5	3.5	0.5	0.5	0.5	0.5	1.0	1.0	1.5	1.5	0.5	0.5	0.5	0.5	0.5	3.5	3.5	3.0	2.5	1.0	0.5	0.5	0.5	0.5	3.0	1.0
10	0.5	0.5	0.5	3.5	1.0	3.5	0.5	0.5	0.5	0.5	0.5	1.0	0.5	2.5	0.5	1.0	1.0	0.5	0.5	1.5	0.5	0.5	1.5	1.0	1.5	0.5	0.5	0.5	1.5	1.0
11	0.5	2.5	0.5	0.5	1.5	0.5	0.5	0.5	0.5	1.0	0.5	0.5	0.5	3.0	0.5	0.5	2.0	0.5	1.0	1.0	0.5	0.5	0.5	2.0	0.5	0.5	0.5	1.0	0.5	1.0
12	2.5	0.5	0.5	1.0	1.0	0.5	0.5	0.5	0.5	0.5	0.5	0.5	0.5	1.0	0.5	0.5	3.5	0.5	0.5	0.5	0.5	0.5	0.5	2.0	0.5	0.5	0.5	1.5	2.5	1.0
13	0.5	0.5	0.5	0.5	0.5	0.5	0.5	0.5	0.5	0.5	1.0	0.5	0.5	1.0	0.5	1.0	0.5	0.5	0.5	1.5	0.5	0.5	0.5	1.5	3.5	0.5	0.5	1.5	1.0	0.5
14	0.5	0.5	0.5	0.5	0.5	0.5	0.5	0.5	0.5	0.5	0.5	1.0	1.0	0.5	0.5	0.5	0.5	0.5	0.5	1.5	0.5	0.5	0.5	1.5	0.5	0.5	0.5	1.0	3.5	0.5
15	0.5	0.5	1.5	0.5	1.5	0.5	0.5	0.5	0.5	0.5	0.5	1.5	1.0	0.5	0.5	0.5	0.5	0.5	0.5	3.0	0.5	0.5	0.5	1.5	0.5	0.5	0.5	2.0	1.5	1.0
πa	$1.99			$ .76			$2.66			$ .88			$ .24			$1.84			$3.02			$1.87			$2.60			$ .73		
πb	1.61			1.86			1.75			2.25			1.49			.76			.00			1.88			1.26			.50		
πc	1.75			1.51			2.35			1.21			2.86			1.74			.75			.77			1.52			2.45		

Key: PB = Practice bids
Pa = Price choice by player a
T = Transactions
πa = Profit to player a

293

Appendix XVI

EXPERIMENT 16

OLIGOPOLY

Duopoly, Complete Information, Price Variation

Instructions
Profit Table
Complete Results for Subjects

Instructions

The National Science Foundation, the Ford Foundation, and the Office of Naval Research have provided funds for the conduct of research regarding economic decisions. If you follow instructions carefully and make appropriate decisions, you may earn an appreciable amount of money.

We will give you $2.50 of capital to start with. *You may keep this money plus all that you earn during the session.* It is possible to end the session with considerably more than $2.50. However, you can lose part or all of the $2.50 you are given if your decisions are not made carefully, but you cannot lose more than that amount. The session will be stopped, if, at any time, you should happen to lose all of your earnings as well as the $2.50 in capital.

You will be paired at random with one other person. *You will not see this person or speak with him at any time.* You will never know the identity of your counterpart, nor will he be aware of yours.

You and your anonymous counterpart will engage in a series of transactions by means of written bids. Imagine that you and he are engaged in selling some standardized commodity. *You must bid on each transaction.* The bids are in terms of the price you will charge for the commodity for that transaction.

You will be furnished with a table showing various levels of profit or loss you can attain. Down the left-hand side of the table are listed the various

294

prices that you may set for the commodity for a given transaction.   Your counterpart has a table identical to the one which you have.   The figures within the body of the table represent the profits that you can make depending on the prices bid by you and your counterpart.   For example, on a given transaction you might select a price of 2.0; you would receive one of the profits in the fourth row.   Since you are bidding with one other player, his price decisions affect your profits.   If you name a price of 2.0 for the given transaction and your counterpart selects a price higher than yours, then you would receive a profit of 67¢ and he would incur a loss of 25¢ for that transaction.   If he had also bid 2.0 for that transaction then you would each have received a profit of 27¢.   Had your counterpart selected a price lower than your bid of 2.0, then you would have lost 25¢ and he would have made money on the transaction.

The process is started by each player selecting and recording a price in the space provided for that purpose on the yellow sheet you received.   You may select any price on the left-hand side of the table; then record your selection.   An experimental assistant will then inform you of the price choice made by the other person as well as your profit or loss for that transaction.   You should record both your counterpart's price bid and your profit or loss from the transaction on your yellow sheet.

The process is repeated over and over.   The players may select the same price each time; they do not have to do so, however.   You will be given a few minutes for each decision.   You will have three practice trials so that you may become accustomed to using the profit tables.

For each transaction you will record the price you selected, the price your counterpart selected, and your profit or loss from that transaction.   At the end of the session we will add up your profit column and give you that amount of money, or take back any losses you incurred, up to the $2.50 you received initially.   This will be done in separate counting rooms, so you will not see the person with whom you have been bidding.

Are there any questions?

Table of Profit to Seller A

My price	Profit when I have the lower price	Profit when I am tied for low price	Loss when I have the higher price
0.5	.13	.00	
1.0	.35	.11	−.25
1.5	.53	.20	−.25
2.0	.67	.27	−.25
2.5	.77	.32	−.25
3.0	.83	.35	−.25
3.5	.85	.36	−.25
4.0	.83	.35	−.25
4.5	.77	.32	−.25
5.0		.27	−.25

EXPERIMENT 16   Price Bids and Total Profits

Group number

	39		40		41		42		43		44		45		46		47		48		49		50		51		52		53		54		55	
PB	Pa	Pb	Pa	Pb	Pa	Pb	Pa	Pb	Pa	Pb	Pa	Pb	Pa	Pb	Pa	Pb	Pa	Pb	Pa	Pb	Pa	Pb	Pa	Pb	Pa	Pb	Pa	Pb	Pa	Pb	Pa	Pb	Pa	Pb
A	3.5	3.5	3.5	3.5	2.0	3.0	3.5	3.5	2.0	3.5	3.0	3.5	3.5	3.5	3.0	3.0	3.5	3.5	3.5	2.0	1.5	2.5	2.0	2.0	0.5	1.5	5.0	3.0	3.5	3.5	3.5	4.0	3.5	3.5
B	3.0	3.0	3.0	3.5	3.5	3.5	2.5	2.5	2.5	3.5	3.0	4.0	3.5	2.5	3.0	3.0	3.5	3.5	2.5	3.0	3.5	0.5	2.0	2.0	4.5	1.0	3.5	3.5	3.0	4.0	3.5	3.5	3.0	3.3
C	3.5	3.5	3.5	3.5	2.0	3.0	2.5	2.5	3.0	4.0	3.0	4.5	2.0	3.0	3.0	3.0	3.5	3.5	3.0	2.5	1.5	4.5	2.0	2.0	3.5	2.5	4.5	3.0	3.5	3.5	3.5	3.5	4.0	3.5
T																																		
1	3.5	3.5	2.0	3.5	1.0	3.0	1.0	4.0	1.5	3.0	1.5	1.0	1.5	3.0	1.0	1.5	1.5	3.5	2.0	3.0	3.5	1.5	2.0	2.0	1.5	1.5	2.0	3.0	2.5	1.5	3.5	3.5	3.5	3.5
2	3.0	2.5	1.5	2.5	1.5	3.5	1.5	1.5	1.5	2.0	2.0	2.0	2.0	2.5	2.0	1.5	2.5	1.5	2.0	2.0	1.5	3.5	2.0	2.0	2.0	2.0	3.0	3.0	2.5	3.0	3.5	3.5	3.5	3.5
3	1.5	3.0	1.0	1.5	1.0	3.0	1.0	0.5	2.0	2.0	2.0	1.5	2.0	1.5	2.5	1.5	3.0	1.5	2.0	2.0	2.0	1.5	2.0	2.0	2.0	2.5	3.0	3.0	2.5	2.5	3.5	3.5	3.5	3.5
4	0.5	0.5	3.0	3.0	3.5	3.5	2.5	2.0	2.5	1.5	1.5	1.5	2.0	1.0	1.5	1.5	3.5	1.5	1.5	2.0	1.5	3.0	2.0	2.0	1.5	1.0	3.0	3.0	2.0	2.0	3.5	3.5	3.5	3.5
5	0.5	2.0	1.0	0.5	1.5	3.0	0.5	0.5	1.0	3.0	1.5	1.0	1.0	1.0	2.0	2.0	2.0	2.0	2.0	2.0	3.5	3.0	2.0	2.0	1.0	3.0	3.0	3.0	3.0	2.0	3.5	3.5	3.5	3.5
6	0.5	2.0	2.0	2.0	1.0	0.2	0.5	0.5	2.0	3.0	1.0	3.0	1.5	1.0	2.0	1.5	3.5	1.5	2.5	2.5	3.5	3.5	2.0	2.0	0.5	1.5	3.0	3.0	3.0	3.0	3.5	3.5	3.5	3.5
7	2.5	0.5	0.5	0.5	0.5	1.0	1.5	0.5	1.5	1.5	1.0	1.0	1.0	1.5	1.5	1.5	1.5	1.0	3.0	3.0	1.5	3.5	3.5	1.0	1.0	1.5	3.5	3.0	3.0	4.0	3.5	3.5	3.5	3.5
8	0.5	0.5	2.5	1.5	0.5	0.5	0.5	0.5	1.5	1.5	1.0	1.5	2.0	1.0	1.5	1.5	1.5	1.5	3.0	2.0	3.0	3.0	3.5	3.5	1.5	1.0	3.0	3.0	3.0	3.0	3.5	3.5	3.5	3.5
9	0.5	0.5	2.0	2.0	0.5	0.5	1.5	0.5	1.5	2.5	0.5	1.0	1.0	1.0	2.0	2.0	1.0	1.5	2.5	2.5	3.0	3.5	3.5	3.5	1.0	1.5	3.0	3.0	3.0	4.0	3.5	3.5	3.5	3.5
10	0.5	0.5	1.0	0.5	2.5	0.5	0.5	0.5	1.0	1.0	1.0	1.0	1.0	1.0	2.0	1.0	1.5	1.0	2.0	2.0	2.0	3.5	3.0	3.0	0.5	1.0	3.0	3.0	3.0	3.0	3.5	3.5	3.5	3.5
11	0.5	0.5	0.5	0.5	1.0	0.5	0.5	0.5	2.0	1.5	1.0	0.5	3.5	1.0	1.5	2.5	1.5	0.5	2.0	2.5	3.0	2.0	3.5	2.0	1.5	1.0	3.0	3.0	2.0	3.0	3.5	3.5	3.5	3.5
12	0.5	0.5	1.0	0.5	1.0	0.5	0.5	0.5	1.5	1.5	0.5	0.5	2.0	1.5	1.5	2.0	3.5	1.5	2.5	2.0	2.0	3.5	3.5	3.0	2.5	1.5	3.0	3.0	2.5	3.5	3.5	3.5	3.5	3.5
13	0.5	0.5	0.5	0.5	1.0	0.5	0.5	0.5	1.0	1.0	0.5	1.0	1.5	1.5	1.0	1.5	1.5	3.0	2.0	2.0	2.0	3.0	2.0	3.5	4.0	1.5	3.0	3.0	2.5	2.5	3.5	3.5	3.5	3.5
14	0.5	0.5	0.5	0.5	0.5	0.5	0.5	0.5	0.5	0.5	1.0	0.5	1.5	1.0	1.0	1.5	1.5	3.0	2.0	2.0	3.5	3.5	3.5	3.5	3.5	3.5	3.0	3.0	2.5	4.0	3.5	3.5	3.5	3.5
15	0.5	0.5	1.0	0.5	0.5	0.5	3.5		1.5		0.5		1.0		2.0	2.5	1.0	0.5	1.5	1.5	3.0	2.0	1.5	1.5	1.5	1.5	3.0	2.5	2.5	1.5	2.5	1.0	2.5	2.0
πa	$2.92		$2.69		$4.36		$2.11		$4.08		$1.96		$4.35		$8.67		$5.14		$5.67		$6.79		$6.61		$2.30		$7.47		$7.06		$7.89		$7.29	
πb	3.16		2.33		1.14		3.11		5.04		3.74		4.31		.53		3.08		6.83		5.11		6.01		5.68		7.57		5.08		7.29		8.21	

Key: PB = Practice bids
Pa = Price choice by player a
T = Transactions
πa = Profit to player a

297

Appendix XVII

OLIGOPOLY

Duopoly, Incomplete Information, Quantity Variation Replication of Experiment 7
Triopoly, Incomplete Information, Quantity Variation Replication of Experiment 8

Instructions Same as for Experiments 7 and 8
Profit Table
Complete Results for Subjects

Table of Profit to Seller A

Quantity produced

	8	9	10	11	12	13	14	15	16	17	18	19
8	1408	1548	1680	1804	1920	2028	2128	2220	2304	2380	2448	2508
9	1376	1512	1640	1760	1872	1976	2072	2160	2240	2317	2376	2432
10	1344	1476	1600	1716	1824	1924	2016	2100	2176	2244	2304	2356
11	1312	1440	1560	1672	1776	1872	1960	2040	2112	2176	2232	2280
12	1280	1404	1520	1628	1728	1820	1904	1980	2048	2108	2160	2204
13	1248	1368	1480	1584	1680	1768	1848	1920	1984	2040	2088	2128
14	1216	1332	1440	1540	1632	1716	1792	1860	1920	1972	2016	2052
15	1184	1296	1400	1496	1584	1664	1736	1800	1856	1904	1944	1976
16	1152	1260	1360	1452	1536	1612	1680	1740	1792	1836	1872	1900
17	1120	1224	1320	1408	1488	1560	1624	1680	1728	1768	1800	1824
18	1088	1188	1280	1364	1440	1508	1568	1620	1664	1700	1728	1748
19	1056	1152	1240	1320	1392	1456	1512	1560	1600	1632	1656	1672
20	1024	1116	1200	1276	1344	1404	1456	1500	1536	1564	1584	1596
21	992	1080	1160	1232	1296	1352	1400	1440	1472	1496	1512	1520
22	960	1044	1120	1188	1248	1300	1344	1380	1408	1428	1440	1444
23	928	1008	1080	1144	1200	1248	1288	1320	1344	1360	1368	1368
24	896	972	1040	1100	1152	1196	1232	1260	1280	1292	1296	1292
25	864	936	1000	1056	1104	1144	1176	1200	1216	1224	1224	1216
26	832	900	960	1012	1056	1092	1120	1140	1152	1156	1152	1140
27	800	864	920	968	1008	1040	1064	1080	1088	1088	1080	1064
28	768	828	880	924	960	988	1008	1020	1024	1020	1008	988
29	736	792	840	880	912	936	952	960	960	952	936	912
30	704	756	800	836	864	884	896	900	896	884	864	836
31	672	720	760	792	816	832	840	840	832	816	792	760
32	640	684	720	748	768	780	784	780	768	748	720	684
33	608	648	680	704	720	728	728	720	704	680	648	608
34	576	612	640	660	672	676	672	660	640	612	576	532
35	544	576	600	616	624	624	616	600	576	544	504	456
36	512	540	560	572	576	572	560	540	512	476	432	380

Quantity produced by seller A's competition

by seller A

20	21	22	23	24	25	26	27	28	29	30	31	32
2560	2604	2640	2668	2688	2700	2704	2700	2688	2668	2640	2604	2560
2480	2520	2552	2576	2592	2600	2600	2592	2576	2552	2520	2480	2432
2400	2436	2464	2484	2496	2500	2496	2484	2464	2436	2400	2356	2304
2320	2352	2376	2392	2400	2400	2392	2376	2352	2320	2280	2232	2176
2240	2268	2288	2300	2304	2300	2288	2268	2240	2204	2160	2108	2048
2160	2184	2200	2208	2208	2200	2184	2160	2128	2088	2040	1984	1920
2080	2100	2112	2116	2112	2100	2080	2052	2016	1972	1920	1860	1792
2000	2016	2024	2024	2016	2000	1976	1944	1904	1856	1800	1736	1664
1920	1932	1936	1932	1920	1900	1872	1836	1792	1740	1680	1612	1536
1840	1848	1848	1840	1824	1800	1768	1728	1680	1624	1560	1488	1408
1760	1764	1760	1748	1728	1700	1664	1620	1568	1508	1440	1364	1280
1680	1680	1672	1656	1632	1600	1560	1512	1456	1392	1320	1240	1152
1600	1596	1584	1564	1536	1500	1456	1404	1344	1276	1200	1116	1024
1520	1512	1496	1472	1440	1400	1352	1296	1232	1160	1080	992	896
1440	1428	1408	1380	1344	1300	1248	1188	1120	1044	960	868	768
1360	1344	1320	1288	1248	1200	1144	1080	1008	928	840	744	640
1280	1260	1232	1196	1152	1100	1040	972	896	812	720	620	512
1200	1176	1144	1104	1056	1000	936	864	784	696	600	496	384
1120	1092	1056	1012	960	900	832	756	672	580	480	372	256
1040	1008	968	920	864	800	728	648	560	464	360	248	128
960	924	880	828	768	700	624	540	448	348	240	124	000
880	840	792	736	672	600	520	432	336	232	120	000	−128
800	756	704	644	576	500	416	324	224	116	000	−124	−256
720	672	616	552	480	400	312	216	112	000	−120	−248	−384
640	588	528	460	384	300	208	108	000	−116	−240	−372	−512
560	504	440	368	288	200	104	000	−112	−232	−360	−496	−640
480	420	352	276	192	100	000	−108	−224	−348	−480	−620	−768
400	336	264	184	96	000	−104	−216	−336	−464	−600	−744	−896
320	252	176	92	00	−100	−208	−324	−448	−580	−720	−868	−1024

Table of Profit to Seller A (Continued)

Quantity produced

	8	9	10	11	12	13	14	15	16	17	18	19
37	480	504	520	528	528	520	504	480	448	408	360	304
38	448	468	480	484	480	468	448	420	384	340	288	228
39	416	432	440	440	432	416	392	360	320	272	216	152
40	384	396	400	396	384	364	336	300	256	204	144	76
41	352	360	360	352	336	312	280	240	192	136	72	00
42	320	324	320	308	288	260	224	180	128	68	00	−76
43	288	288	280	264	240	208	168	120	64	00	−72	−152
44	256	252	240	220	192	156	112	60	00	−68	−144	−228
45	224	216	200	176	144	104	56	00	−64	−136	−216	−304
46	192	180	160	132	96	52	00	−60	−128	−204	−288	−380
47	160	144	120	88	48	00	−56	−120	−192	−272	−360	−456
48	128	108	80	44	00	−52	−112	−180	−256	−340	−432	−532
49	96	72	40	00	−48	−104	−168	−240	−320	−408	−504	−608
50	64	36	00	−44	−96	−156	−224	−300	−384	−476	−576	−684
51	32	00	−40	−88	−144	−208	−280	−360	−448	−544	−648	−760
52	00	−36	−80	−132	−192	−260	−336	−420	−512	−612	−720	−836
53	−32	−72	−120	−176	−240	−312	−392	−480	−576	−680	−792	−912
54	−64	−108	−160	−220	−288	−364	−448	−540	−640	−748	−864	−988
55	−96	−144	−200	−264	−336	−416	−504	−600	−704	−816	−936	−1064
56	−128	−180	−240	−308	−384	−468	−560	−660	−768	−884	−1008	−1140
57	−160	−216	−280	−352	−432	−520	−616	−720	−832	−952	−1080	−1216
58	−192	−252	−320	−396	−480	−572	−672	−780	−896	−1020	−1152	−1292
59	−224	−288	−360	−440	−528	−624	−728	−840	−960	−1088	−1224	−1368
60	−256	−324	−400	−484	−576	−676	−784	−900	−1024	−1156	−1296	−1444
61	−288	−360	−440	−528	−624	−728	−840	−960	−1088	−1224	−1368	−1520
62	−320	−396	−480	−572	−672	−780	−896	−1020	−1152	−1292	−1440	−1596
63	−352	−432	−520	−616	−720	−832	−952	−1080	−1216	−1360	−1512	−1672
64	−384	−468	−560	−660	−768	−884	−1008	−1140	−1280	−1428	−1584	−1748

Quantity produced by seller A's competition

by seller A

20	21	22	23	24	25	26	27	28	29	30	31	32
240	168	88	00	−96	−200	−312	−432	−560	−696	−840	−992	−1152
160	84	00	−92	−192	−300	−416	−540	−672	−812	−960	−1116	−1280
80	00	−88	−184	−288	−400	−520	−648	−784	−928	−1080	−1240	−1408
00	−84	−176	−276	−384	−500	−624	−756	−896	−1044	−1200	−1364	−1536
−80	−168	−264	−368	−480	−600	−728	−864	−1008	−1160	−1320	−1488	−1664
−160	−252	−352	−460	−576	−700	−832	−972	−1120	−1276	−1440	−1612	−1792
−240	−336	−440	−552	−672	−800	−936	−1080	−1232	−1392	−1560	−1736	−1920
−320	−420	−528	−644	−768	−900	−1040	−1188	−1344	−1508	−1680	−1860	−2048
−400	−504	−616	−736	−864	−1000	−1144	−1296	−1456	−1624	−1800	−1984	−2176
−480	−588	−704	−828	−960	−1100	−1248	−1404	−1568	−1740	−1920	−2108	−2304
−560	−672	−792	−920	−1056	−1200	−1352	−1512	−1680	−1856	−2040	−2232	−2432
−640	−756	−880	−1012	−1152	−1300	−1456	−1620	−1792	−1972	−2160	−2356	−2560
−720	−840	−968	−1104	−1248	−1400	−1560	−1728	−1904	−2088	−2280	−2480	−2688
−800	−924	−1056	−1196	−1344	−1500	−1664	−1836	−2016	−2204	−2400	−2604	−2816
−880	−1008	−1144	−1288	−1440	−1600	−1768	−1944	−2128	−2320	−2520	−2728	−2944
−960	−1092	−1232	−1380	−1536	−1700	−1872	−2052	−2240	−2436	−2640	−2852	−3072
−1040	−1176	−1320	−1472	−1632	−1800	−1976	−2160	−2352	−2552	−2760	−2976	−3200
−1120	−1260	−1408	−1564	−1728	−1900	−2080	−2268	−2464	−2668	−2880	−3100	−3328
−1200	−1344	−1496	−1656	−1824	−2000	−2184	−2376	−2576	−2784	−3000	−3224	−3456
−1280	−1428	−1584	−1748	−1920	−2100	−2288	−2484	−2688	−2900	−3120	−3348	−3584
−1360	−1512	−1672	−1840	−2016	−2200	−2392	−2592	−2800	−3016	−3240	−3472	−3712
−1440	−1596	−1760	−1932	−2112	−2300	−2496	−2700	−2912	−3132	−3360	−3596	−3840
−1520	−1680	−1848	−2024	−2208	−2400	−2600	−2808	−3024	−3248	−3480	−3720	−3968
−1600	−1764	−1936	−2116	−2304	−2500	−2704	−2916	−3136	−3364	−3600	−3844	−4096
−1680	−1848	−2024	−2208	−2400	−2600	−2808	−3024	−3248	−3480	−3720	−3968	−4224
−1760	−1932	−2112	−2300	−2496	−2700	−2912	−3132	−3360	−3596	−3840	−4092	−4352
−1840	−2016	−2200	−2392	−2592	−2800	−3016	−3240	−3472	−3712	−3960	−4216	−4480
−1920	−2100	−2288	−2484	−2688	−2900	−3120	−3348	−3584	−3828	−4080	−4340	−4608

EXPERIMENT 17   Quantity Bids: Replication of Experiment 7

	Group							
	1		2		3		4	
PB	Qa	Qb	Qa	Qb	Qa	Qb	Qa	Qb
A	22	20	25	19	26	23	20	21
B	20	30	27	23	25	19	26	15
C			24	26	26	18	28	25
T								
1	17	25	20	22	20	22	18	21
2	26	23	18	16	25	25	15	21
3	19	21	20	15	8	24	20	20
4	21	22	21	20	26	20	19	20
5	18	21	24	23	29	22	19	20
6	20	23	23	17	15	22	20	20
7	18	23	19	22	22	25	20	20
8	19	23	24	22	26	20	20	20
9	19	24	22	24	26	21	20	20
10	18	22	23	23	26	18	19	20
11	19	22	25	19	26	22	20	20
12	19	22	23	22	23	17	19	20
13	19	21	21	23	23	25	20	20
14	19	21	22	22	19	20	19	20
15	19	21	24	21	19	21	20	20
16	19	21	20	23	20	19	19	20
17	19	22	22	22	20	23	20	20
18	19	22	20	22	18	20	19	20
19	19	22	24	21	18	22	21	20
20	19	21	20	23	32	20	19	20
21	19	21	24	22	26	23	21	20
22	19	21	23	21	26	19	19	20

Key: PB = Practice bids
Qa = Quantity produced by player a
T = Transactions

EXPERIMENT 17   Quantity Bids: Replication of Experiment 8

		Group·										
		5			6			7			8	
PB	Qa	Qb	Qc	Qa	Qb	Qc	Qa	Qb	Qc	Qa	Qb	Qc
A	17	20	8	22	17	15	20	12	16	20	13	17
B	19	12	8	13	20	13	25	11	14	15	12	20
C	19	18	17	22	22	16	8	19	22	15	12	21
T												
1	14	20	17	15	18	12	15	19	11	20	16	14
2	11	15	12	16	25	12	16	19	16	25	13	21
3	10	20	10	12	17	11	18	20	11	15	13	19
4	12	17	15	14	20	11	18	21	25	14	14	8
5	15	13	13	13	18	10	18	20	19	16	11	8
6	15	8	8	21	17	11	8	20	19	16	22	12
7	17	17	9	15	12	13	10	21	17	16	18	16
8	14	19	10	13	20	12	11	20	13	16	13	16
9	22	21	14	16	18	13	14	19	18	16	15	11
10	13	15	8	15	15	10	22	20	24	14	17	8
11	16	21	8	14	11	11	15	20	11	15	12	22
12	15	17	10	15	18	12	13	20	8	15	13	14
13	16	16	11	15	17	10	14	20	8	15	15	10
14	19	20	10	14	16	12	14	20	15	15	18	16
15	18	17	11	14	14	13	13	19	22	25	17	16
16	14	17	15	18	18	14	13	20	15	25	15	9
17	20	15	8	17	15	14	15	20	24	25	15	16
18	21	16	10	17	20	14	13	19	22	20	12	14
19	15	16	12	17	17	13	13	18	16	20	12	14
20	14	16	11	15	16	12	13	17	16	20	12	8
21	17	18	8	15	25	13	13	16	15	20	13	16
Bonus awards	3	2			1							
1	15	16	13	15	14	10	16	16	15	15	15	14
2	17	16	11	14	15	11	14	20	15	15	16	16
3	17	17	12	15	16	15	15	20	15	15	15	14
4	13	16	13	15	22	14	17	19	14	15	17	15
5	19	16	12	16	17	12	15	20	13	15	16	16

Key: PB = Practice bids

Qa = Quantity produced by player a

T = Transactions

EXPERIMENT 17 Quantity Bids: Duopoly with Special Bonus Instructions

	Group									
	9		10		11		12		13, mixed	
PB	Qa	Qb	Qa	Qb	Qa	Qb	Qa	Qb	Qa	Qb
A	15	20	15	14	23	21	8	25	26	20
B	21	23	14	14	15	19	30	26	26	20
C	21	22	16	23	24	20	20	17	19	14
T										
1	20	19	15	25	21	19	23	19	20	24
2	20	20	18	23	20	19	20	16	18	20
3	21	19	20	21	20	20	19	20	26	16
4	20	20	22	20	21	20	18	18	28	18
5	21	20	23	19	20	20	21	21	22	16
6	21	20	24	18	21	19	20	20	21	19
7	21	19	25	20	21	20	18	20	26	22
8	20	19	24	22	20	20	24	21	22	17
9	21	19	22	24	21	20	19	17	20	20
10	21	20	17	26	18	19	22	20	26	18
11	20	21	16	28	21	20	20	19	21	22
12	20	22	18	23	20	20	19	18	21	20
13	20	20	19	25	21	20	20	20	20	19
14	20	20	18	26	21	20	21	18	20	16
15	20	23	24	23	21	19	20	19	20	20
16	21	23	26	25	19	20	22	20	16	20
17	20	21	17	25	20	20	19	21	20	17
18	20	20	15	25	19	20	20	20	20	19
19	20	20	18	25	21	20	20	21	20	20
20	20	21	17	24	20	19	21	20	22	22
21	20	20	17	24	20	20	19	19	19	19
22	25	20	17	23	20	20	20	20	20	21

Key: PB = Practice bids
Qa = Quantity choice by player a
T = Transactions

Index